The Plain

WILLIAM HAZLITT

The Plain Speaker

The Key Essays

Introduced by Tom Paulin
Edited by Duncan Wu

BLACKWELL
Publishers

First published 1998

2 4 6 8 10 9 7 5 3 1

Blackwell Publishers Ltd
108 Cowley Road
Oxford OX4 1JF
UK

Blackwell Publishers Inc.
350 Main Street
Malden, Massachusetts 02148
USA

British Library Cataloguing in Publication Data
A CIP catalogue record for this book is available from the British Library.

Library of Congress Cataloging-in-Publication Data

Hazlitt, William, 1778–1830.
      [Plain speaker.   Selections]
      The plain speaker: the key essays / William Hazlitt; introduced
   by Tom Paulin; edited by Duncan Wu.
         p.   cm.
      A selection from the two-volume work.
      Includes bibliographical references and index.
      ISBN 0–631–21056–3 (alk. paper). — ISBN 0–631–21057–1 (alk. paper)
      1. English literature—19th century—History and criticism—Theory, etc.
   2. England—Civilization—18th century. I. Wu, Duncan. II. Title.
   PR4771.W8   1999
   824′.7—dc21
                                                                          98–21304
                                                                          CIP

Typeset in 10.5 on 12.5 pt Galliard
by Ace Filmsetting Ltd, Frome, Somerset
Printed in Great Britain by MPG Books Ltd, Bodmin, Cornwall

This book is printed on acid-free paper

Contents

Introduction

Tom Paulin

Sometimes books disappear from the cultural memory: they fall out
of the literary canon and continue their slow descent through ob-
livion until, with luck, they are rescued and restored, maybe for a
generation, maybe for longer. Hazlitt's *The Plain Speaker* is one such
lost text, and as Hazlitt's critical genius is now being rediscovered
after a long period of neglect, it seems appropriate to bring this collection back into print. Though some of the essays have dated –
Hazlitt's demolition of a phrenologist called Spurzheim, for example – others are among his greatest and deserve fresh attention. The
opening essay – 'On the Prose-Style of Poets' – is seminal, for it
concentrates a lifetime's meditation on the nature of prose and sets
out what is in effect a poetics of prose. This essay was last reprinted
more than twenty-five years ago in Christopher Salvesen's selection
of Hazlitt, but it is seldom referred to by critics interested in the
nature of prose – indeed, such critics are themselves extremely rare;
it's as if Orwell's dictum that good prose should be like a window-
pane has discouraged any attempt to see prose as anything other
than the vehicle of ideas. That good prose has shape, form, pattern,
beauty or, in Hazlitt's term, *momentum*, is an idea that is absent in
most critical discussion.

Central to Hazlitt's aesthetic is the argument that poets cannot
write good prose, and it is through his analysis of what is absent from
their attempts at prose that he shows what ideally ought to shape
good writing: 'Their style halts, totters, is loose, disjointed, and

without expressive pauses or rapid movements' (p. 1) – a sentence which animates Hazlitt's critical argument like a type of cartoon metaphor, and which depends for its structure on the several *t* sounds and on the way in which 'loose', 'pauses' and 'move' chime together. He can almost guess, Hazlitt says, that Sir Walter Scott is a writer of 'ambling verses' because the 'march' of his style has a 'desultory vacillation and want of firmness' (p. 1). Often, as I've noted, it's the *t* sounds in Hazlitt that brace his sentences, as in this dedication to the journalist and editor John Hunt: 'THE tried, steady, zealous, and conscientious advocate of the liberty of his country, and the rights of mankind'. This sentence begins the dedication to *Political Essays*, a collection published in 1819, seven years before *The Plain Speaker*. Like the later volume, *Political Essays* affirms the integrity of the plain spoken, and it does so in a manner that is consciously nativist, consciously English, or 'old English' as Hazlitt would prefer to describe this quality of muscular directness and accuracy. As he explains in 'Old English Writers and Speakers', the mark of the 'genuine English intellect' is the way it constantly combines, as Fielding and Hogarth do, 'truth of external observation with strength of internal meaning'. Rather like T. S. Eliot, who stole the concept of dissociation of sensibility from Hazlitt's account of the seventeenth-century Puritan Bulstrode Whitelocke, he believes that the English intellect has suffered division and decline from the middle of the seventeenth century. After the Restoration, Hazlitt argues that 'the grave, enthusiastic, puritanical, "prick-eared" style became quite exploded'. What replaced it was a 'gay and piquant' style that reflected courtly conversation and polished manners, and which was borrowed from the French. Milton alone stood out as a 'partisan' of the old Elizabethan school. Then after the Williamite Revolution of 1688, we 'sobered down' into a 'strain of greater demureness, and into a Dutch or German fidelity of imitation of domestic manners and individual character'.

The reference to Dutch or German fidelity alludes to a passage in one of the poet William Shenstone's letters which haunted Hazlitt and which lies behind the adjective 'plain' in the title of this collection:

> I think *poets* are *Tories* by nature, supposing them to be by nature poets. – The love of an individual person or family, that has worn a crown for many successions, is an inclination greatly adapted to the

fanciful tribe. On the other hand, mathematicians, abstract-reasoners, of no manner of attachment to persons, at least to the *visible* part of them, but prodigiously devoted to the ideas of virtue, liberty, and so forth, are generally *Whigs*. It happens agreeably enough to this maxim, that the Whigs are friends to that wise, plodding, unpoetical people the Dutch. – The Tories, on the other hand, are taken mightily with that showy ostentatious nation the French. Foxhunters, that reside among the beauties of nature, and bid defiance to art, in short, that have intellects of a poetical *turn*, are frequently Tories; citizens, merchants, etc. that scarce see what nature is, and consequently have no pretensions to a poetical estate, are, I think, generally argumentative and Whiggish.

Hazlitt quotes part of this letter in an earlier collection, *Table-Talk*, and for him prose writers, like the Dutch, live on the plains and appear incapable of reaching the sublime heights that poetry aspires to. Hazlitt feels deep down that prose is inferior to poetry – it is plodding, unimaginative, abstract – but at an even deeper level of his sensitive imaginative pride in his own art he feels that, yes, prose is an art form, a separate, unique, autarkic form that needs recognition, that needs to shake off the inferiority complex implicit in the pejorative term 'to prose'. He needs to express the spirit of great prose scaling the heights, and he does so in a complex, bravura passage in 'The Prose-Style of Poets':

It has always always appeared to me that the most perfect prose-style, the most powerful, the most dazzling, the most daring, that which went the nearest to the verge of poetry, and yet never fell over, was Burke's. It has the solidity, and sparkling effect of the diamond: all other *fine writing* is like French paste or Bristol-stones in the comparison. Burke's style is airy, flighty, adventurous, but it never loses sight of the subject; nay, is always in contact with, and derives its increased or varying impulse from it. It may be said to pass yawning gulfs 'on the unsteadfast footing of a spear': still it has an actual resting-place and tangible support under it – it is not suspended on nothing. It differs from poetry, as I conceive, like the chamois from the eagle: it climbs to an almost equal height, touches upon a cloud, overlooks a precipice, is picturesque, sublime – but all the while, instead of soaring through the air, it stands upon a rocky cliff, clambers up by abrupt and intricate ways, and browses on the roughest bark, or crops the tender flower. The principle which guides his pen is truth, not beauty – not pleasure, but power. He has no choice, no selection of subject to flatter the reader's idle taste, or assist his own fancy: he must take what comes, and make the most of it. He works the most striking effects out of the most unpromising materials, by the mere activity of his mind. He rises with the lofty, descends with the mean, luxuriates in beauty, gloats over deformity. It is all the same to him, so that he loses no particle of the exact, characteristic, extreme impression of the thing he writes about, and that he communicates this to the reader, after exhausting every possible mode of illustration, plain or abstracted, figurative or literal. (p. 7)

The chamois is his symbol for the spirit of prose: its leaping delicacy and wild alpine grace are the equivalent of the nightingale's darkling song.

Burke's style is Hazlitt's inspiration, and throughout his writing career he turns to Burke whom he obsessively and at times extravagantly castigates, praises, denounces and admires. His mixed, highly complicated, attitude to Burke's style shows in the way the term 'Bristol stone' seems to define all that Burke's style is not, until we remember that Burke was MP for Bristol, then he lost his seat when he asserted the principle that a member of parliament must vote according to his conscience, not according to the wishes of his constituents. The image is in a sense contradictory, and when we trace the image of Burke's prose passing yawning gulfs, 'on the unsteadfast footing of a spear' we can see a similar contradiction. Hazlitt catches the style's headlong momentum by alluding to Worcester's speech to the angry Hotspur early in *Henry IV, Part 1*:

Worcester: And now I will unclasp a secret book,
    And to your quick-conceiving discontents
    I'll read you matter deep and dangerous,
    As full of peril and adventurous spirit
    As to o'erwalk a current roaring loud
    On the unstedfast footing of a spear.
Hotspur: If he fall in, good night, or sink, or swim!
    Send danger from the east unto the west,
    So honour cross it from the north to south,
    And let them grapple. O, the blood more stirs
    To rouse a lion than to start a hare!

So Burke is vehement, impatient, combative, headstrong, morally passionate and wildly impolitic like Hotspur – his prose style is a weapon unstably bridging the current of history. He, too, is a doomed, chivalric anachronism, loud and noisy and undeviating like the river. The single line of Shakespeare catches the propulsive, balancing-by-keeping-moving and therefore potentially unbalanced nature of Burke's armed style. Placed in context, the line keys a whole composite of qualities, chief among them the noise, the rush, the danger in the historical process.

There is a similar image in Hazlitt's 1817 character of Burke, where he argues that it is Burke's

> impatience to transfer his conceptions entire, living, in all their rapidity, strength, and glancing variety, to the minds of others, that constantly pushes him to the verge of extravagance, and yet supports him there in dignified security –

> > Never so sure our rapture to create,
> > As when he treads the brink of all we hate.

What he's stressing is the current of existential danger in Burke's style, the way he is forever on the brink of transgressing barriers, and the excitement this creates in the reader through the animation of his language, its direct intensity.

Anticipating his remark that prose works its most striking effects out of 'the most unpromising materials', Hazlitt immediately offers an image of its self-delighting airiness in that other cliffhanging passage I quoted from earlier:

> It differs from poetry, as I conceive, like the chamois from the eagle: it climbs to an almost equal height, touches upon a cloud, overlooks a precipice, is picturesque, sublime – but all the while, instead of soaring through the air, it stands upon a rocky cliff, clambers up by abrupt and intricate ways, and browses on the roughest bark, or crops the tender flower. The principle which guides his pen is truth, not beauty – not pleasure, but power. (p. 7)

The image of the Coriolanian eagle he has applied to Burke's style elsewhere, but here he denies it in order to offer the more

interesting figure of the chamois, whose Alpine habitat immediately
introduces the idea of the Romantic poet, an idea which also counters
his argument that this prose is not quite poetry (the subtle rhyme
browses flower power assists the contradiction). There is a similar moment in a novel Hazlitt knew and admired, Godwin's *St Leon*, where
the central character climbs up into the Alps:

> The wildness of an untamed and savage scene best accorded with the
> temper of my mind. I sprung from cliff to cliff among the points of
> the rock. I rushed down precipices that to my sobered sense appeared
> in a manner perpendicular, and only preserved my life, with a sort of
> inborn and unelective care, by catching at the roots and shrubs which
> occasionally broke the steepness of the descent. I hung over the tops
> of the rocks still more fearful in their declivities, and courted the gid-
> diness and whirls of spirit which such spectacles are accustomed to
> produce.

Even closer, though, is this speech which Caesar delivers early in *Antony
and Cleopatra*:

> Antony,
> Leave thy lascivious wassails. When thou once
> Was beaten from Modena, and where thou slew'st
> Hirtius and Pansa, consuls, at thy heel
> Did famine follow, whom thou fought'st against
> (Though daintily brought up) with patience more
> Than savages would suffer. Thou didst drink
> The stale of horses and the gilded puddle
> Which beasts would cough at. Thy palate then did
>   deign
> The roughest berry on the rudest hedge.
> Yea, like the stag when snow the pasture sheets,
> The barks of trees thou browsed. On the Alps
> It is reported thou didst eat strange flesh,
> Which some did die to look on. And all this
> (It wounds thine honor that I speak it now)
> Was borne so like a soldier that thy cheek
> So much as lanked not.

Hazlitt's chamois, like Antony, browses on the bark of trees – noticing the allusion we see that Hazlitt's symbol isn't simply irenic, because there is a mighty general shadowing it, in fact there are two generals. We are back with Napoleon, crossing the Alps, on his way to conquer Italy.

For Hazlitt, a historical prose style is constantly moving, changing, taking risks, pushing against obstacles. As readers, he asks us to admire and enjoy the expressive movement of prose. Citing the etymologist and radical politician Horne Tooke, he explains how true prose is textured by speech and conversation:

> Horne Tooke used to maintain that no one could write a good prose style, who was not accustomed to express himself *viva voce*, or to talk in company. He argued that this was the fault of Addison's prose, and that its smooth, equable uniformity, and want of sharpness and spirit, arose from his not having familiarized his ear to the sound of his own voice, or at least only among friends and admirers, where there was but little collision, dramatic fluctuation, or sudden contrariety of opinion to provoke animated discussion, and give birth to different intonations and lively transitions of speech. His style (in this view of it) was not indented, nor did it project from the surface. There was no stress laid on one word more than another – it did not hurry on or stop short, or sink or swell with the occasion: it was throughout equally insipid, flowing, and harmonious, and had the effect of a studied recitation rather than of a natural discourse. (pp. 2–3)

The 'lively transitions' of speech, the 'indented' nature of true prose, is imaged in the later passage by the leaping chamois clambering up a rocky cliff 'by abrupt and intricate ways'. And the image of the chamois browsing on the 'roughest bark' is another image of the indented texture of prose, as well as an image of the fact that the prose writer has to deal with 'dry matters of fact and close reasoning' – has to 'marshal' facts, as we say, like a general. In a sense, prose is rather like Louis Simpson's definition of American poetry:

> Whatever it is, it must have
> A stomach that can digest
> Rubber, coal, uranium, moons, poems.

Like the shark, it contains a shoe.
It must swim for miles through the desert
Uttering cries that are almost human.

As Hazlitt says of Burke, he had to 'treat of political questions, mixed modes, abstract ideas' – these are the pieces of dry, very rough bark, the chunks of rubber and scrap metal, that prose must both digest and embody.

If we consider the idea that this aesthetic of prose involves a concept of recycling various different and recalcitrant forms of discourse, then a passage in 'The Old Age of Artists' reveals how great criticism uses illustration and image in the manner of symbolist poetry to represent its essence, its unique self:

Mr Fuseli's conversation is more striking and extravagant, but less pleasing and natural than Mr Northcote's. He deals in paradoxes and caricatures. He talks allegories and personifications, as he paints them. You are sensible of effort without any repose – no careless pleasantry – no traits of character or touches from nature – everything is laboured or overdone. His ideas are gnarled, hard, and distorted, like his features – his theories stalking and straddle-legged, like his gait – his projects aspiring and gigantic, like his gestures – his performance uncouth and dwarfish, like his person. His pictures are also like himself, with eyeballs of stone stuck in rims of tin, and muscles twisted together like ropes or wires. Yet Fuseli is undoubtedly a man of genius, and capable of the most wild and grotesque combinations of fancy. It is a pity that he ever applied himself to painting, which must always be reduced to the test of the senses. He is a little like Dante or Ariosto, perhaps; but no more like Michael Angelo, Raphael, or Correggio, than I am. Nature, he complains, puts him out. Yet he can laugh at artists who 'paint ladies with iron lapdogs', and he describes the great masters of old in words or lines full of truth, and glancing from a pen or tongue of fire. I conceive any person would be more struck with Mr Fuseli at first sight, but would wish to visit Mr Northcote oftener. There is a bold and startling outline in his style of talking, but not the delicate finishing or bland tone that there is in that of the latter. Whatever there is harsh or repulsive about him is, however, in a great degree carried off by his animated foreign accent and broken English, which give character where there is none, and soften its asperities where it is too abrupt and violent. (pp. 72–3)

This is a very interesting sketch of Fuseli, one of the many passages in Hazlitt's criticism which use his own experience as a portrait painter as the basis for his prose aesthetic.

The Shandyish dashes appropriately give a spoken improvisatory texture to the sentence, an extempore effect that's developed further when he suddenly makes the artist into a kind of Frankensteinian monster whose pictures are also 'like himself'. Like a modernist sculpture, a piece of *bricolage*, Fuseli lurches into a kind of artificial life.

This characterization of Fuseli is a brief, dashed-off moment in the essay, but I want to consider it at some length because it may be another figure for Hazlitt's critical art. Like Frankenstein, like Fuseli, he seeks to make something out of pre-existing materials – books, plays, pictures, allusions, quotations, critical terms, all sorts of phrases and scraps. What he designs isn't planned *a priori*, but comes into existence spontaneously. His centos or critical collages are thrown together quickly from bits and pieces that are to hand.

Here it's worth considering this technique in relation to more recent accounts of the nature of literary criticism. In particular, Gérard Genette's discussion of its relationship to Claude Lévi-Strauss's definition of mythical thought as a kind of *bricolage* that always makes use of materials and tools that, unlike those of the engineer, say, 'were not intended for the task in hand'. Applying this insight to the practice of literary criticism, Genette points out that literary criticism distinguishes itself formally from, say, art criticism or music criticism by the fact that it uses the same materials – writing – as the works with which it is concerned. It is therefore a 'metalanguage' or 'discourse upon a discourse', as Barthes terms it. Which means that original writers belong to nature, critics to culture. Hazlitt's obsession with 'nature' as a critical term represents his agonized desire to cross the apparently absolute divide between the two. Fuseli, in his characterization of him, becomes a figure for the critic who takes, say, a sentence from Burke, a phrase from Milton, an image from Shakespeare, an account of a painting by Poussin, and binds them together into an argument about, say, the nature of prose style. Those same images might also be applied in an essay on Indian jugglers, Kean's Iago, or the ignorance of the learned, or what ever subject he happens to be addressing and where they might be appropriate – or might be made to appear appropriate.

If we set to one side the concept of the original, fixed aesthetic masterpiece and concentrate on the argument's process, on the business of assembling a paragraph or an essay, we can watch the critical act taking place as a form of creativity, rather than as a subsidiary gesture. It's like pasting up a collage or making a bowl out of *papier mâché* or having a conversation in a studio.

Commenting on this concept of *bricolage*, Amit Chaudhuri describes how the plaster original of Picasso's sculpture *The She-Goat* was constructed from a wicker-basket, palm leaves, scraps of iron and ceramic pots which represented the goat's belly, backbone, ribs, shoulder and udder. What is remarkable, Chaudhuri notes, is that even in the 'finished' – really never finished – product, the 'materials of creation', the process of construction and making, the peculiar pathos and joy of gradual creation, are left open to view. The effect of this is to deny the idea that the final structure came into perfect form by inspiration, genius or 'an automatic authorial magic.' For example, when Lawrence describes a bat as having 'long, black paper ears' or a tortoise as having a mouth like 'sudden curved scissors,' he's substituting improvisation and process for static description. If we compare this anti-aesthetic with Hazlitt's characterization of Fuseli, we may note that while he immediately adds that Fuseli is 'undoubtedly a man of genius', he has raised the question of improvisation in a manner which denies traditional ideas of pure, plenary inspiration. What he communicates is the hectic, driven nature of the creative process – its use of the makeshift, the ready-to-hand.

Ted Hughes similarly celebrates Shakespeare's gift for improvising language, and in *Moortown Diary* praises his father-in-law, the farmer Jack Orchard, who was 'equal to any job, any crisis, using the most primitive means, adapting and improvising with any old bit of metal'. And we can see this all-off-the-top-of-the-head spontaneity in Lawrence's line 'I say untarnished, but I mean opaque' – a perfect iambic pentameter disguised as a sudden second-thought revision interjected immediately after the slightly sluggish lines which open 'Bare Fig Trees':

Fig-trees, weird fig-trees
Made of thick, smooth silver,
Made of sweet, untarnished silver in the sea-southern air –
I say untarnished, but I mean opaque.

Lawrence abandons these lines by suddenly substituting 'opaque' for 'untarnished', and so making the poem run in a much more natural and improvised manner, while at the same time stressing the metallic, man-made and therefore not in the least natural qualities of the fig trees.

If we take Hughes on the way farmers adapt old metal scraps, Hazlitt on the tin-like Fuseli, Lawrence on silver-smooth fig trees, as symbolic of the process of creating a work of art or a critical essay, then we can see that they share an aim to break down the barrier between criticism and artistic creation. The dissenting culture that nurtured them is suspicious of finished or overly perfect works of art, and values instead the utile, the recycled, the improvised and economical. Hazlitt wasn't good with money, but he was able to circulate and recirculate the wealth of quotations he had banked from his early reading. The Kurt Schwitters of literary criticism, he pastes up his centos and abandons them rapidly. But he can make repeated lines from Shakespeare or Burke sound like his own signature phrases. Curiously, T. S. Eliot does something similar in *The Waste Land*, where a line from Marvell can reverberate with a snatch of overheard conversation or a fragment of stage dialogue to produce an effect that's meant to resemble an orchestra tuning up, an effect which in turn alludes for support to a modernist musical composition Eliot admired enormously – Stravinsky's *Rite of Spring*. Despite the apparently recondite or élitist nature of the references in Eliot, the cento is a highly democratic form of art because it transforms bits and pieces of cultural scrap into a new type of broken or dissonant form, which allows the audience to participate in the process of assembling the diverging components.

In his account of Lawrence's imagination, Chaudhuri argues that the dichotomy which 'almost always' exists in Western culture between the interpretative and aesthetic functions is often 'dissolved' in Lawrence's writing. Instead, his criticism '*enters*, textually, the work being looked at, plays with it, imitates it, takes on its characteristics,' so that interpretation can't stay separate from creativity. Chaudhuri's comment issues from an impatience with the founding tropes of Western criticism – sight and hearing. Following Derrida, he argues that those senses are 'antithetical to desire' and naturally lend themselves to 'distancing, clarity, logic, perspective,

and the ideal'. The more physically immediate senses which are
excluded as 'tropes of understanding' – touch and taste – would
lend themselves to an aesthetic of 'sensation, collision, eroticism
and the surface'. Hazlitt's frequent invocation of the body in his
criticism, his pervasive recourse to boxing and racket playing as
figures for prose style, are an attempt to put sensation and physical
impact at the centre of his writing – every word should be a blow,
every hit should tell. And, as we have seen in 'The Prose-Style of
Poets', Addison's prose is not 'indented' and does not 'project
from the surface'. The sensuous texture communicates that erotics
of prose style which is such a rubbed, tactile feature of Hazlitt's
writing and which links him to Hindu aesthetics. Both Chaudhuri
and Hazlitt use the term 'collision' to express the at times erotic
abrasiveness this aesthetic values. Chaudhuri points out that in Indian poetry, painting and music, the operative critical term is *rasa*
or 'juice'. The person who responds to a work of art would inevita-
bly taste its juice or flavour, and here, 'taste' relates less to the up-
per-class British usage, than to appetite, so this is an aesthetic that
'admits of desire'.

Interestingly, Hazlitt in his criticism of contemporary utilitarian
reformers argues that their 'intellectual food does not assimilate with
the juices of the mind'. Similarly, in the dialogue essay 'On Envy' he
praises Northcote's manner of discussing Titian: 'your discourse has
an extreme unction about it, a marrowiness like his colouring' (p.
84). The idea of the unguent, the oily, the juicy, must have been
current in Hazlitt's circle because it's also present in an epicurean
letter Charles Lamb wrote to his friend, the Orientalist Thomas
Manning, in which he savours 'the unctuous and palate-soothing
flesh of geese wild and tame'.

Although the adjective is now wholly pejorative, it previously sig-
nified deep spiritual feeling and was associated with the sacred: 'But
ye have an unction from the Holy One, and ye know all things'. As
Hazlitt employs it, unctuousness is a quality that opposes the 'dry,
meagre, penurious' imagination which he dislikes in 'captious and
scrutinizing' Protestant culture (p. 138). In the same essay, 'Hot
and Cold', he contrasts north European repugnance and shame with
the behaviour of southern Europeans:

The Italians, Spaniards, and people of the south swarm alive without
being sick or sorry at the circumstance: they hunt the accustomed
prey in each other's tangled locks openly in the streets and on the
highways, without manifesting shame or repugnance: combs are an
invention of our northern climes. Now I can comprehend this, when
I look at the dirty, dingy, greasy, sunburnt complexion of an Italian
peasant or beggar, whose body seems alive all over with a sort of tingling, oily sensation, so that from any given particle of his shining skin
to the beast 'whose name signifies love' the transition is but small.
This populousness is not unaccountable where all teems with life, where
all is glowing and in motion, and every pore thrills with an exuberance of feeling. Not so in the dearth of life and spirit, in the drossy,
dry, material texture, the clear complexions and fair hair of the Saxon
races, where the puncture of an insect's sting is a solution of their
personal identity, and the idea of life attached to and courting an
intimacy with them in spite of themselves, naturally produces all the
revulsions of the most violent antipathy and nearly drives them out of
their wits. How well the smooth ivory comb and auburn hair agree –
while the Greek *dandy*, on entering a room, applies his hand to brush
a cloud of busy stragglers from his hair like powder, and gives himself
no more concern about them than about the motes dancing in the
sunbeams! The dirt of the Italians is as it were baked into them, and
so ingrained as to become a part of themselves, and occasion no discontinuity of their being. (pp. 131–2)

It's important, as I've argued, to trace Hazlitt's quotations, because
they are often more than merely decorative – instead, they take us
into the deepest recesses of his imagination. In this passage, he is
discussing the erotic fascination he feels for all that is dirty, dingy,
greasy, sunburnt, southern, and he introduces an allusion to this passage from *The Merry Wives of Windsor*:

Slender: They may give their dozen white luces in their coat.
Shallow: It is an old coat.
Evans: The dozen white louses do become an old coat well.
        It agrees well, passant; it is a familiar beast to man, and signifies
love.
Shallow: The luce is the fresh fish. The salt fish is an old coat.
                        (Shakespeare, *The Merry Wives of Windsor* I. i. 15–21)

Alluding to Evans's statement, Hazlitt uses Shakespeare as a way of imbuing his observations with authority, familiarity and a witty suggestiveness.

Elsewhere, Hazlitt praises the 'heavy, dingy, slimy effect' of various oil paints, and he also remarks on the 'tingling' effect on the eye that Titian's paintings have, so he is drawing on both the materials from which art is made, as well as on the erotic experience of creating and experiencing art. As always in Hazlitt, the body is a figure for prose, and it is significant that he states 'an author had better try the effect of his sentences on his stomach rather than his ear'. For Hazlitt, good prose is like boxing: 'every word should be a blow: every thought should instantly grapple with its fellow'. The tiny, almost invisible pararhyme *blow/fellow* makes this into the prose equivalent of a rhyming couplet, though really, as we have seen with Lawrence's 'Bare Fig Trees', it's with free verse that the true analogy lies. But the problem is that to imagine a poetics of free verse is to contemplate an even more unvisited subject than the aesthetics of prose style. We arrive here at something that feels like the margins of criticism, an area that may seem defunct, almost hopelessly old-fashioned, yet at the same time is one that contains the possibility of extending the sensuous pleasure we take in art by finding a vocabulary for the *techne* of prose.

Again and again, Hazlitt's image for prose writing is that of a journey, i.e. a process that by its very nature is incomplete. Take his criticism of Coleridge's prose:

> The simple truth does not satisfy him – no direct proposition fills up the moulds of his understanding. All is foreign, far-fetched, irrelevant, laboured, unproductive. To read one of his disquisitions is like hearing the variations to a piece of music without the score. Or, to vary the simile, he is not like a man going a journey by the stage-coach along the high road, but is always getting into a balloon, and mounting into the air, above the plain ground of prose. (p. 13)

The Plain Speaker takes its stand on that plain ground – it can do no other – and it seeks always to give a grounded quality, a being to prose which in its combination of the abstract and the concrete perhaps needs the terms *Grund* and *Dasein* to express Hazlitt's aesthetic of the 'severity' of prose composition. This aesthetic produces terms such as 'momentum', 'vehemence', 'natural', 'direct', 'spirited', 'elasticity', and it insists that the prose writer's task precludes 'continual beauty'. Prose is disjunctive, not all of a piece – it has to dig ditches, crush rock, or in Yeats's image for the fascinating difficulties of verse-writing, 'lash, strain, sweat and jolt/As though it dragged road-metal'.

But if prose cannot be continuously beautiful, it does not 'preclude continual ingenuity, force, originality'. The writer of prose

> works the most striking effects out of the most unpromising materials, by the mere activity of his mind. He rises with the lofty, descends with the mean, luxuriates in beauty, gloats over deformity. It is all the same to him, so that he loses no particle of the exact, characteristic, extreme impression of the thing he writes about . . . (p. 7)

For Hazlitt, the prose writer 'always mingles clay with his gold', and often separates truth from 'mere pleasure'. What he is delineating is in a sense a puritan anti-poetics of prose where 'nothing can be admitted by way of ornament or relief, that does not add new force or clearness to the original conception' (p. 8). It is an ethic of continual aspiration – stretch, elasticity, sinew, muscle, are the images he often employs for the process which is prose composition. That process is given a physical feel, a grounded or worked-in quality, like when we roll putty till it gets warm, sweaty, linseedy, before we press it round a new pane of glass in a window-frame. Thus, Burke's execution, 'like that of all good prose, savours of the texture of what he describes, and his pen slides or drags over the ground of his subject, like the painter's pencil' (p. 10). By 'pencil' Hazlitt means brush – the prose writer is like a painter working oil into his canvas and enjoying the mesh of hair, oil, pigment, rough canvas.

All the essays in *The Plain Speaker* are on one level rhapsodies to prose composition – they invite us to share the critic's enjoyment of his art, and they ask us to share the texture of his prose so that 'every pore thrills with an exuberance of feeling'. Where a poet, Hazlitt argues, is the 'slave of his style', the prose writer is the 'master of his materials'.

It is the heated, active struggle with those materials that fascinates Hazlitt, and in 'Application to Study' he extemporizes a hymn to that process:

I do not conceive rapidity of execution necessarily implies slovenliness or crudeness. On the contrary, I believe it is often productive both of sharpness and freedom. The eagerness of composition strikes out sparkles of fancy, and runs the thoughts more naturally and closely into one another. There may be less formal method, but there is more life, and spirit, and truth. In the play and agitation of the mind, it runs over, and we dally with the subject, as the glass-blower rapidly shapes the vitreous fluid. A number of new thoughts rise up spontaneously, and they come in the proper places, because they arise from the occasion. They are also sure to partake of the warmth and vividness of that ebullition of mind, from which they spring. *Spiritus precipitandus est.* In these sort of voluntaries in composition, the thoughts are worked up to a state of projection: the grasp of the subject, the presence of mind, the flow of expression must be something akin to *extempore* speaking; or perhaps such bold but finished draughts may be compared to *fresco* paintings, which imply a life of study and great previous preparation, but of which the execution is momentary and irrevocable. I will add a single remark on a point that has been much disputed. Mr Cobbett lays it down that the first word that occurs is always the best. I would venture to differ from so great an authority. Mr Cobbett himself indeed writes as easily and as well as he talks; but he perhaps is hardly a rule for others without his practice and without his ability. In the hurry of composition three or four words may present themselves, one on the back of the other, and the last may be the best and right one. I grant thus much, that it is in vain to seek for the word we want, or endeavour to get at it second-hand, or as a paraphrase on some other word – it must come of itself, or arise out of an immediate impression or lively intuition of the subject; that is, the proper word must be suggested immediately by the thoughts, but it need not be presented as soon as called for. It is the same in trying to recollect the names of places, persons, etc. We cannot force our memory; they must come of themselves by natural association, as it were; but they may occur to us when we least think of it, owing to some casual circumstance or link of connection, and long after we have given up the search. Proper expressions rise to the surface from the heat and fermentation of the mind, like bubbles on an agitated stream. It is this which produces a clear and sparkling style. (pp. 60–1)

The illuminated transparency – a magic lantern slide – and the fragile glistening bubble made of glass or water are favourite images in Hazlitt for journalism. They catch its written-to-the-moment ephemerality,

and belong to a symbolic network which seeks to invest prose composition with power and authority. We imagine the poet in a lonely
tower, but Hazlitt wants us to have a vision of the journalist writing
to a deadline, committed to keeping free speech alive. The prose
writer – plain-spoken, unbuttoned, direct, emphatic – is therefore a
civic hero for Hazlitt. He asks us to see the critic and journalist as the
fiery heart of a living culture, and he asks us to participate in the
'stimulus of writing' which is like the 'stimulus of intoxication'.

> While we are engaged in any work, we are thinking of the subject, and
> cannot stop to admire ourselves; and when it is done, we look at it
> with comparative indifference. I will venture to say, that no one but a
> pedant ever read his own works regularly through. They are not *his* –
> they are become mere words, wastepaper, and have none of the glow,
> the creative enthusiasm, the vehemence, and natural spirit with which
> he wrote them. When we have once committed our thoughts to pa-
> per, written them fairly out, and seen that they are right in the print-
> ing, if we are in our right wits, we have done with them forever. I
> sometimes try to read an article I have written in some magazine or
> review (for when they are bound up in a volume, I dread the very
> sight of them) but stop after a sentence or two, and never recur to the
> task. I know pretty well what I have to say on the subject, and do not
> want to go to school to myself. It is the worst instance of the *bis
> repetita crambe* in the world. I do not think that even painters have
> much delight in looking at their works after they are done. While they
> are in progress, there is a great degree of satisfaction in considering
> what has been done, or what is still to do – but this is hope, is reverie,
> and ceases with the completion of our efforts. I should not imagine
> Raphael or Correggio would have much pleasure in looking at their
> former works, though they might recollect the pleasure they had had
> in painting them; they might spy defects in them (for the idea of un-
> attainable perfection still keeps pace with our actual approaches to it),
> and fancy that they were not worthy of immortality. The greatest por-
> trait-painter the world ever saw used to write under his pictures,
> '*Titianus faciebat*', signifying that they were imperfect; and in his let-
> ter to Charles V accompanying one of his most admired works, he
> only spoke of the time he had been about it. (p. 99)

Frequently, Hazlitt employs Titian's signature as a symbol of the
unfinished process which is prose composition. The analogy for me

is with action painting: 'I don't paint nature', Jackson Pollock said, 'I am nature'. At some deep level, the Scots–Irish culture which formed the painter and the critic shape this insistence on intense, natural action.

What Hazlitt aims for is a style which, as he says of his hero Burke, is 'communicative, diffuse, magnificent'. By reclaiming *The Plain Speaker* – by inhabiting these essays – we begin to bring one of the masters of English prose back into the light.

Editor's Note

William Hazlitt (1778–1830)

William Hazlitt was born on 10 April 1778, in Maidstone in Kent,[1] where his father, William Hazlitt Sr (1737–1820), was a Unitarian minister. Hazlitt Sr was the correspondent of two distinguished fellow-Unitarians, Richard Price and Benjamin Franklin, and it was no doubt at their urging that, in 1783, the family moved to America, where he preached at Philadelphia and Boston. Returning in 1784, they settled in Wem, Shropshire, where Hazlitt's education was supervised by his father. At fifteen he went to the Unitarian College in Hackney to prepare for the ministry. He read widely in philosophy, from Locke to Godwin, and came under the influence of radical thinkers like Helvetius and Holbach. This led him to renounce all expectation of a life in the ministry for a career as a philosopher, for which he returned to Wem in 1797.

On 14 January 1798 Coleridge preached a sermon at the Unitarian chapel in Shrewsbury; Hazlitt (aged 17) was there to hear him, and fell under his spell immediately. Coleridge spent the following night with the Hazlitts, and the next morning received a letter from the Wedgwoods offering him an annuity of £150 a year for life, thus relieving him from the need to become a minister.[2] Coleridge re-

---

1 The Unitarian chapel where Hazlitt Sr preached still stands, and the local museum contains a number of his son's paintings.
2 All this is related, more effectively, by Hazlitt, in 'My First Acquaintance with Poets', *Romanticism: An Anthology (Second Edition)* ed. Duncan Wu (Oxford, 1998), pp. 600–10.

turned to Nether Stowey, urging Hazlitt to visit him there. Hazlitt did so, and through him met Wordsworth and Charles Lamb – with the latter making a friendship that would change his life for ever. To Alfoxden he brought the manuscript of his *Essay on the Principles of Human Action* (published 1805), a lengthy disquisition on some of the ideas in David Hartley's *Observations on Man* (1749, 1791) that underlay *The Recluse*. He seems to have discussed it at some length with Wordsworth, appearing 'somewhat unreasonably attached to modern books of moral philosophy'; their exchanges provided the inspiration for Wordsworth's *Expostulation and Reply* and *The Tables Turned*.

By this time Hazlitt wanted to be a painter, and studied with his elder brother John, who was a pupil of Reynolds. During the Peace of Amiens, 1802–3, he went to Paris and copied a number of paintings in the Louvre. In 1808 he married Sarah Stoddart, a friend of the Lambs, and at her cottage in Winterslow, near Salisbury, he began to write. In 1812 he moved his wife and son to London, where he delivered lectures, first on philosophy and then on literature, all of which he published subsequently. At around this time he relinquished his hope of being a painter. Instead, he made his name writing parliamentary reports and theatrical criticism for the *Morning Chronicle*; his drama reviews were collected in 1818 as *A View of the English Stage* – unquestionably the most important book about drama in the Romantic period. It contains the best record we have of the performances of Kean, Macready, Kemble and Siddons.

Further commissions poured in, and Hazlitt became one of the most sought-after journalists in the field, being recruited by Leigh Hunt for *The Examiner* and John Scott for the *London Magazine*. It was not just that he had developed one of the most delicious prose styles in literature, but that his judgements on whatever topic – philosophical, political, cultural, literary – were sharp, shrewd and brilliantly expressed. He possessed, above all, a precision of manner and thought with which he was able to trace the exact profile of the various intellects of the age. No other non-fiction prose writer had the same flawless combination of wit and technique. A series of unmatched collections of essays and lectures poured from him in the first decades of the nineteenth century – notably, *Characters of Shakespeare's Plays* (1817), *The Round Table* (1817, with Leigh Hunt),

Lectures on the English Poets (1818), *Lectures on the English Comic Writers* (1819), *Political Essays* (1819), *Lectures on the Dramatic Literature of the Age of Elizabeth* (1821), *Table-Talk* (1821–2), *Liber Amoris* (1823), *The Spirit of the Age* (1825) and *The Plain Speaker* (1826). He placed enormous hope in his final work, the huge four-volume *Life of Napoleon* (1826–30). It was largely quarried from the work of others, but those passages by Hazlitt are written with his distinctive brilliance. He died having just completed it, in 1830, destitute, but with his old friend, Charles Lamb, at his side. He was 52.

The Plain Speaker

The Plain Speaker (1826) is written with characteristic passion, and displays Hazlitt's erudition and wit to fine effect in some of his most important essays: 'On the Prose-Style of Poets', 'On the Conversation of Authors', 'On Reason and Imagination' and 'On Envy', to name just a few. And yet most of its component parts were written during a period of immense turmoil and unhappiness in Hazlitt's life. In mid-August 1820 Hazlitt took up his new lodgings in 9 Southampton Buildings, where his landlord was a tailor called Walker. It was on the 16th that he first saw his landlord's daughter, Sarah.[3] He seems to have fallen in love with her immediately, and in the following year sought to divorce his wife, so as to marry her. The divorce, which he obtained in Scotland, was granted only after a series of tormenting delays and legal tangles, on 17 July 1822, by which time he was beginning to suspect that Sarah was not seriously interested in him. On 29 July he discovered confirmation of her preference for another of her father's lodgers, Tomkins. This story is told in painful detail by Hazlitt in *Liber Amoris* (1823), which draws freely on letters written while these events were taking place. The clean break that is implied in the closing pages of that volume never took place, however; Hazlitt continued to be tortured by his obsession. As late as March 1823 he arranged for a friend to attempt to seduce her in order to obtain final, conclusive proof that Sarah was no longer inclined towards him.

---

3 By far the most sympathetic and perceptive account of this meeting is provided by Stanley Jones, *Hazlitt: A Life* (Oxford, 1989), pp. 310–14.

It was one thing to have written about these matters, but something quite else to publish the result. He must have known he was taking a risk: after years of castigating Tory politicians and placemen, Hazlitt had accumulated a large party of political enemies who wasted no time in using *Liber Amoris* as a weapon against him. Even though it had been issued anonymously, Hazlitt's identity was soon revealed, and the volume brought down upon him a firestorm of vilification and invective. He married a second time and left the country for an extended tour of the Continent. While in Paris he published some of the *Plain Speaker* essays in a volume called *Table-Talk* (2 vols, Paris, 1825). He kept working on the volume, and on his return set about the publication of *The Plain Speaker* in London. By this time, though young by twentieth-century standards, he was depressed and in poor health. *The Plain Speaker* was to be his last original collection of essays.

The Work and its Reception

The Plain Speaker was published on 28 April 1826[4] in two volumes. Keynes suggests that a large edition was printed and issued in a variety of bindings. But sales were bad; it was still available in 1840, when Templeman reduced its price from 24 shillings to 11 shillings.[5] It remains something of a mystery as to why such an important volume should have dropped still-born from the press. Certainly, Hazlitt had many enemies in the literary world, who, three years after the publication of *Liber Amoris*, would have taken pleasure in seeing *The Plain Speaker* fail. If this was their intention, it may be that they decided to damn it by ignoring it; I have managed to locate only five reviews, a very low number for a work of this kind.[6] Of the few critics

---

4 The dating is Stanley Jones's; see *Analytical and Enumerative Bibliography* 6 (1982), p. 276.
5 See Geoffrey Keynes, *Bibliography of William Hazlitt* (2nd edn, Godalming, 1981), p. 98.
6 *Monthly Review* 3rd ser., 2 (June 1826), pp. 113–22; *Atlas* (28 May 1826), pp. 26–7; *Companion* (12, 19 March 1828), pp. 113–28, 129–36 [by Leigh Hunt]; *Monthly Magazine* 2 (June 1826), pp. 206–7; *Star Chamber* 1 (17 May 1826), p. 105.

who did devote some space to a consideration of it, only one (Leigh Hunt) was remotely favourable. At any rate, *The Plain Speaker* received little attention on its first appearance, and, perhaps as a result, has never generated the same interest as *The Spirit of the Age*, *Liber Amoris* or even *The Round Table*. A second edition was edited by William Hazlitt Jr in 1851, and a third, edited by William Carew Hazlitt, in 1870. Since then, its only appearance besides the various collected editions of Hazlitt's works has been in the Everyman edition of 1928 (notes by Waller and Glover, introduction by P. P. Howe).

Only the best of the essays from the collection are presented here. In selecting them, we have given priority to those which reflect the central preoccupations of Hazlitt as a writer, and which are most likely to interest readers today. We have therefore had no qualms about omitting the essays on phrenology ('On Dr Spurzheim's Theory', 'On Dreams'), for instance, or those which relate only tangentially to the central themes of the book ('On Personal Character', 'On Respectable People', 'On Jealousy and Spleen of Party'). It is our hope that the final selection preserves the overall structure, and reflects the rich diversity of argument, of the two-volume collection from which it derives. The wider circulation of its essential contents will, we hope, encourage readers to seek out the complete *Plain Speaker* in the nine volume *Selected Writings of William Hazlitt* currently being prepared for publication by Pickering and Chatto in 1998.

Editorial Principles

The present text is designed for the use of students and the general reader, and editorial procedures are geared accordingly. The first edition of 1826 provides copy-text, but is not followed unquestioningly. Hazlitt took considerable care over his punctuation, and it has provided the basis for that of the present text. It is lightened where it might be thought too heavy for modern tastes; for instance, the dashes that Hazlitt sometimes placed after his full stops have been removed, as well as the less necessary commas and exclamation marks. However, editorial intervention has been conservative; Hazlitt's punctuation has remained the touchstone of the present text.

Orthography is modernized except in the case of proper nouns; thus, 'burthen' is modernized to 'burden', while 'Woolstonecroft' (for Wollstonecraft) is allowed to stand. Pervasive initial capitals have been eliminated, except where they are deployed for obvious rhetorical effect. Similarly, Hazlitt's italics have not been removed, and I have in fact italicized names of journals, novels and the like. Small capitals (often used as an alternative for italics) are retained only for effect; they are more usually rendered as italics. Rare typographical errors in the text have been silently corrected. I have not hesitated to fill blanks when the intended word is known; thus, 'L——' is turned into 'Lamb', and 'C——', 'Coleridge'. Words and phrases in languages other than English have not been emended in any way.

Although this is a selected text, the sequence of the essays is that of the 1826 edition, and all essays are complete in themselves. Dates of composition, where they can be verified, are provided underneath the title of each, with details of first publication, where applicable. As space is at a premium, this edition carries no annotation; those seeking the keys to Hazlitt's allusions, echoes, borrowings, and information concerning some of the events and issues mentioned along the way, will find a full set of notes in the Pickering and Chatto *Selected Writings of William Hazlitt*, where it comprises volume eight.

Further Reading

William Hazlitt ed. Harold Bloom (New York, 1986)
David Bromwich, *Hazlitt: The Mind of a Critic* (New York and Oxford, 1983)
Stanley Jones, *Hazlitt: A Life* (Oxford, 1991)
P.P. Howe, *The Life of William Hazlitt* (3rd edn, London, 1947)
Roy Park, *Hazlitt and the Spirit of the Age* (Oxford, 1971) .
Tom Paulin, *The Day-Star of Liberty: William Hazlitt and Radical Style* (London, 1998)

Acknowledgements

This edition derives from a lavishly annotated 'ideal' text, during work on which I incurred a number of debts to friends and colleagues, whom it is my pleasure to thank: John Beer, Heather and Robin Jackson, Michael Sharp, Brendan McLaughlin and David Chandler. I wish to thank Tina Gee, Curator of Keats House, Hampstead, and The Corporation of London, for permission to publish an extract from Reynolds's letter to Mary Leigh, 28 April 1817, in Appendix III. Stanley Jones has proved the most trustworthy of guides, and I am deeply grateful to him for the scholarly information he has vouchsafed to me on numerous matters concerning *The Plain Speaker* and Hazlitt in general. Tom Paulin initiated my work on Hazlitt and has proved an invaluable source of encouragement and support throughout.

My greatest debts are to the British Academy, which provided me with a research grant that freed me from tutorial responsibilities during work on this volume, and to Richard Cronin, my head of department at the University of Glasgow, and my colleagues there, who tolerated my absence with such good grace.

On the Prose-Style of Poets

COMPOSED AUGUST 1822

'Do you read or sing? If you sing, you sing very ill!'

I have but an indifferent opinion of the prose-style of poets: not that it is not sometimes good, nay, excellent; but it is never the better, and generally the worse from the habit of writing verse. Poets are winged animals, and can cleave the air, like birds, with ease to themselves and delight to the beholders; but like those 'feathered, two-legged things', when they light upon the ground of prose and matter-of-fact, they seem not to have the same use of their feet.

What is a little extraordinary, there is a want of *rhythmus* and cadence in what they write without the help of metrical rules. Like persons who have been accustomed to sing to music, they are at a loss in the absence of the habitual accompaniment and guide to their judgement. Their style halts, totters, is loose, disjointed, and without expressive pauses or rapid movements. The measured cadence and regular *sing-song* of rhyme or blank verse have destroyed, as it were, their natural ear for the mere characteristic harmony which ought to subsist between the sound and the sense. I should almost guess the author of *Waverley* to be a writer of ambling verses from the desultory vacillation and want of firmness in the march of his style. There is neither *momentum* nor elasticity in it; I mean as to the *score*, or effect upon the ear. He has improved since in his other works: to be sure, he has had practice enough.[1] Poets either get into this incoherent, undetermined, shuffling style, made up of 'unpleasing flats and sharps', of unaccountable starts and pauses, of doubtful odds and ends, flirted about like straws in a gust of wind; or, to avoid it and steady themselves, mount into a sustained and measured prose (like the translation of Ossian's *Poems*, or some parts of Shaftesbury's *Characteristics*) which is more odious still, and as bad as being at sea in a calm. Dr Johnson's style (particularly in his *Rambler*) is not free from the last objection. There is a tune in it, a mechanical recurrence of the same rise and fall in the clauses of his sentences, independent of any reference to the meaning of the text, or progress or inflection of the sense. There is the alternate roll of his cumbrous cargo of words; his periods complete their revolutions at certain stated intervals, let the matter be longer or shorter, rough or smooth, round or square, different or the same. This monotonous and balanced mode of composition may be compared to that species of portrait-painting which prevailed about a century ago, in which each face was cast in a regular and preconceived mould. The eyebrows were arched mathematically as if with a pair of compasses, and the distances between the nose and mouth, the forehead and chin, determined according to a 'foregone conclusion', and the features of the identical individual were afterwards accommodated to them, how they could![2]

Horne Tooke used to maintain that no one could write a good prose style, who was not accustomed to express himself *viva voce*, or to talk in company. He argued that this was the fault of Addison's prose, and that its smooth, equable uniformity, and want of sharpness and spirit, arose from his not having familiarized his ear to the sound of his own voice, or at least only among friends and admirers, where there was but little collision, dramatic fluctuation, or sudden contrariety of opinion to provoke animated discussion, and give birth to different intonations and lively transitions of speech. His style (in this view of it) was not indented, nor did it project from the surface. There was no stress laid on one word more than another – it did not

1   Is it not a collateral proof that Sir Walter Scott is the author of *Waverley*, that ever since these novels began to appear, his Muse has been silent, till the publication of *Halidon-Hill*?
2   See the portraits of Kneller, Richardson, and others.

hurry on or stop short, or sink or swell with the occasion: it was throughout equally insipid, flowing, and harmonious, and had the effect of a studied recitation rather than of a natural discourse. This would not have happened (so the Member for Old Sarum contended) had Addison laid himself out to argue at his club, or to speak in public; for then his ear would have caught the necessary modulations of sound arising out of the feeling of the moment, and he would have transferred them unconsciously to paper. Much might be said on both sides of this question:[3] but Mr Tooke was himself an unintentional confirmation of his own argument; for the tone of his written compositions is as flat and unraised as his manner of speaking was hard and dry. Of the poet it is said by someone, that

> He murmurs by the running brooks
> A music sweeter than their own.

On the contrary, the celebrated person just alluded to might be said to grind the sentences between his teeth, which he afterwards committed to paper, and threw out crusts to the critics, or *bon-mots* to the Electors of Westminster (as we throw bones to the dogs) without altering a muscle, and without the smallest tremulousness of voice or eye.[4] I certainly so far agree with the above theory as to conceive that no style is worth a farthing that is not calculated to be read out, or that is not allied to spirited conversation: but I at the same time think the process of modulation and inflection may be quite as complete, or more so, without the external enunciation; and that an author had better try the effect of his sentences on his stomach than on his ear. He may be deceived by the last, not by the first. No person, I imagine, can dictate a good style; or spout his own compositions with impunity. In the former case, he will flounder on

3 Goldsmith was not a talker, though he blurted out his good things now and then: yet his style is gay and voluble enough. Pope was also a silent man; and his prose is timid and constrained, and his verse inclining to the monotonous.

4 As a singular example of steadiness of nerves, Mr Tooke on one occasion had got upon the table at a public dinner to return thanks for his health having been drank. He held a bumper of wine in his hand, but he was received with considerable opposition by one party, and at the end of the disturbance, which lasted for a quarter of an hour, he found the wine glass still full to the brim.

before the sense or words are ready, sooner than suspend his voice in air; and in the latter, he can supply what intonation he pleases, without consulting his readers. Parliamentary speeches sometimes read well aloud; but we do not find, when such persons sit down to write, that the prose-style of public speakers and great orators is the best, most natural, or varied of all others. It has almost always either a professional twang, a mechanical rounding off, or else is stunted and unequal. Charles Fox was the most rapid and even *hurried* of speakers; but his written style halts and creeps slowly along the ground.[5] A speaker is necessarily kept within bounds in expressing certain things, or in pronouncing a certain number of words, by the limits of the breath or power of respiration: certain sounds are observed to join in harmoniously or happily with others: an emphatic phrase must not be placed, where the power of utterance is enfeebled or exhausted, etc. All this must be attended to in writing (and will be so unconsciously by a practised hand), or there will be *hiatus in manuscriptis*. The words must be so arranged, in order to make an efficient readable style, as 'to come trippingly off the tongue'. Hence it seems that there is a natural measure of prose in the feeling of the subject and the power of expression in the voice, as there is an artificial one of verse in the number and co-ordination of the syllables; and I conceive that the trammels of the last do not (where they have been long worn) greatly assist the freedom or the exactness of the first.

Again, in poetry, from the restraints in many respects, a greater number of inversions, or a latitude in the transposition of words is

5   I have been told, that when Sheridan was first introduced to Mr Fox, what cemented an immediate intimacy between them was the following circumstance. Mr Sheridan had been the night before to the House of Commons; and being asked what his impression was, said he had been principally struck with the difference of manner between Mr Fox and Lord Stormont. The latter began by declaring in a slow, solemn, drawling, nasal tone that 'when he considered the enormity and the unconstitutional tendency of the measures just proposed, he was hurried away in a torrent of passion and a whirlwind of impetuosity', pausing between every word and syllable; while the first said (speaking with the rapidity of lightning, and with breathless anxiety and impatience), that 'such was the magnitude, such the importance, such the vital interest of this question, that he could not help imploring, he could not help abjuring the House to come to it with the utmost calmness, the utmost coolness, the utmost deliberation.' This trait of discrimination instantly won Mr Fox's heart.

allowed, which is not conformable to the strict laws of prose. Consequently, a poet will be at a loss, and flounder about for the common or (as we understand it) *natural* order of words in prose-composition. Dr Johnson endeavoured to give an air of dignity and novelty to his diction by affecting the order of words usual in poetry. Milton's prose has not only this drawback, but it has also the disadvantage of being formed on a classic model. It is like a fine translation from the Latin; and indeed, he wrote originally in Latin. The frequency of epithets and ornaments, too, is a resource for which the poet finds it difficult to obtain an equivalent. A direct, or simple prose-style seems to him bald and flat; and, instead of forcing an interest in the subject by severity of description and reasoning, he is repelled from it altogether by the absence of those obvious and meretricious allurements, by which his senses and his imagination have been hitherto stimulated and dazzled. Thus there is often at the same time a want of splendour and a want of energy in what he writes, without the invocation of the Muse – *invita Minervâ*. It is like setting a ropedancer to perform a tumbler's tricks – the hardness of the ground jars his nerves; or it is the same thing as a painter's attempting to carve a block of marble for the first time – the coldness chills him, the colourless uniformity distracts him, the precision of form demanded disheartens him. So in prose-writing, the severity of composition required damps the enthusiasm, and cuts off the resources of the poet. He is looking for beauty, when he should be seeking for truth; and aims at pleasure, which he can only communicate by increasing the sense of power in the reader. The poet spreads the colours of fancy, the illusions of his own mind, round every object, *ad libitum*; the prose-writer is compelled to extract his materials patiently and bit by bit, from his subject. What he adds of ornament, what he borrows from the pencil, must be sparing, and judiciously inserted. The first pretends to nothing but the immediate indulgence of his feelings: the last has a remote practical purpose. The one strolls out into the adjoining fields or groves to gather flowers: the other has a journey to go, sometimes through dirty roads, and at others through untrodden and difficult ways. It is this effeminacy, this immersion in sensual ideas, or craving after continual excitement, that spoils the poet for his prose-tasks. He cannot wait till the effect comes of itself, or arises out of the occasion: he must force it upon all occasions, or his spirit droops and flags under a supposed imputation of dullness. He can never drift with the current, but is always hoisting sail, and has his streamers flying. He has got a striking simile on hand; he *lugs* it in with the first opportunity, and with little connection, and so defeats his object. He has a story to tell: he tells it in the first page, and where it would come in well, has nothing to say; like Goldsmith, who having to wait upon a Noble Lord, was so full of himself and of the figure he should make, that he addressed a set speech, which he had studied for the occasion, to his Lordship's butler, and had just ended as the nobleman made his appearance. The prose ornaments of the poet are frequently beautiful in themselves, but do not assist the subject. They are pleasing excrescences – hindrances, not helps in an argument. The reason is, his embellishments in his own walk grow out of the subject by natural association; that is, beauty gives birth to kindred beauty, grandeur leads the mind on to greater grandeur. But in treating a common subject, the link is truth, force of illustration, weight of argument, not a graceful harmony in the immediate ideas; and hence the obvious and habitual clue which before guided him is gone, and he hangs on his patchwork, tinsel finery at random, in despair, without propriety, and without effect. The poetical prose-writer stops to describe an object, if he admires it, or thinks it will bear to be dwelt on: the genuine prose-writer only alludes to or characterizes it in passing, and with reference to his subject. The prose-writer is master of his materials: the poet is the slave of his style. Everything showy, everything extraneous tempts him, and he reposes idly on it: he is bent on pleasure, not on business. He aims at effect, at captivating the reader, and yet is contented with commonplace ornaments, rather than none. Indeed, this last result must necessarily follow, where there is an ambition to shine, without the effort to dig for jewels in the mine of truth. The habits of a poet's mind are not those of industry or research: his images come to him, he does not go to them; and in prose-subjects, and dry matters of fact and close reasoning, the natural stimulus that at other times warms and rouses, deserts him altogether. He sees no unhallowed visions, he is inspired by no day-dreams. All is tame, literal, and barren, without the Nine. Nor does he collect his strength to strike fire from the flint by the sharpness of collision, by the eagerness of his blows. He gathers roses, he steals colours from the rainbow. He lives on nectar and ambrosia. He 'treads the primrose path of dalliance', or ascends 'the highest heaven of invention', or falls flat to the ground. *He is nothing, if not fanciful!*

I shall proceed to explain these remarks, as well as I can, by a few instances in point.

It has always appeared to me that the most perfect prose-style, the most powerful, the most dazzling, the most daring, that which went the nearest to the verge of poetry, and yet never fell over, was Burke's. It has the solidity, and sparkling effect of the diamond: all other *fine writing* is like French paste or Bristol-stones in the comparison. Burke's style is airy, flighty, adventurous, but it never loses sight of the subject; nay, is always in contact with, and derives its increased or varying impulse from it. It may be said to pass yawning gulfs 'on the unsteadfast footing of a spear': still it has an actual resting-place and tangible support under it – it is not suspended on nothing. It differs from poetry, as I conceive, like the chamois from the eagle: it climbs to an almost equal height, touches upon a cloud, overlooks a precipice, is picturesque, sublime – but all the while, instead of soaring through the air, it stands upon a rocky cliff, clambers up by abrupt and intricate ways, and browses on the roughest bark, or crops the tender flower. The principle which guides his pen is truth, not beauty – not pleasure, but power. He has no choice, no selection of subject to flatter the reader's idle taste, or assist his own fancy: he must take what comes, and make the most of it. He works the most striking effects out of the most unpromising materials, by the mere activity of his mind. He rises with the lofty, descends with the mean, luxuriates in beauty, gloats over deformity. It is all the same to him, so that he loses no particle of the exact, characteristic, extreme impression of the thing he writes about, and that he communicates this to the reader, after exhausting every possible mode of illustration, plain or abstracted, figurative or literal. Whatever stamps the original image more distinctly on the mind, is welcome. The nature of his task precludes continual beauty; but it does not preclude continual ingenuity, force, originality. He had to treat of political questions, mixed modes, abstract ideas, and his fancy (or poetry, if you will) was engrafted on these artificially, and as it might sometimes be thought, violently, instead of growing naturally out of them, as it would spring of its own accord from individual objects and feelings. There is a resistance in the *matter* to the illustration applied to it – the concrete and abstract are hardly co-ordinate; and therefore it is that, when the first difficulty is overcome, they must agree more closely in the essential qualities, in order that the coincidence may be complete. Otherwise, it is good for nothing; and you justly charge the author's style with being loose, vague, flaccid, and imbecile. The poet has been said

> To make us heirs
> Of truth and pure delight in endless lays.

Not so the prose-writer, who always mingles clay with his gold, and often separates truth from mere pleasure. He can only arrive at the last through the first. In poetry, one pleasing or striking image obviously suggests another: the increasing the sense of beauty or grandeur is the principle of composition: in prose, the professed object is to impart conviction, and nothing can be admitted by way of ornament or relief, that does not add new force or clearness to the original conception. The two classes of ideas brought together by the orator or impassioned prose-writer, to wit, the general subject and the particular image, are so far incompatible, and the identity must be more strict, more marked, more determinate, to make them coalesce to any practical purpose. Every word should be a blow: every thought should instantly grapple with its fellow. There must be a weight, a precision, a conformity from association in the tropes and figures of animated prose to fit them to their place in the argument, and make them *tell*, which may be dispensed with in poetry, where there is something much more congenial between the subject-matter and the illustration–

> Like beauty making beautiful old rime!

What can be more remote, for instance, and at the same time more apposite, more *the same*, than the following comparison of the English Constitution to 'the proud Keep of Windsor', in the celebrated *Letter to a Noble Lord*?

'Such are *their* ideas; such *their* religion, and such *their* law. But as to *our* country and *our* race, as long as the well-compacted structure of our church and state, the sanctuary, the holy of holies of that ancient law, defended by reverence, defended by power – a fortress at once and a temple[6] – shall stand inviolate on the brow of the British Sion; as long as the British Monarchy – not more limited than fenced by the orders of the State – shall, like the proud Keep of Windsor, rising in the majesty of proportion, and girt with the double belt of its kindred and coeval towers; as long as this awful structure shall oversee and guard the subjected land, so long the mounds and dykes of the low, fat, Bedford level will have nothing to fear from all the pickaxes of all the levellers of France. As long as our Sovereign Lord the King, and his faithful subjects, the Lords and Commons of this realm – the triple cord which no man can break; the solemn, sworn, constitutional frank-pledge of this nation; the firm guarantees of each other's being, and each other's rights; the joint and several securities, each in its place and order, for every kind and every quality of property and of dignity – as long as these endure, so long the Duke of Bedford is safe: and we are all safe together – the high from the blights of envy and the spoliations of rapacity; the low from the iron hand of oppression and the insolent spurn of contempt. Amen! and so be it: and so it will be,

Dum domus Æneæ Capitoli immobile axum Accolet; imperiumque pater Romanus habebit.

Nothing can well be more impracticable to a simile than the vague and complicated idea which is here embodied in one; yet how finely, how nobly it stands out, in natural grandeur, in royal state, with double barriers round it to answer for its identity, with 'buttress, frieze, and coigne of 'vantage' for the imagination to 'make its pendant bed and procreant cradle', till the idea is confounded with the object representing it – the wonder of a kingdom; and then how striking, how determined the descent, 'at one fell swoop', to the 'low, fat, Bedford level!' Poetry would have been bound to maintain a certain decorum, a regular balance between these two ideas; sterling prose throws aside all such idle respect to appearances, and with its pen, like a sword, 'sharp and sweet', lays open the naked truth!

6 '*Templum in modum arcis.*' TACITUS of the Temple of Jerusalem.

The poet's Muse is like a mistress, whom we keep only while she is young and beautiful, *durante bene placito*; the Muse of prose is like a wife, whom we take during life, *for better for worse*. Burke's execution, like that of all good prose, savours of the texture of what he describes, and his pen slides or drags over the ground of his subject, like the painter's pencil. The most rigid fidelity and the most fanciful extravagance meet, and are reconciled in his pages. I never pass Windsor but I think of this passage in Burke, and hardly know to which I am indebted most for enriching my moral sense, that or the fine picturesque stanza in Gray,

> From Windsor's heights the expanse below
> Of mead, of lawn, of wood survey, etc.

I might mention that the so much admired description in one of the India speeches, of Hyder Ally's army (I think it is) which 'now hung like a cloud upon the mountain, and now burst upon the plain like a thunderbolt', would do equally well for poetry or prose. It is a bold and striking illustration of a naturally impressive object. This is not the case with the Abbe Sieyes's far-famed 'pigeon-holes', nor with the comparison of the Duke of Bedford to 'the Leviathan, tumbling about his unwieldy bulk in the ocean of royal bounty'. Nothing here saves the description but the force of the invective; the startling truth, the vehemence, the remoteness, the aptitude, the perfect peculiarity and coincidence of the allusion. No writer would ever have thought of it but himself; no reader can ever forget it. What is there in common, one might say, between a Peer of the Realm, and 'that sea-beast', of those

> Created hugest that swim the ocean-stream?

Yet Burke has knit the two ideas together, and no man can put them asunder. No matter how slight and precarious the connection, the length of line it is necessary for the fancy to give out in keeping hold of the object on which it has fastened, he seems to have 'put his hook in the nostrils' of this enormous creature of the crown, that empurples all its track through the glittering expanse of a profound and restless imagination!

In looking into the *Iris* of last week, I find the following passages, in an article on the death of Lord Castlereagh.

'The splendour of Majesty leaving the British metropolis, careering along the ocean, and landing in the capital of the North, is distinguished only by glimpses through the dense array of clouds in which Death hid himself, while he struck down to the dust the stateliest courtier near the throne, and the broken train of which pursues and crosses the Royal progress wherever its glories are presented to the eye of imagination. . . .

'The same indefatigable mind – a mind of all work – which thus ruled the Continent with a rod of iron, the sword – within the walls of the House of Commons ruled a more distracted region with a more subtle and finely-tempered weapon, the tongue; and truly, if this *was* the only weapon his Lordship wielded there, where he had daily to encounter, and frequently almost alone, enemies more formidable than Buonaparte, it must be acknowledged that he achieved greater victories than Demosthenes or Cicero ever gained in far more easy fields of strife; nay, he wrought miracles of speech, outvying those miracles of song, which Orpheus is said to have performed, when not only men and brutes, but rocks, woods, and mountains, followed the sound of his voice and lyre. . . .

'But there was a worm at the root of the gourd that flourished over his head in the brightest sunshine of a court; both perished in a night, and in the morning, that which had been his glory and his shadow, covered him like a shroud; while the corpse, notwithstanding all his honours, and titles, and offices, lay unmoved in the place where it fell, till a judgment had been passed upon him, which the poorest peasant escapes when he dies in the ordinary course of nature.'

Sheffield Advertiser, Aug. 20, 1822

This, it must be confessed, is very unlike Burke: yet Mr Montgomery is a very pleasing poet, and a strenuous politician. The whole is *travelling out of the record*, and to no sort of purpose. The author is constantly getting away from the impression of his subject, to envelop himself in a cloud of images, which weaken and perplex, instead of adding force and clearness to it. Provided he is figurative, he does not care how commonplace or irrelevant the figures are, and he wanders on, delighted in a labyrinth of words, like a truant school-boy, who is only glad to have escaped from his task. He has a very slight hold of his subject, and is tempted to let it go for any fallacious ornament of style. How obscure and circuitous is the allusion to 'the clouds in which Death hid himself, to strike down the stateliest courtier near the throne!' How hackneyed is the reference to Demosthenes and Cicero, and how utterly quaint and unmeaning is the ringing the changes upon Orpheus and his train of men, beasts, woods, rocks, and mountains in connection with Lord Castlereagh! But he is better pleased with this classical fable than with the death of the Noble Peer, and delights to dwell upon it, to however little use. So he is glad to take advantage of the scriptural idea of a gourd; not to enforce, but as a relief to his reflections; and points his conclusion with a puling sort of commonplace, that a peasant, who dies a natu-ral death, has no Coroner's Inquest to sit upon him. All these are the faults of the ordinary poetical style. Poets think they are bound, by the tenor of their indentures to the Muses, to 'elevate and surprise' in every line; and not having the usual resources at hand in common or abstracted subjects, aspire to the end without the means. They make, or pretend, an extraordinary interest where there is none. They are ambitious, vain, and indolent – more busy in preparing idle orna-ments, which they take their chance of bringing in somehow or other, than intent on eliciting truths by fair and honest enquiry. It should seem as if they considered prose as a sort of waiting-maid to poetry, that could only be expected to wear her mistress's cast-off finery. Poets have been said to succeed best in fiction; and the account here given may in part explain the reason. That is to say, they must choose their own subject, in such a manner as to afford them continual op-portunities of appealing to the senses and exciting the fancy. Dry details, abstruse speculations, do not give scope to vividness of de-scription; and, as they cannot bear to be considered dull, they be-come too often affected, extravagant, and insipid.

I am indebted to Mr Coleridge for the comparison of poetic prose to the second-hand finery of a lady's maid (just made use of). He himself is an instance of his own observation, and (what is even worse) of the opposite fault – an affectation of quaintness and originality. With bits of tarnished lace and worthless frippery, he assumes a sweeping oriental costume, or borrows the stiff dresses of our ancestors, or starts an eccentric fashion of his own. He is swelling and turgid – everlastingly aiming to be greater than his subject; filling his fancy with fumes and vapours in the pangs and throes of miraculous parturition, and bringing forth only *still births*. He has an incessant craving, as it were, to exalt every idea into a metaphor, to expand every sentiment into a lengthened mystery, voluminous and vast, confused and cloudy. His style is not succinct, but encumbered with a train of words and images that have no practical, and only a possible relation to one another – that add to its stateliness, but impede its march. One of his sentences winds its 'forlorn way obscure' over the page like a patriarchal procession with camels laden, wreathed turbans, household wealth, the whole riches of the author's mind poured out upon the barren waste of his subject. The palm-tree spreads its sterile branches overhead, and the land of promise is seen in the distance. All this is owing to his wishing to overdo everything – to make something more out of everything than it is, or than it is worth. The simple truth does not satisfy him – no direct proposition fills up the moulds of his understanding. All is foreign, far-fetched, irrelevant, laboured, unproductive. To read one of his disquisitions is like hearing the variations to a piece of music without the score. Or, to vary the simile, he is not like a man going a journey by the stage-coach along the high-road, but is always getting into a balloon, and mounting into the air, above the plain ground of prose. Whether he soars to the empyrean, or dives to the centre (as he sometimes does), it is equally to get away from the question before him, and to prove that he owes everything to his own mind. His object is to invent; he scorns to imitate. The business of prose is the contrary. But Mr Coleridge is a poet, and his thoughts are free.

I think the poet laureate is a much better prose-writer. His style has an antique quaintness, with a modern familiarity. He has just a sufficient sprinkling of *archaisms*, of allusions to old Fuller, and Burton, and Latimer, to set off or qualify the smart flippant tone of his apologies for existing abuses, or the ready, galling virulence of his personal invectives. Mr Southey is a faithful historian, and no inefficient partisan. In the former character, his mind is tenacious of facts; and in the latter, his spleen and jealousy prevent the 'extravagant and erring spirit' of the poet from losing itself in Fancy's endless maze. He 'stoops to *earth*', at least, and prostitutes his pen to some purpose (not at the same time losing his own soul, and gaining nothing by it) – and he vilifies reform, and praises the reign of George III in good set terms, in a straightforward, intelligible, practical, pointed way. He is not buoyed up by conscious power out of the reach of common apprehensions, but makes the most of the obvious advantages he possesses. You may complain of a pettiness and petulance of manner, but certainly there is no want of spirit or facility of execution. He does not waste powder and shot in the air, but loads his piece, takes a level aim, and hits his mark. One would say (though his Muse is ambidexter) that he wrote prose with his right hand; there is nothing awkward, circuitous, or feeble in it. 'The words of Mercury are harsh after the songs of Apollo': but this would not apply to him. His prose lucubrations are pleasanter reading than his poetry. Indeed, he is equally practised and voluminous in both; and it is no improbable conjecture, that Mr Southey may have had some idea of rivalling the reputation of Voltaire in the extent, the spirit, and the versatility of his productions in prose and verse, except that he has written no tragedies but *Wat Tyler*!

To my taste, the author of *Rimini*, and editor of the *Examiner*, is among the best and least corrupted of our poetical prose-writers. In his light but well-supported columns we find the raciness, the sharpness, and sparkling effect of poetry, with little that is extravagant or far-fetched, and no turgidity or pompous pretension. Perhaps there is too much the appearance of relaxation and trifling (as if he had escaped the shackles of rhyme), a caprice, a levity, and a disposition to innovate in words and ideas. Still the genuine master-spirit of the prose-writer is there; the tone of lively, sensible conversation; and this may in part arise from the author's being himself an animated talker. Mr Hunt wants something of the heat and earnestness of the political partisan; but his familiar and miscellaneous papers have all the ease, grace, and point of the best style of essay-writing. Many of his effusions in the *Indicator* show, that if he had devoted himself exclusively to that mode of writing, he inherits more of the spirit of Steele than any man since his time.

Lord Byron's prose is bad; that is to say, heavy, laboured, and coarse: he tries to knock someone down with the butt-end of every line, which defeats his object – and the style of the author of *Waverley* (if he comes fairly into this discussion), as mere style, is villainous. It is pretty plain he is a poet; for the sound of names runs mechanically in his ears, and he rings the changes unconsciously on the same words in a sentence, like the same rhymes in a couplet.

Not to spin out this discussion too much, I would conclude by observing, that some of the old English prose-writers (who were not poets) are the best, and, at the same time, the most *poetical* in the favourable sense. Among these we may reckon some of the old divines, and Jeremy Taylor at the head of them. There is a flush like the dawn over his writings; the sweetness of the rose, the freshness of the morning dew. There is a softness in his style, proceeding from the tenderness of his heart: but his head is firm, and his hand is free. His materials are as finely wrought up as they are original and attractive in themselves. Milton's prose-style savours too much of poetry, and, as I have already hinted, of an imitation of the Latin. Dryden's is perfectly unexceptionable, and a model, in simplicity, strength, and perspicuity, for the subjects he treated of.

On the Conversation of Authors

FIRST PUBLISHED *LONDON MAGAZINE*,
SEPTEMBER 1820

An author is bound to write – well or ill, wisely or foolishly: it is his trade. But I do not see that he is bound to talk, any more than he is bound to dance, or ride, or fence better than other people. Reading, study, silence, thought, are a bad introduction to loquacity. It would be sooner learnt of chambermaids and tapsters. He understands the art and mystery of his own profession, which is book-making: what right has anyone to expect or require him to do more – to make a bow gracefully on entering or leaving a room, to make love charmingly, or to make a fortune at all? In all things there is a division of labour. A lord is no less amorous for writing ridiculous love-letters, nor a General less successful for wanting wit and honesty. Why then may not a poor author say nothing, and yet pass muster? Set him on the top of a stagecoach, he will make no figure; he is *mum-chance*, while the slang-wit flies about as fast as the dust, with the crack of the whip and the clatter of the horses' heels: put him in a ring of boxers, he is a poor creature—

And of his port as meek as is a maid.

Introduce him to a tea-party of milliner's girls, and they are ready to split their sides with laughing at him: over his bottle, he is dry: in the drawing-room, rude or awkward: he is too refined for the vulgar, too clownish for the fashionable: – 'he is one that cannot make a good leg, one that cannot eat a mess of broth cleanly, one that cannot ride a horse without spur-galling, one that cannot salute a woman, and look on her directly': – in courts, in camps, in town and country, he is a cypher or a butt: he is good for nothing but a laughing-stock or a scarecrow. You can scarcely get a word out of him for love or money. He knows nothing. He has no notion of pleasure or business, or of what is going on in the world; he does not understand cookery (unless he is a doctor in divinity) nor surgery, nor chemistry (unless he is a *quidnunc*) nor mechanics, nor husbandry and tillage (unless he is as great an admirer of Tull's *Husbandry*, and has profited as much by it as the philosopher of Botley) – no, nor music, painting, the drama, nor the fine arts in general.

'What the deuce is it then, my good sir, that he does understand, or know any thing about?'

'BOOKS, VENUS, BOOKS!'

'What books?'

'Not receipt-books, Madona, nor account-books, nor books of pharmacy, or the veterinary art (they belong to their respective callings and handicrafts) but books of liberal taste and general knowledge.'

'What do you mean by that general knowledge which implies not a knowledge of things in general, but an ignorance (by your own account) of every one in particular: or by that liberal taste which scorns the pursuits and acquirements of the rest of the world in succession, and is confined exclusively, and by way of excellence, to what nobody takes an interest in but yourself, and a few idlers like yourself? Is this what the critics mean by the *belles-lettres*, and the study of humanity?'

Book-knowledge, in a word, then, is knowledge *communicable by books*: and it is general and liberal for this reason, that it is intelligible and interesting on the bare suggestion. That to which anyone feels a romantic attachment, merely from finding it in a book, must be interesting in itself: that which he instantly forms a lively and entire conception of, from seeing a few marks and scratches upon paper, must be taken from common nature: that which, the first time you meet with it, seizes upon the attention as a curious speculation, must exercise the general faculties of the human mind. There are certain broader aspects of society and views of things common to every subject, and more or less cognizable to every mind; and these the scholar treats and founds his claim to general attention upon them, without being chargeable with pedantry. The minute descriptions of fishing-tackle, of baits and flies in Walton's *Complete Angler*, make that work a great favourite with sportsmen: the alloy of an amiable humanity, and the modest but touching descriptions of familiar incidents and rural objects scattered through it, have made it an equal favourite with every reader of taste and feeling. Montaigne's *Essays*, Dilworth's *Spelling Book*, and Fearn's *Treatise on Contingent Remainders*, are all equally books, but not equally adapted for all classes of readers. The two last are of no use but to schoolmasters and lawyers: but the first is a work we may recommend to anyone to read who has ever thought at all, or who would learn to think justly on any subject. Persons of different trades and professions – the mechanic, the shopkeeper, the medical practitioner, the artist, etc. may all have great knowledge and ingenuity in their several vocations, the details of which will be very edifying to themselves, and just as incomprehensible to their neighbours: but over and above this professional and technical knowledge, they must be supposed to have a stock of common sense and common feeling to furnish subjects for common conversation, or to give them any pleasure in each other's company. It is to this common stock of ideas, spread over the surface, or striking its roots into the very centre of society, that the popular writer appeals, and not in vain; for he finds readers. It is of this finer essence of wisdom and humanity, 'etherial mould, sky-tinctured', that books of the better sort are made. They contain the language of thought. It must happen that, in the course of time and the variety of human capacity, some persons will have struck out finer observations, reflections, and sentiments than others. These they have committed to books of memory, have bequeathed as a lasting legacy to posterity; and such persons have become standard authors. We visit at the shrine, drink in some measure of the inspiration, and cannot easily 'breathe in other air less pure, accustomed to immortal fruits'. Are we to be blamed for this, because the vulgar and illiterate do not always understand us? The fault is rather in them, who are 'confined and cabin'd in', each in their own particular sphere and compartment of ideas, and have not the same refined medium of communication or abstracted topics of discourse. Bring a number of literary, or of illiterate persons together, perfect strangers to each other, and see which party will make the best company. 'Verily, we have our reward.' We have made our election, and have no reason to repent it, if we were wise. But the misfortune is, we wish to have all the advantages on one side. We grudge, and cannot reconcile it to ourselves, that anyone 'should go about to cozen fortune, without the stamp of learning!' We think 'because we are *scholars*, there shall be no more cakes and ale!' We don't know how to account for it, that barmaids should gossip, or ladies whisper, or bullies roar, or fools laugh, or knaves thrive, without having gone through the same course of select study that we have! This vanity is preposterous, and carries its own punishment with it. Books are a world in themselves, it is true; but they are not the only world. The world itself is a volume larger than all the libraries in it. Learning is a sacred deposit from the experience of ages; but it has not put all future experience on the shelf, or debarred the common herd of mankind from the use of their hands, tongues, eyes, ears, or understandings. Taste is a luxury for the privileged few: but it would be hard upon those who have not the same standard of refinement in their own minds that we suppose ourselves to have, if this should prevent them from having recourse, as usual, to their old frolics, coarse jokes, and horseplay, and getting through the wear and tear of the world, with such homely sayings and shrewd helps as they may. Happy is it, that the mass of mankind eat and drink, and sleep, and perform their several tasks, and do as they like without us – caring nothing for our scribblings, our carpings, and our quibbles; and moving on the same, in spite of our fine-spun distinctions, fantastic theories, and lines of demarcation, which are like the chalk-figures drawn on ballroom floors to be danced out before morning! In the field opposite the window where I write this, there is a country-girl picking stones: in the one next it, there are several poor women weeding the blue and red flowers from the corn: farther on, are two boys, tending a flock of sheep. What do they know or care about what I am writing about them, or ever will – or what would they be the better for it, if they did? Or why need we despise

> The wretched slave,
> Who like a lackey, from the rise to the set,
> Sweats in the eye of Phœbus, and all night
> Sleeps in Elysium; next day, after dawn,
> Doth rise, and help Hyperion to his horse;
> And follows so the ever-running year
> With profitable labour to his grave?

Is not this life as sweet as writing ephemerides? But we put that which flutters the brain idly for a moment, and then is heard no more, in competition with nature, which exists every where, and lasts always. We not only underrate the force of nature, and make too much of art – but we also overrate our own accomplishments and advantages derived from art. In the presence of clownish ignorance, or of persons without any great pretensions, real or affected, we are very much inclined to take upon ourselves, as the virtual representatives of science, art, and literature. We have a strong itch to show off and do the honours of civilization for all the great men whose works we have ever read, and whose names our auditors have never heard of, as noblemen's lackeys, in the absence of their masters, give themselves airs of superiority over everyone else. But though we have read Congreve, a stagecoachman may be an over-match for us in wit: though we are deep-versed in the excellence of Shakspeare's colloquial style, a village beldam may outscold us: though we have read Machiavel in the original Italian, we may be easily outwitted by a clown: and though we have cried our eyes out over the *New Eloise*, a poor shepherd-lad, who hardly knows how to spell his own name, may 'tell his tale, under the hawthorn in the dale', and prove a more thriving wooer. What then is the advantage we possess over the meanest of the mean? Why this, that we have read Congreve, Shakspeare, Machiavel, the *New Eloise* – not that we are to have their wit, genius, shrewdness, or melting tenderness.

From speculative pursuits we must be satisfied with speculative benefits. From reading, too, we learn to write. If we have had the pleasure of studying the highest models of perfection in their kind, and can hope to leave anything ourselves, however slight, to be looked upon as a model, or even a good copy in its way, we may think ourselves pretty well off, without engrossing all the privileges of learning, and all the blessings of ignorance into the bargain.

It has been made a question whether there have not been individuals in common life of greater talents and powers of mind than the most celebrated writers – whether, for instance, such or such a Liverpool merchant, or Manchester manufacturer, was not a more sensible man than Montaigne, of a longer reach of understanding than the Viscount of St Albans. There is no saying, unless some of these illustrious obscure had communicated their important discoveries to the world. But then they would have been authors! On the other hand, there is a set of critics who fall into the contrary error; and suppose that unless the proof of capacity is laid before all the world, the capacity itself cannot exist; looking upon all those who have not commenced authors, as literally 'stocks and stones, and worse than senseless things'. I remember trying to convince a person of this class, that a young lady, whom he knew something of, the niece of a celebrated authoress, had just the same sort of fine *tact* and ironical turn in conversation, that her relative had shown in her writings when young. The only answer I could get was an incredulous smile, and the observation that when she wrote anything as good as ——, or ——, he might think her as clever. I said all I meant was, that she had the same family talents, and asked whether he thought that if Miss Burney had not been very clever, as a mere girl, before she wrote her novels, she would ever have written them? It was all in vain. He still stuck to his text, and was convinced that the niece was a little fool compared to her aunt at the same age; and if he had known the aunt formerly, he would have had just the same opinion of *her*. My friend was one of those who have a settled persuasion that it is the book that makes the author, and not the author the book. That's a strange opinion for a great philosopher to hold. But he wilfully shuts his eyes to the germs and indistinct workings of genius, and treats them with supercilious indifference, till they stare him in the face through the press; and then takes cognizance only of the overt acts and published evidence. This is neither a proof of wisdom, nor the way to be wise. It is partly pedantry and prejudice, and partly feebleness of judgement and want of magnanimity. He dare as little commit himself on the character of books, as of individuals, till they are stamped by the public. If you show him any work for his approbation, he asks, 'Whose is the superscription?' He judges of genius by its shadow, reputation – of the metal by the coin. He is just the reverse of another person whom I know – for, as Godwin never allows a particle of merit to anyone till it is acknowledged by the whole world, Coleridge withholds his tribute of applause from every person, in whom any mortal but himself can descry the least glimpse of understanding. He would be thought to look farther into a mill-stone than anybody else. He would have others see with his eyes, and take their opinions from him on trust, in spite of their senses. The more obscure and defective the indications of merit, the greater his sagacity and candour in being the first to point them out. He looks upon what he nicknames *a man of genius*, but as the breath of his nostrils, and the clay in the potter's hands. If any such inert, unconscious mass, under the fostering care of the modern Prometheus, is kindled into life, begins to see, speak, and move, so as to attract the notice of other people, our jealous patroniser of latent worth in that case throws aside, scorns, and hates his own handiwork; and deserts his intellectual offspring from the moment they can go alone and shift for themselves. But to pass on to our more immediate subject.

The conversation of authors is not so good as might be imagined: but, such as it is (and with rare exceptions) it is better than any other. The proof of which is, that, when you are used to it, you cannot put up with any other. That of mixed company becomes utterly intoler-able – you cannot sit out a common tea and card party, at least, if they pretend to talk at all. You are obliged in despair to cut all your old acquaintance who are not *au fait* on the prevailing and most smartly contested topics, who are not imbued with the high gusto of criticism and *virtù*. You cannot bear to hear a friend whom you have not seen for many years, tell at how much a yard he sells his laces and tapes, when he means to move into his next house, when he heard last from his relations in the country, whether trade is alive or dead, or whether Mr Such-a-one gets to look old. This sort of neighbourly gossip will not go down after the high-raised tone of literary conver-sation. The last may be very absurd, very unsatisfactory, and full of turbulence and heart-burnings; but it has a zest in it which more ordinary topics of news or family-affairs do not supply. Neither will the conversation of what we understand by *gentlemen* and men of fashion, do after that of men of letters. It is flat, insipid, stale, and unprofitable, in the comparison. They talk about much the same things, pictures, poetry, politics, plays; but they do it worse, and at a sort of vapid secondhand. They, in fact, talk out of newspapers and magazines, what *we write there*. They do not feel the same interest in the subjects they affect to handle with an air of fashionable conde-scension, nor have they the same knowledge of them, if they were ever so much in earnest in displaying it. If it were not for the wine and the dessert, no author in his senses would accept an invitation to a well-dressed dinner-party, except out of pure good nature and un-willingness to disoblige by his refusal. Persons in high life talk almost entirely by rote. There are certain established modes of address, and certain answers to them expected as a matter of course, as a point of etiquette. The studied forms of politeness do not give the greatest possible scope to an exuberance of wit or fancy. The fear of giving offence destroys sincerity, and without sincerity there can be no true enjoyment of society, nor unfettered exertion of intellectual activity. Those who have been accustomed to live with the great are hardly considered as conversible persons in literary society. They are not to be talked with, any more than puppets or echoes. They have no opin-ions but what will please; and you naturally turn away, as a waste of time and words, from attending to a person who just before assented to what you said, and whom you find, the moment after, from some-thing that unexpectedly or perhaps by design drops from him, to be of a totally different way of thinking. This *bush-fighting* is not re-garded as fair play among scientific men. As fashionable conversa-tion is a sacrifice to politeness, so the conversation of low life is nothing but rudeness. They contradict you without giving a reason, or if they do, it is a very bad one – swear, talk loud, repeat the same thing fifty times over, get to calling names, and from words proceed to blows. You cannot make companions of servants, or persons in an inferior station in life. You may talk to them on matters of business, and what they have to do for you (as lords talk to bruisers on subjects of *fancy*, or country-squires to their grooms on horse-racing) but out of that narrow sphere, to any general topic, you cannot lead them; the con-versation soon flags, and you go back to the old question, or are obliged to break up the sitting for want of ideas in common. The conversation of authors is better than that of most professions. It is better than that of lawyers, who talk nothing but *double entendre* – than that of physicians, who talk of the approaching deaths of the College, or the marriage of some new practitioner with some rich widow – than that of divines, who talk of the last place they dined at – than that of University men, who make stale puns, repeat the refuse of the London newspapers, and affect an ignorance of Greek and mathematics – it is better than that of players, who talk of nothing but the greenroom, and rehearse the scholar, the wit, or the fine gentleman, like a part on the stage – or than that of ladies, who, whatever you talk of, think of nothing, and expect you to think of nothing, but themselves. It is not easy to keep up a conversation with women in company. It is thought a piece of rudeness to differ from them: it is not quite fair to ask them a reason for what they say. You are afraid of pressing too hard upon them: but where you cannot differ openly and unreservedly, you cannot heartily agree. It is not so in France. There the women talk of things in general, and reason better than the men in this country. They are mistresses of the intellectual foils. They are adepts in all the topics. They know what is to be said for and against all sorts of questions, and are lively and full of mischief into the bargain. They are very subtle. They put you to your trumps immediately. Your logic is more in requisition even than your gallantry. You must argue as well as bow yourself into the good graces of these modern Amazons. What a situation for an Englishman to be placed in![1]

The fault of literary conversation in general is its too great tenaciousness. It fastens upon a subject, and will not let it go. It resembles a battle rather than a skirmish, and makes a toil of a pleasure. Perhaps it does this from necessity, from a consciousness of wanting the more familiar graces, the power to sport and trifle, to touch lightly and adorn agreeably, every view or turn of a question *en passant*, as it arises. Those who have a reputation to lose are too ambitious of shining, to please. 'To excel in conversation', said an ingenious man,

---

1   The topics of metaphysical argument having got into female society in France, is a proof how much they must have been discussed there generally, and how unfounded the charge is which we bring against them of excessive thoughtlessness and frivolity. The French (taken all together) are a more sensible, reflecting, and better informed people than the English.

'one must not be always striving to say good things: to say one good thing, one must say many bad, and more indifferent ones.' This desire to shine without the means at hand, often makes men silent:

> The fear of being silent strikes us dumb.

A writer who has been accustomed to take a connected view of a difficult question, and to work it out gradually in all its bearings, may be very deficient in that quickness and ease, which men of the world, who are in the habit of hearing a variety of opinions, who pick up an observation on one subject, and another on another, and who care about none any farther than the passing away of an idle hour, usually acquire. An author has studied a particular point – he has read, he has enquired, he has thought a great deal upon it: he is not contented to take it up casually in common with others, to throw out a hint, to propose an objection: he will either remain silent, uneasy, and dissatisfied, or he will begin at the beginning and go through with it to the end. He is for taking the whole responsibility upon himself. He would be thought to understand the subject better than others, or indeed would show that nobody else knows anything about it. There are always three or four points on which the literary novice at his first outset in life fancies he can enlighten every company, and bear down all opposition: but he is cured of this Quixotic and pugnacious spirit, as he goes more into the world, where he finds that there are other opinions and other pretensions to be adjusted besides his own. When this asperity wears off, and a certain scholastic precocity is mellowed down, the conversation of men of letters becomes both interesting and instructive. Men of the world have no fixed principles, no groundwork of thought: mere scholars have too much an object, a theory always in view, to which they wrest everything, and not infrequently, common sense itself. By mixing with society, they rub off their hardness of manner, and impracticable, offensive singularity, while they retain a greater depth and coherence of understanding. There is more to be learnt from them than from their books. This was a remark of Rousseau's, and it is a very true one. In the confidence and unreserve of private intercourse, they are more at liberty to say what they think, to put the subject in different and opposite points of view, to illustrate it more briefly and pithily by familiar expressions, by an appeal to individual character and personal knowledge – to bring in the limitation, to obviate misconception, to state difficulties on their own side of the argument, and answer them as well as they can. This would hardly agree with the prudery, and somewhat ostentatious claims of authorship. Dr Johnson's conversation in Boswell's *Life* is much better than his published works: and the fragments of the opinions of celebrated men, preserved in their letters or in anecdotes of them, are justly sought after as invaluable for the same reason. For instance, what a fund of sense there is in Grimm's *Memoirs!* We thus get at the essence of what is contained in their more laboured productions, without the affectation or formality. Argument, again, is the death of conversation, if carried on in a spirit of hostility: but discussion is a pleasant and profitable thing, where you advance and defend your opinions as far as you can, and admit the truth of what is objected against them with equal impartiality; in short, where you do not pretend to set up for an oracle, but freely declare what you really know about any question, or suggest what has struck you as throwing a new light upon it, and let it pass for what it is worth. This tone of conversation was well described by Dr Johnson, when he said of some party at which he had been present the night before – 'We had good talk, sir!' As a general rule, there is no conversation worth anything but between friends, or those who agree in the same leading views of a subject. Nothing was ever learnt by either side in a dispute. You contradict one another, will not allow a grain of sense in what your adversary advances, are blind to whatever makes against yourself, dare not look the question fairly in the face, so that you cannot avail yourself even of your real advantages, insist most on what you feel to be the weakest points of your argument, and get more and more absurd, dogmatical, and violent every moment. Disputes for victory generally end to the dissatisfaction of all parties; and the one recorded in *Gil Blas* breaks up just as it ought. I once knew a very ingenious man, than whom, to take him in the way of common chit-chat or fireside gossip, no one could be more entertaining or rational. He would make an apt classical quotation, propose an explanation of a curious passage in Shakespeare's *Venus and Adonis*, detect a metaphysical error in Locke, would infer the volatility of the French character from the chapter in Sterne where the Count mistakes the feigned name of Yorick for a proof of his being the identical imaginary character in *Hamlet* (*Et vous êtes Yorick!*) – thus confounding words with things twice over – but let a difference of opinion be once hitched in, and it was all over with him. His only object from that time was to shut out common sense, and to be proof against conviction. He would argue the most ridiculous point (such as that there were two original languages) for hours together, nay, through the horologe. You would not suppose it was the same person. He was like an obstinate runaway horse, that takes the bit in his mouth, and becomes mischievous and unmanageable. He had made up his mind to one thing, not to admit a single particle of what anyone else said for or against him. It was all the difference between a man drunk or sober, sane or mad. It is the same when he once gets the pen in his hand. He has been trying to prove a contradiction in terms for the ten last years of his life, *viz.* that the Bourbons have the same right to the throne of France that the Brunswick family have to the throne of England. Many people think there is a want of honesty or a want of understanding in this. There is neither. But he will persist in an argument to the last pinch; he will yield, in absurdity, to no man!

This litigious humour is bad enough: but there is one character still worse, that of a person who goes into company, not to contradict, but to *talk at* you. This is the greatest nuisance in civilized society. Such a person does not come armed to defend himself at all points, but to unsettle, if he can, and throw a slur on all your favourite opinions. If he has a notion that anyone in the room is fond of poetry, he immediately volunteers a contemptuous tirade against the idle jingle of verse. If he suspects you have a delight in pictures, he endeavours, not by fair argument, but by a side-wind, to put you out of conceit with so frivolous an art. If you have a taste for music, he does not think much good is to be done by this tickling of the ears. If you speak in praise of a comedy, he does not see the use of wit: if you say you have been to a tragedy, he shakes his head at this mockery of human misery, and thinks it ought to be prohibited. He tries to find out beforehand whatever it is that you take a particular pride or pleasure in, that he may annoy your self-love in the tenderest point (as if he were probing a wound) and make you dissatisfied with yourself and your pursuits for several days afterwards. A person might as well make a practice of throwing out scandalous aspersions against your dearest friends or nearest relations, by way of ingratiating himself into your favour. Such ill-timed impertinence is 'villainous, and shows a pitiful ambition in the fool that uses it'.

The soul of conversation is sympathy. Authors should converse chiefly with authors, and their talk should be of books. 'When Greek meets Greek, then comes the tug of war.' There is nothing so pedantic as pretending not to be pedantic. No man can get above his pursuit in life: it is getting above himself, which is impossible. There is a freemasonry in all things. You can only speak to be understood, but this you cannot be, except by those who are in the secret. Hence an argument has been drawn to supersede the necessity of conversation altogether; for it has been said, that there is no use in talking to people of sense, who know all that you can tell them, nor to fools, who will not be instructed. There is, however, the smallest encouragement to proceed, when you are conscious that the more you really enter into a subject, the farther you will be from the comprehension of your hearers – and that the more proofs you give of any position, the more odd and out-of-the-way they will think your notions. Coleridge is the only person who can talk to all sorts of people, on all sorts of subjects, without caring a farthing for their understanding one word he says – and *he* talks only for admiration and to be listened to, and accordingly the least interruption puts him out. I firmly believe he would make just the same impression on half his audiences, if he purposely repeated absolute nonsense with the same voice and manner and inexhaustible flow of undulating speech! In general, wit shines only by reflection. You must take your cue from your company – must rise as they rise, and sink as they fall. You must see that your good things, your knowing allusions, are not flung away, like the pearls in the adage. What a check it is to be asked a foolish question; to find that the first principles are not understood! You are thrown on your back immediately, the conversation is stopped like a country-dance by those who do not know the figure. But when a set of adepts, of *illuminati*, get about a question, it is worthwhile to hear them talk. They may snarl and quarrel over it, like dogs; but they pick it bare to the bone, they masticate it thoroughly.

The Same Subject Continued

This was the case formerly at Lamb's – where we used to have many lively skirmishes at their Thursday evening parties. I doubt whether the small-coal man's musical parties could exceed them. Oh! for the pen of John Buncle to consecrate a *petit souvenir* to their memory! – There was Lamb himself, the most delightful, the most provoking, the most witty and sensible of men. He always made the best pun, and the best remark in the course of the evening. His serious conversation, like his serious writing, is his best. No one ever stammered out such fine, piquant, deep, eloquent things in half a dozen half-sentences as he does. His jests scald like tears: and he probes a question with a play upon words. What a keen, laughing, hare-brained vein of home-felt truth! What choice venom! How often did we cut into the haunch of letters, while we discussed the haunch of mutton on the table! How we skimmed the cream of criticism! How we got into the heart of controversy! How we picked out the marrow of authors! 'And, in our flowing cups, many a good name and true was freshly remembered.' Recollect (most sage and critical reader) that in all this I was but a guest! Need I go over the names? They were but the old everlasting set – Milton and Shakespeare, Pope and Dryden, Steele and Addison, Swift and Gay, Fielding, Smollett, Sterne, Richardson, Hogarth's prints, Claude's landscapes, the cartoons at Hampton Court, and all those things, that, having once been, must ever be. The Scotch novels had not then been heard of: so we said nothing about them. In general, we were hard upon the moderns.

The author of the *Rambler* was only tolerated in Boswell's *Life* of him; and it was as much as anyone could do to edge in a word for Junius. Lamb could not bear *Gil Blas*. This was a fault. I remember the greatest triumph I ever had was in persuading him, after some years' difficulty, that Fielding was better than Smollett. On one occasion, he was for making out a list of persons famous in history that one would wish to see again – at the head of whom were Pontius Pilate, Sir Thomas Browne, and Dr Faustus – but we blackballed most of his list! But with what a gusto would he describe his favourite authors, Donne, or Sir Philip Sidney, and call their most crabbed passages *delicious*! He tried them on his palate as epicures taste olives, and his observations had a smack in them, like a roughness on the tongue. With what discrimination he hinted a defect in what he admired most – as in saying that the display of the sumptuous banquet in *Paradise Regained* was not in true keeping, as the simplest fare was all that was necessary to tempt the extremity of hunger – and stating that Adam and Eve in *Paradise Lost* were too much like married people. He has furnished many a text for Coleridge to preach upon. There was no fuss or cant about him: nor were his sweets or his sours ever diluted with one particle of affectation. I cannot say that the party at Lamb's were all of one description. There were honorary members, lay-brothers. Wit and good fellowship was the motto inscribed over the door. When a stranger came in, it was not asked, 'Has he written anything?' – we were above that pedantry; but we waited to see what he could do. If he could take a hand at piquet, he was welcome to sit down. If a person liked anything, if he took snuff heartily, it was sufficient. He would understand, by analogy, the pungency of other things, besides Irish blackguard, or Scotch rappee. A character was good anywhere, in a room or on paper. But we abhorred insipidity, affectation, and fine gentlemen. There was one of our party who never failed to mark 'two for his Nob' at cribbage, and he was thought no mean person. This was Ned Phillips, and a better fellow in his way breathes not. There was Rickman, who asserted some incredible matter of fact as a likely paradox, and settled all controversies by an *ipse dixit*, a *fiat* of his will, hammering out many a hard theory on the anvil of his brain – the Baron Munchausen of politics and practical philosophy: there was Captain Burney, who had you at an advantage by never understanding you: there was

Jem White, the author of *Falstaff's Letters*, who the other day left this dull world to go in search of more kindred spirits, 'turning like the latter end of a lover's lute': there was Ayrton, who sometimes dropped in, the Will Honeycomb of our set – and Mrs Reynolds, who being of a quiet turn, loved to hear a noisy debate. An utterly uninformed person might have supposed this a scene of vulgar confusion and uproar. While the most critical question was pending, while the most difficult problem in philosophy was solving, Phillips cried out, 'That's game', and Martin Burney muttered a quotation over the last remains of a veal pie at a side-table. Once, and once only, the literary interest overcame the general. For Coleridge was riding the high German horse, and demonstrating the categories of the transcendental philosophy to the author of *The Road to Ruin*; who insisted on his knowledge of German, and German metaphysics, having read the *Critique of Pure Reason* in the original. 'My dear Mr Holcroft', said Coleridge, in a tone of infinitely provoking conciliation, 'you really put me in mind of a sweet pretty German girl, about fifteen, that I met with in the Hartz forest in Germany – and who one day, as I was reading the *Limits of the Knowable and the Unknowable*, the profoundest of all his works, with great attention, came behind my chair, and leaning over, said, What, *you* read Kant? Why, *I* that am a German born, don't understand him!' This was too much to bear, and Holcroft, starting up, called out in no measured tone, 'Mr Coleridge, you are the most eloquent man I ever met with, and the most troublesome with your eloquence!' Phillips held the cribbage-peg that was to mark him game, suspended in his hand; and the whist table was silent for a moment. I saw Holcroft downstairs, and, on coming to the landing-place in Mitre Court, he stopped me to observe, that 'he thought Mr Coleridge a very clever man, with a great command of language, but that he feared he did not always affix very precise ideas to the words he used'. After he was gone, we had our laugh out, and went on with the argument on the nature of reason, the imagination, and the will. I wish I could find a publisher for it: it would make a supplement to the *Biographia Literaria* in a volume and a half octavo.

Those days are over! An event, the name of which I wish never to mention, broke up our party, like a bombshell thrown into the room: and now we seldom meet——

Like angels' visits, short and far between.

There is no longer the same set of persons, nor of associations. Lamb does not live where he did. By shifting his abode, his notions seem less fixed. He does not wear his old snuff-coloured coat and breeches. It looks like an alteration in his style. An author and a wit should have a separate costume, a particular cloth: he should present something positive and singular to the mind, like Mr Douce of the Museum. Our faith in the religion of letters will not bear to be taken to pieces, and put together again by caprice or accident. Leigh Hunt goes there sometimes. He has a fine vinous spirit about him, and tropical blood in his veins: but he is better at his own table. He has a great flow of pleasantry and delightful animal spirits: but his hits do not tell like Lamb's; you cannot repeat them the next day. He requires not only to be appreciated, but to have a select circle of admirers and devotees, to feel himself quite at home. He sits at the head of a party with great gaiety and grace; has an elegant manner and turn of features; is never at a loss – *aliquando sufflaminandus erat* – has continual sportive sallies of wit of fancy; tells a story capitally; mimics an actor, or an acquaintance to admiration; laughs with great glee and good humour at his own or other people's jokes; understands the point of an equivoque, or an observation immediately; has a taste and knowledge of books, of music, of medals; manages an argument adroitly; is genteel and gallant, and has a set of bye-phrases and quaint allusions always at hand to produce a laugh: if he has a fault, it is that he does not listen so well as he speaks, is impatient of interruption, and is fond of being looked up to, without considering by whom. I believe, however, he has pretty well seen the folly of this. Neither is his ready display of personal accomplishment and variety of resources an advantage to his writings. They sometimes present a desultory and slip-shod appearance, owing to this very circumstance. The same things that tell, perhaps, best, to a private circle round the fireside, are not always intelligible to the public, nor does he take pains to make them so. He is too confident and secure of his audience. That which may be entertaining enough with the assistance of a certain liveliness of manner, may read very flat on paper, because it is abstracted from all the circumstances that had set it off to advantage. A writer should recollect that he has only to trust to the immediate impression of words, like a musician who sings without the accompaniment of an instrument. There is nothing to help out, or slubber over, the defects of the voice in the one case, nor of the style in the other. The reader may, if he pleases, get a very good idea Leigh Hunt's conversation from a very agreeable paper he has lately published, called the *Indicator*, than which nothing can be more happily conceived or executed.

The art of conversation is the art of hearing as well as of being heard. Authors in general are not good listeners. Some of the best talkers are, on this account, the worst company; and some who are very indifferent, but very great talkers, are as bad. It is sometimes wonderful to see how a person, who has been entertaining or tiring a company by the hour together, drops his countenance as if he had been shot, or had been seized with a sudden lockjaw, the moment anyone interposes a single observation. The best converser I know is, however, the best listener. I mean Mr Northcote, the painter. Painters by their profession are not bound to shine in conversation, and they shine the more. He lends his ear to an observation, as if you had brought him a piece of news, and enters into it with as much avidity and earnestness, as if it interested himself personally. If he repeats an old remark or story, it is with the same freshness and point as for the first time. It always arises out of the occasion, and has the stamp of originality. There is no parroting of himself. His look is a continual, ever-varying history-piece of what passes in his mind. His face is as a book. There need no marks of interjection or interrogation to what he says. His manner is quite picturesque. There is an excess of character and *naiveté* that never tires. His thoughts bubble up and sparkle, like beads on old wine. The fund of anecdote, the collection of curious particulars, is enough to set up any common retailer of jests, that dines out every day; but these are not strung together like a row of galley-slaves, but are always introduced to illustrate some argument or bring out some fine distinction of character. The mixture of spleen adds to the sharpness of the point, like poisoned arrows. Mr Northcote enlarges with enthusiasm on the old painters, and tells good things of the new. The only thing he ever vexed me in was his liking the *Catalogue Raisonneé*. I had almost as soon hear him talk of Titian's pictures (which he does with tears in his eyes, and looking just like them) as see the originals, and I had rather hear him talk of Sir Joshua's than see them. He is the last of that school who knew Goldsmith and Johnson. How finely he describes Pope! His elegance of mind, his figure, his character were not unlike his own. He does not resemble a modern Englishman, but puts one in mind of a Roman Cardinal or Spanish Inquisitor. I never ate or drank with Mr Northcote; but I have lived on his conversation with undiminished relish ever since I can remember – and when I leave it, I come out into the street with feelings lighter and more etherial than I have at any other time. One of his *tête-à-têtes* would at any time make an essay; but he cannot write himself, because he loses himself in the connecting passages, is fearful of the effect, and wants the habit of bringing his ideas into one focus or point of view. A *lens* is necessary to collect the diverging rays, the refracted and broken angular lights of conversation on paper. Contradiction is half the battle in talking – the being startled by what others say, and having to answer on the spot. You have to defend yourself, paragraph by paragraph, parenthesis within parenthesis. Perhaps it might be supposed that a person who excels in conversation and cannot write, would succeed better in dialogue. But the stimulus, the immediate irritation would be wanting; and the work would read flatter than ever, from not having the very thing it pretended to have.

Lively sallies and connected discourse are very different things. There are many persons of that impatient and restless turn of mind, that they cannot wait a moment for a conclusion, or follow up the thread of any argument. In the hurry of conversation their ideas are somehow huddled into sense; but in the intervals of thought, leave a great gap between. Montesquieu said, he often lost an idea before he could find words for it: yet he dictated, by way of saving time, to an amanuensis. This last is, in my opinion, a vile method, and a solecism in authorship. Horne Tooke, among other paradoxes, used to maintain, that no one could write a good style who was not in the habit of talking and hearing the sound of his own voice. He might as well have said that no one could relish a good style without reading it aloud, as we find common people do to assist their apprehension. But there is a method of trying periods on the ear, or weighing them with the scales of the breath, without any articulate sound. Authors, as they write, may be said to 'hear a sound so fine, there's nothing lives 'twixt it and silence'. Even musicians generally compose in their heads. I agree that no style is good, that is not fit to be spoken or read aloud with effect. This holds true not only of emphasis and cadence, but also with regard to natural idiom and colloquial freedom. Sterne's was in this respect the best style that ever was written. You fancy that you hear the people talking. For a contrary reason, no college man writes a good style, or understands it when written. Fine writing is with him all verbiage and monotony – a translation into classical centos or hexameter lines.

That which I have just mentioned is among many instances I could give of ingenious absurdities advanced by Mr Tooke in the heat and pride of controversy. A person who knew him well, and greatly admired his talents, said of him that he never (to his recollection) heard him defend an opinion which he thought right, or in which he believed him to be himself sincere. He indeed provoked his antagonists into the toils by the very extravagance of his assertions, and the teasing sophistry by which he rendered them plausible. His temper was prompter to his skill. He had the manners of a man of the world, with great scholastic resources. He flung everyone else off his guard, and was himself immovable. I never knew anyone who did not admit his superiority in this kind of warfare. He put a full stop to one of Coleridge's long-winded prefatory apologies for his youth and inexperience, by saying abruptly, 'Speak up, young man!' and, at another time, silenced a learned professor, by desiring an explanation of a word which the other frequently used, and which, he said, he had been many years trying to get at the meaning of – the copulative Is! He was the best intellectual fencer of his day. He made strange havoc of Fuseli's fantastic hieroglyphics, violent humours, and oddity of dialect. Curran, who was sometimes of the same party, was lively and animated in convivial conversation, but dull in argument; nay, averse to anything like reasoning or serious observation, and had the worst taste I ever knew. His favourite critical topics were to abuse Milton's *Paradise Lost*, and *Romeo and Juliet*. Indeed, he confessed a want of sufficient acquaintance with books when he found himself in literary society in London. He and Sheridan once dined at John Kemble's with Mrs Inchbald and Mary Woolstonecroft, when the discourse almost wholly turned on love, 'from noon to dewy eve, a summer's day!' What a subject! What speakers, and what hearers! What would I not give to have been there, had I not learned it all from the bright eyes of Amaryllis, and may one day make a *Table-Talk* of it! Peter Pindar was rich in anecdote and grotesque humour, and profound in technical knowledge both of music, poetry, and painting, but he was gross and overbearing. Wordsworth sometimes talks like a man inspired on subjects of poetry (his own out of the question) – Coleridge well on every subject, and Godwin, on none. To finish this subject – Mrs Montagu's conversation is as fine-cut as her features, and I like to sit in the room with that sort of coronet face. What she says leaves a flavour, like fine green tea. Hunt's is like champagne, and Northcote's like anchovy sandwiches. Haydon's is like a game at trapball: Lamb's like snapdragon: and my own (if I do not mistake the matter) is not very much unlike a game at nine-pins! . . . One source of the conversation of authors, is the character of other authors, and on that they are rich indeed. What things they say! What stories they tell of one another, more particularly of their friends! If I durst only give some of these confidential communications! . . . The reader may perhaps think the foregoing a specimen of them: but indeed he is mistaken.

I do not know of any greater impertinence, than for an obscure individual to set about pumping a character of celebrity. 'Bring him to me', said a Doctor Tronchin, speaking of Rousseau, 'that I may see whether he has any thing in him.' Before you can take measure of the capacity of others, you ought to be sure that they have not taken measure of yours. They may think you a spy on them, and may not like their company. If you really want to know whether another person can talk well, begin by saying a good thing yourself, and you will have a right to look for a rejoinder. 'The best tennis-players', says Sir Fopling Flutter, 'make the best matches'.

> For wit is like a rest
> Held up at tennis, which men do the best
> With the best players.

We hear it often said of a great author, or a great actress, that they are very stupid people in private. But he was a fool that said so. *Tell me your company, and I'll tell you your manners.* In conversation, as in other things, the action and reaction should bear a certain proportion to each other. Authors may, in some sense, be looked upon as foreigners, who are not naturalized even in their native soil. Lamb once came down into the country to see us. He was 'like the most capricious poet Ovid among the Goths'. The country people thought him an oddity, and did not understand his jokes. It would be strange if they had; for he did not make any, while he stayed. But when we crossed the country to Oxford, then he spoke a little. He and the old colleges were hail-fellow well met; and in the quadrangles, he 'walked gowned'.

There is a character of a gentleman; so there is a character of a scholar, which is no less easily recognized. The one has an air of books about him, as the other has of good breeding. The one wears his thoughts as the other does his clothes, gracefully; and even if they are a little old-fashioned, they are not ridiculous: they have had their day. The gentleman shows, by his manner, that he has been used to respect from others: the scholar that he lays claim to self-respect and to a certain independence of opinion. The one has been accustomed to the best company; the other has passed his time in cultivating an intimacy with the best authors. There is nothing forward or vulgar in the behaviour of the one; nothing shrewd or petulant in the obser-vations of the other, as if he should astonish the by-standers, or was astonished himself at his own discoveries. Good taste and good sense, like common politeness, are, or are supposed to be, matters of course. One is distinguished by an appearance of marked attention to every-one present; the other manifests an habitual air of abstraction and absence of mind. The one is not an upstart with all the self-impor-tant airs of the founder of his own fortune; nor the other a self-taught man, with the repulsive self-sufficiency which arises from an ignorance of what hundreds have known before him. We must ex-cuse perhaps a little conscious family-pride in the one, and a little harmless pedantry in the other. As there is a class of the first charac-ter which sinks into the mere gentleman, that is, which has nothing but this sense of respectability and propriety to support it – so the character of a scholar not unfrequently dwindles down into the shadow of a shade, till nothing is left of it but the mere bookworm. There is often something amiable as well as enviable in this last character. I know one such instance, at least. The person I mean has an admira-tion for learning, if he is only dazzled by its light. He lives among old authors, if he does not enter much into their spirit. He handles the covers, and turns over the page, and is familiar with the names and dates. He is busy and self-involved. He hangs like a film and cobweb upon letters, or is like the dust upon the outside of knowledge, which should not be rudely brushed aside. He follows learning as its shadow; but as such, he is respectable. He browses on the husk and leaves of books, as the young fawn browses on the bark and leaves of trees. Such a one lives all his life in a dream of learning, and has never once had his sleep broken by a real sense of things. He believes implicitly in genius, truth, virtue, liberty, because he finds the names of these things in books. He thinks that love and friendship are the finest things imaginable, both in practice and theory. The legend of good women is to him no fiction. When he steals from the twilight of his cell, the scene breaks upon him like an illuminated missal, and all the people he sees are but so many figures in a *camera obscura*. He reads the world, like a favourite volume, only to find beauties in it, or like an edition of some old work which he is preparing for the press, only to make emendations in it, and correct the errors that have inadvertently slipt in. He and his dog Tray are much the same honest, simple-hearted, faithful, affectionate creatures – if Tray could but read! His mind cannot take the impression of vice: but the gentleness of his nature turns gall to milk. He would not hurt a fly. He draws the picture of mankind from the guileless simplicity of his own heart: and when he dies, his spirit will take its smiling leave, without having ever had an ill thought of others, or the consciousness of one in itself!

On Reason and Imagination

COMPOSED PROBABLY BEFORE APRIL 1823

I hate people who have no notion of anything but generalities, and forms, and creeds, and naked propositions, even worse than I dislike those who cannot for the soul of them arrive at the comprehension of an abstract idea. There are those (even among philosophers) who, deeming that all truth is contained within certain outlines and common topics, if you proceed to add colour or relief from individuality, protest against the use of rhetoric as an illogical thing; and if you drop a hint of pleasure or pain as ever entering into 'this breathing world', raise a prodigious outcry against all appeals to the passions.

It is, I confess, strange to me that men who pretend to more than usual accuracy in distinguishing and analysing, should insist that in treating of human nature, of moral good and evil, the nominal differences are alone of any value, or that in describing the feelings and motives of men, anything that conveys the smallest idea of what those feelings are in any given circumstances, or can by parity of reason ever be in any others, is a deliberate attempt at artifice and delusion – as if a knowledge or representation of things as they really exist (rules and definitions apart) was a proportionable departure from the truth. They stick to the table of contents, and never open the volume of the mind. They are for having maps, not pictures of the world we live in: as much as to say that a bird's-eye view of things contains the truth, the whole truth, and nothing but the truth. If you want to look for the situation of a particular spot, they turn to a pasteboard globe, on which they fix their wandering gaze; and because you cannot find the object of your search in their bald 'abridgements', tell you there is no such place, or that it is not worth enquiring after. They had better confine their studies to the celestial sphere and the signs of the zodiac; for there they will meet with no petty details to boggle at, or contradict their vague conclusions. Such persons would make excellent theologians, but are very indifferent philosophers. To pursue this geographical reasoning a little farther. They may say that the map of a county or shire, for instance, is too large, and conveys a disproportionate idea of its relation to the whole. And we say that their map of the globe is too small, and conveys no idea of it at all.

> In the world's volume
> Our Britain shows as of it, but not in it;
> In a great pool a swan's nest:

but is it really so? What! the county is bigger than the map at any rate: the representation falls short of the reality, by a million degrees, and you would omit it altogether in order to arrive at a balance of power in the non-entities of the understanding, and call this keeping within the bounds of sense and reason; and whatever does not come within those self-made limits is to be set aside as frivolous or monstrous. But 'there are more things between heaven and earth than were ever dreamt of in this philosophy'. They cannot get them all in, *of the size of life*, and therefore they reduce them on a graduated scale, till they think they can. So be it, for certain necessary and general purposes, and in compliance with the infirmity of human intellect: but at other times, let us enlarge our conceptions to the dimensions of the original objects; nor let it be pretended that we have outraged truth and nature, because we have encroached on your diminutive mechanical standard. There is no language, no description that can strictly come up to the truth and force of reality: all we have to do is to guide our descriptions and conclusions by the reality. A certain proportion must be kept: we must not invert the rules of moral perspective. Logic should enrich and invigorate its decisions by the use of imagination; as rhetoric should be governed in its application, and guarded from abuse by the checks of the understanding. Neither, I apprehend, is sufficient alone. The mind can conceive only one or a few things in their integrity: if it proceeds to more, it must have recourse to artificial substitutes, and judge by comparison merely. In the former case, it may select the least worthy, and so distort the truth of things, by giving a hasty preference: in the latter, the danger is that it may refine and abstract so much as to attach no idea at all to them, corresponding with their practical value, or their influence on the minds of those concerned with them. Men act from individual impressions; and to know mankind, we should be acquainted with nature. Men act from passion; and we can only judge of passion by sympathy. Persons of the dry and husky class above spoken of, often seem to think even nature itself an interloper on their flimsy theories. They prefer the shadows in Plato's cave to the actual objects without it. They consider men 'as mice in an air-pump', fit only for their experiments; and do not consider the rest of the universe, or 'all the mighty world of eye and ear', as worth any notice at all. This is making short, but not sure work. Truth does not lie *in vacuo*, any more than in a well. We must improve our concrete experience of persons and things into the contemplation of general rules and principles; but without being grounded in individual facts and feelings, we shall end as we began, in ignorance.

It is mentioned in a short account of *The Last Moments of Mr Fox*, that the conversation at the house of Lord Holland (where he died) turning upon Mr Burke's style, that Noble Person objected to it as too gaudy and meretricious, and said that it was more profuse of flowers than fruit. On which Mr Fox observed, that though this was a common objection, it appeared to him altogether an unfounded one; that on the contrary, the flowers often concealed the fruit beneath them, and the ornaments of style were rather an hindrance than an advantage to the sentiments they were meant to set off. In confirmation of this remark, he offered to take down the book, and translate a page anywhere into his own plain, natural style; and by his doing so, Lord Holland was convinced that he had often missed the thought from having his attention drawn off to the dazzling imagery. Thus people continually find fault with the colours of style as incompatible with the truth of the reasoning, but without any foundation whatever. If it were a question about the figure of two triangles, and any person were to object that one triangle was green and the other yellow, and bring this to bear upon the acuteness or obtuseness of the angles, it would be obvious to remark that the colour had nothing to do with the question. But in a dispute whether two objects are coloured alike, the discovery, that one is green and the other yellow, is fatal. So with respect to moral truth (as distinct from mathematical), whether a thing is good or evil, depends on the quantity of passion, of feeling, of pleasure and pain connected with it, and with which we must be made acquainted in order to come to a sound conclusion, and not on the enquiry, whether it is round or square. Passion, in short, is the essence, the chief ingredient in moral truth; and the warmth of passion is sure to kindle the light of imagination on the objects around it. The 'words that glow' are almost inseparable from the 'thoughts that burn'. Hence logical reason and practical truth are *disparates*. It is easy to raise an outcry against violent invectives, to talk loud against extravagance and enthusiasm, to pick a quarrel with everything but the most calm, candid, and qualified statement of facts: but there are enormities to which no words can do adequate justice. Are we then, in order to form a complete idea of them, to omit every circumstance of aggravation, or to suppress every feeling of impatience that arises out of the details, lest we should be accused of giving way to the influence of prejudice and passion? This would be to falsify the impression altogether, to misconstrue reason, and fly in the face of nature. Suppose, for instance, that in the discussions on the slave-trade, a description to the life was given of the horrors of the *Middle Passage* (as it was termed), that you saw the manner in which thousands of wretches, year after year, were stowed together in the hold of a slave-ship, without air, without light, without food, without hope, so that what they suffered in reality was brought home to you in imagination, till you felt in sickness of heart as one of them, could it be said that this was a prejudging of the case, that your knowing the extent of the evil disqualified you from pronouncing sentence upon it, and that your disgust and abhorrence were the effects of a heated imagination? No. Those evils that inflame the imagination and make the heart sick, ought not to leave the head cool. This is the very test and measure of the degree of the enormity, that it involuntarily staggers and appals the mind. If it were a common iniquity, if it were slight and partial, or necessary, it would not have this effect; but it very properly carries away the feelings, and (if you will) overpowers the judgement, because it is a mass of evil so monstrous and unwarranted as not to be endured, even in thought. A man on the rack does not suffer the less, because the extremity of anguish takes away his command of feeling and attention to appearances. A pang inflicted on humanity is not the less real, because it stirs up sympathy in the breast of humanity. Would you tame down the glowing language of justifiable passion into that of cold indifference, of self-complacent, sceptical reasoning, and thus take out the sting of indignation from the mind of the spectator? Not, surely, till you have removed the nuisance by the levers that strong feeling alone can set at work, and have thus taken away the pang of suffering that caused it! Or say that the question were proposed to you, whether, on some occasion, you should thrust your hand into the flames, and were coolly told that you were not at all to consider the pain and anguish it might give you, nor suffer yourself to be led away by any such idle appeals to natural sensibility, but to refer the decision to some abstract, technical ground of propriety, would you not laugh in your adviser's face? Oh! no; where our own interests are concerned, or where we are sincere in our professions of regard, the pretended distinction between sound judgement and lively imagination is quickly done away with. But I would not wish a better or more philosophical standard of morality, than that we should think and feel towards others as we should, if it were our own case. If we look for a higher standard than this, we shall not find it; but shall lose the substance for the shadow! Again, suppose an extreme or individual instance is brought forward in any general question, as that of the cargo of sick slaves that were thrown overboard as so much *live lumber* by the captain of a Guinea vessel, in the year 1775, which was one of the things that first drew the attention of the public to this nefarious traffic,[1] or the practice of suspending contumacious negroes in cages to have their eyes pecked out, and to be devoured alive by birds of prey – does this form no rule, because the mischief is solitary or excessive? The rule is absolute; for we feel that nothing of the kind could take place, or be tolerated for an instant, in any system that was not rotten at the core. If such things are ever done in any circumstances with impunity, we know what must be done every day under the same sanction. It shows that there is an

---

1 See *Memoirs of Granville Sharp*, by Prince Hoare, Esq.

utter deadness to every principle of justice or feeling of humanity; and where this is the case, we may take out our tables of abstraction, and set down what is to follow through every gradation of petty, galling vexation, and wanton, unrelenting cruelty. A state of things, where a single instance of the kind can possibly happen without exciting general consternation, ought not to exist for half an hour. The parent, hydra-headed injustice ought to be crushed at once with all its viper brood. Practices, the mention of which makes the flesh creep, and that affront the light of day, ought to be put down the instant they are known, without enquiry and without repeal.

There was an example of eloquent moral reasoning connected with this subject, given in the work just referred to, which was not the less solid and profound, because it was produced by a burst of strong personal and momentary feeling. It is what follows: 'The name of a person having been mentioned in the presence of Naimbanna (a young African chieftain), who was understood by him to have publicly asserted something very degrading to the general character of Africans, he broke out into violent and vindictive language. He was immediately reminded of the Christian duty of forgiving his enemies; upon which he answered nearly in the following words: "If a man should rob me of my money, I can forgive him; if a man should shoot at me, or try to stab me, I can forgive him; if a man should sell me and all my family to a slave-ship, so that we should pass all the rest of our days in slavery in the West Indies, I can forgive him; but" (added he, rising from his seat with much emotion) "if a man takes away the character of the people of my country, I never can forgive him." Being asked why he would not extend his forgiveness to those who took away the character of the people of his country, he answered: "If a man should try to kill me, or should sell me and my family for slaves, he would do an injury to as many as he might kill or sell; but if anyone takes away the character of black people, that man injures black people all over the world; and when he has once taken away their character, there is nothing which he may not do to black people ever after. That man, for instance, will beat black men, and say, *Oh, it is only a black man, why should not I beat him?* That man will make slaves of black people; for, when he has taken away their character; he will say, *Oh, they are only black people, why should not I make them slaves?* That man will take away all the people of Africa if he can catch them; and if you ask him, But why do you take away all these people? he will say, *Oh! they are only black people – they are not like white people – why should I not take them?* That is the reason why I cannot forgive the man who takes away the character of the people of my country;"' *Memoirs of Granville Sharp*, p. 369.

I conceive more real light and vital heat is thrown into the argument by this struggle of natural feeling to relieve itself from the weight of a false and injurious imputation, than would be added to it by twenty volumes of tables and calculations of the *pros* and *cons* of right and wrong, of utility and inutility, in Mr Bentham's handwriting. In allusion to this celebrated person's theory of morals, I will here go a step farther, and deny that the dry calculation of consequences is the sole and unqualified test of right and wrong; for we are to take into the account (as well) the reaction of these consequences upon the mind of the individual and the community. In morals, the cultivation of a *moral sense* is not the last thing to be attended to – nay, it is the first. Almost the only unsophisticated or spirited remark that we meet with in Paley's *Moral Philosophy*, is one which is also to be found in Tucker's *Light of Nature* – namely, that in dispensing charity to common beggars we are not to consider so much the good it may do the object of it, as the harm it will do the person who refuses it. A sense of compassion is involuntarily excited by the immediate appearance of distress, and a violence and injury is done to the kindly feelings by withholding the obvious relief, the trifling pittance in our power. This is a remark, I think, worthy of the ingenious and amiable author from whom Paley borrowed it. So with respect to the atrocities committed in the slave-trade, it could not be set up as a doubtful plea in their favour, that the actual and intolerable sufferings inflicted on the individuals were compensated by certain advantages in a commercial and political point of view – in a moral sense they *cannot* be compensated. They hurt the public mind: they harden and sear the natural feelings. The evil is monstrous and palpable; the pretended good is remote and contingent. In morals, as in philosophy, *De non apparentibus et non existentibus eaden est ratio.* What does not touch the heart, or come home to the feelings, goes comparatively for little or nothing. A benefit that exists merely in possibility, and is judged of only by the forced dictates of the understanding, is not a set-off against an evil (say of equal magnitude in itself) that strikes upon the senses, that haunts the imagination, and lacerates the human heart. A spectacle of deliberate cruelty, that shocks everyone that sees and hears of it, is not to be justified by any calculations of cold-blooded self-interest – is not to be permitted in any case. It is prejudged and self-condemned. Necessity has been therefore justly called 'the tyrant's plea'. It is no better with the mere doctrine of utility, which is the sophist's plea. Thus, for example, an infinite number of lumps of sugar put into Mr Bentham's artificial ethical scales would never weigh against the pounds of human flesh, or drops of human blood, that are sacrificed to produce them. The taste of the former on the palate is evanescent; but the others sit heavy on the soul. The one are an object to the imagination: the others only to the understanding. But man is an animal compounded both of imagination and understanding; and, in treating of what is good for man's nature, it is necessary to consider both. A calculation of the mere ultimate advantages, without regard to natural feelings and affections, may improve the external face and physical comforts of society, but will leave it heartless and worthless in itself. In a word, the sympathy of the individual with the consequences of his own act is to be attended to (no less than the consequences themselves) in every sound system of morality; and this must be determined by certain natural laws of the human mind, and not by rules of logic or arithmetic.

The aspect of a moral question is to be judged of very much like the face of a country, by the projecting points, by what is striking and memorable, by that which leaves traces of itself behind, or 'casts its shadow before'. Millions of acres do not make a picture; nor the calculation of all the consequences in the world a sentiment. We must have some outstanding object for the mind, as well as the eye, to dwell on and recur to – something marked and decisive to give a tone and texture to the moral feelings. Not only is the attention thus roused and kept alive; but what is most important as to the principles of action, the desire of good or hatred of evil is powerfully excited. But all individual facts and history come under the head of what these people call *Imagination*. All full, true, and particular accounts they consider as romantic, ridiculous, vague, inflammatory. As a case in point, one of this school of thinkers declares that he was qualified to write a better *History of India* from having never been there than if he had, as the last might lead to local distinctions or party-prejudices; that is to say, that he could describe a country better at second-hand than from original observation, or that from having seen no one object, place, or person, he could do ampler justice to the whole. It might be maintained, much on the same principle, that an artist would paint a better likeness of a person after he was dead, from description or different sketches of the face, than from having seen the individual living man. On the contrary, I humbly conceive that the seeing half a dozen wandering Lascars in the streets of London gives one a better idea of the soul of India, that cradle of the world, and (as it were) garden of the sun, than all the charts, records, and statistical reports that can be sent over, even under the classical administration of Mr Canning. *Ex uno omnes.* One Hindu differs more from a citizen of London than he does from all other Hindus; and by seeing the two first, man to man, you know comparatively and essentially what they are, nation to nation. By a very few specimens you fix the great leading differences, which are nearly the same throughout. Any one thing is a better representative of its kind, than all the words and definitions in the world can be. The sum total is indeed different from the particulars; but it is not easy to guess at any general result, without some previous induction of particulars and appeal to experience.

What can we reason, but from what we know?

Again, it is quite wrong, instead of the most striking illustrations of human nature, to single out the stalest and tritest, as if they were most authentic and infallible; not considering that from the extremes you may infer the means, but you cannot from the means infer the extremes in any case. It may be said that the extreme and individual cases may be retorted upon us – I deny it, unless it be with truth. The imagination is an *associating* principle; and has an instinctive perception when a thing belongs to a system, or is only an exception to it. For instance, the excesses committed by the victorious besiegers of a town do not attach to the nation committing them, but to the nature of that sort of warfare, and are common to both sides. They may be struck off the score of national prejudices. The cruelties exercised upon slaves, on the other hand, grow out of the

relation between master and slave; and the mind intuitively revolts at
them as such. The cant about the horrors of the French Revolution
is mere cant – everybody knows it to be so: each party would have
retaliated upon the other: it was a civil war, like that for a disputed
succession: the general principle of the right or wrong of the change
remained untouched. Neither would these horrors have taken place,
except from Prussian manifestos, and treachery within: there were
none in the American, and have been none in the Spanish Revolution. The massacre of St Bartholomew arose out of the principles of
that religion which exterminates with fire and sword, and keeps no
faith with heretics. If it be said that nicknames, party watchwords,
bugbears, the cry of 'No Popery', etc. are continually played off upon
the imagination with the most mischievous effect, I answer that most
of these bugbears and terms of vulgar abuse have arisen out of abstruse speculation or barbarous prejudice, and have seldom had their
root in real facts or natural feelings. Besides, are not general topics,
rules, exceptions, endlessly bandied to and fro, and balanced one
against the other by the most learned disputants? Have not three-
fourths of all the wars, schisms, heart-burnings in the world begun
on mere points of controversy? There are two classes whom I have
found given to this kind of reasoning against the use of our senses
and feelings in what concerns human nature, *viz*, knaves and fools.
The last do it, because they think their own shallow dogmas settle all
questions best without any farther appeal; and the first do it, because
they know that the refinements of the head are more easily got rid of
than the suggestions of the heart, and that a strong sense of injustice, excited by a particular case in all its aggravations, tells more
against them than all the distinctions of the jurists. Facts, concrete
existences, are stubborn things, and are not so soon tampered with
or turned about to any point we please, as mere names and abstrac-
tions. Of these last it may be said,

> A breath can *mar* them, as a breath has made:

and they are liable to be puffed away by every wind of doctrine, or
baffled by every plea of convenience. I wonder that Rousseau gave
into this cant about the want of soundness in rhetorical and imaginative reasoning; and was so fond of this subject, as to make an abridg-

ment of Plato's rhapsodies upon it, by which he was led to expel poets from his commonwealth. Thus two of the most flowery writers are those who have exacted the greatest severity of style from others. Rousseau was too ambitious of an exceedingly technical and scientific mode of reasoning, scarcely attainable in the mixed questions of human life, (as may be seen in his *Social Contract* – a work of great ability, but extreme formality of structure) and it is probable he was led into this error in seeking to overcome his too great warmth of natural temperament and a tendency to indulge merely the impulses of passion. Burke, who was a man of fine imagination, had the good sense (without any of this false modesty) to defend the moral uses of the imagination, and is himself one of the grossest instances of its abuse.

It is not merely the fashion among philosophers – the poets also have got into a way of scouting individuality as beneath the sublimity of their pretensions, and the universality of their genius. The philosophers have become mere logicians, and their rivals mere rhetoricians; for as these last must float on the surface, and are not allowed to be harsh and crabbed and recondite like the others, by leaving out the individual, they become commonplace. They cannot reason, and they must declaim. Modern tragedy, in particular, is no longer like a vessel making the voyage of life, and tossed about by the winds and waves of passion, but is converted into a handsomely constructed steam-boat, that is moved by the sole expansive power of words. Lord Byron has launched several of these ventures lately (if ventures they may be called) and may continue in the same strain as long as he pleases. We have not now a number of *dramatis personae* affected by particular incidents and speaking according to their feelings, or as the occasion suggests, but each mounting the rostrum, and delivering his opinion on fate, fortune, and the entire consummation of things. The individual is not of sufficient importance to occupy his own thoughts or the thoughts of others. The poet fills his page with *grandes pensées*. He covers the face of nature with the beauty of his sentiments and the brilliancy of his paradoxes. We have the subtleties of the head, instead of the workings of the heart, and possible justifications instead of the actual motives of conduct. This all seems to proceed on a false estimate of individual nature and the value of human life. We have been so used to count by millions of late, that we think the units that compose them nothing; and are so prone to trace remote principles, that we neglect the immediate results. As an instance of the opposite style of dramatic dialogue, in which the persons speak for themselves, and to one another, I will give, by way of illustration, a passage from an old tragedy, in which a brother has just caused his sister to be put to a violent death.

> *Bosola*:   Fix your eye here.
> *Ferdinand*:   Constantly.
> *Bosola*:   Do you not weep?
>   Other sins only speak; murther shrieks out:
>   The element of water moistens the earth;
>   But blood flies upwards, and bedews the heavens.
> *Ferdinand*:   Cover her face: mine eyes dazzle; she died young.
> *Bosola*:   I think not so: her infelicity
>   Seem'd to have years too many.
> *Ferdinand*:   She and I were twins:
>   And should I die this instant, I had lived
>   Her time to a minute.
>
> *Duchess of Malfy*, Act IV, Scene 2

How fine is the constancy with which he first fixes his eye on the dead body, with a forced courage, and then, as his resolution wavers, how natural is his turning his face away, and the reflection that strikes him on her youth and beauty and untimely death, and the thought that they were twins, and his measuring his life by hers up to the present period, as if all that was to come of it were nothing! Now, I would fain ask whether there is not in this contemplation of the interval that separates the beginning from the end of life, of a life too so varied from good to ill, and of the pitiable termination of which the person speaking has been the wilful and guilty cause, enough to 'give the mind pause?' Is not that revelation as it were of the whole extent of our being which is made by the flashes of passion and stroke of calamity, a subject sufficiently staggering to have place in legitimate tragedy? Are not the struggles of the will with untoward events and the adverse passions of others as interesting and instructive in the representation as reflections on the mutability of fortune or inevitableness of destiny, or on the passions of men in general? The tragic Muse does not merely utter muffled sounds: but we see the paleness on the cheek, and the life-blood gushing from the heart! The interest we take in our own lives, in our successes or disappointments, and the *home* feelings that arise out of these, when well described, are the clearest and truest mirror in which we can see the image of human nature. For in this sense each man is a microcosm. What he is, the rest are – whatever his joys and sorrows are composed of, theirs are the same – no more, no less.

> One touch of nature makes the whole world kin.

But it must be the genuine touch of nature, not the outward flourishes and varnish of art. The spouting, oracular, didactic figure of the poet no more answers to the living man, than the lay-figure of the painter does. We may well say to such a one,

> Thou hast no speculation in those eyes
> That thou dost glare with: thy bones are marrowless,
> Thy blood is cold!

Man is (so to speak) an endless and infinitely varied repetition: and if we know what one man feels, we so far know what a thousand feel in the sanctuary of their being. Our feeling of general humanity is at once an aggregate of a thousand different truths, and it is also the same truth a thousand times told. As is our perception of this original truth, the root of our imagination, so will the force and richness of the general impression proceeding from it be. The boundary of our sympathy is a circle which enlarges itself according to its propulsion from the centre – the heart. If we are imbued with a deep sense of individual weal or woe, we shall be awe-struck at the idea of humanity in general. If we know little of it but its abstract and common properties, without their particular application, their force or degrees, we shall care just as little as we know either about the whole or the individuals. If we understand the texture and vital feeling, we then can fill up the outline, but we cannot supply the former from having the latter given. Moral and poetical truth is like expression in a picture – the one is not to be attained by smearing over a large canvas, nor the other by bestriding a vague topic. In such matters, the most pompous sciolists are accordingly found to be the greatest contemners of human life. But I defy any great tragic writer to despise that nature which he understands, or that heart which he has probed, with all its rich bleeding materials of joy and sorrow. The subject may not be a source of much triumph to him, from its alternate light and shade, but it can never become one of supercilious indifference. He must feel a strong reflex interest in it, corresponding to that which he has depicted in the characters of others. Indeed, the object and end of playing, 'both at the first and now, is to hold the mirror up to nature', to enable us to feel for others as for ourselves, or to embody a distinct interest out of ourselves by the force of imagination and passion. This is summed up in the wish of the poet –

To feel what others are, and know myself a man.

If it does not do this, it loses both its dignity and its proper use.

– On Application to Study –

FIRST PUBLISHED *NEW MONTHLY MAGAZINE*, DECEMBER 1823

No one is idle, who can do anything. It is conscious inability, or the sense of repeated failure, that prevents us from undertaking, or deters us from the prosecution of any work.

Wilson, the painter, might be mentioned as an exception to this rule; for he was said to be an indolent man. After bestowing a few touches on a picture, he grew tired, and said to any friend who called in, 'Now, let us go somewhere!' But the fact is, that Wilson could not finish his pictures minutely; and that those few masterly touches, carelessly thrown in of a morning, were all that he could do. The rest would have been labour lost. Morland has been referred to as another man of genius, who could only be brought to work by fits and snatches. But his landscapes and figures (whatever degree of merit they might possess) were mere hasty sketches; and he could produce all that he was capable of, in the first half-hour, as well as in twenty years. Why bestow additional pains without additional effect? What he did was from the impulse of the moment, from the lively impression of some coarse, but striking object; and with that impulse his efforts ceased, as they justly ought. There is no use in labouring, *invitâ Minerva* – nor any difficulty in it, when the Muse is not averse.

> The labour we delight in physics pain.

Denner finished his unmeaning portraits with a microscope, and without being ever weary of his fruitless task; for the essence of his genius was industry. Sir Joshua Reynolds, courted by the Graces and by Fortune, was hardly ever out of his painting-room; and lamented a few days, at any time spent at a friend's house or at a nobleman's seat in the country, as so much time lost. That darkly illuminated room 'to him a kingdom was'. His pencil was the sceptre that he wielded, and the throne, on which his sitters were placed, a throne for Fame. Here he felt indeed at home; here the current of his ideas flowed full and strong; here he felt most self-possession, most command over others; and the sense of power urged him on to his delightful task with a sort of vernal cheerfulness and vigour, even in the decline of life. The feeling of weakness and incapacity would have made his hand soon falter, would have rebutted him from his object; or had the canvas mocked, and been insensible to his toil, instead of gradually turning to

> A lucid mirror, in which nature saw
> All her reflected features,

he would, like so many others, have thrown down his pencil in despair, or proceeded reluctantly, without spirit and without success. Claude Lorraine, in like manner, spent whole mornings on the banks of the Tiber or in his study, eliciting beauty after beauty, adding touch to touch, getting nearer and nearer to perfection, luxuriating in endless felicity – not merely giving the salient points, but filling up the whole intermediate space with continuous grace and beauty! What farther motive was necessary to induce him to persevere, but the bounty of his fate? What greater pleasure could he seek for, than that of seeing the perfect image of his mind reflected in the work of his hand? But as is the pleasure and the confidence produced by consummate skill, so is the pain and the desponding effect of total failure. When for the fair face of nature, we only see an unsightly blot issuing from our best endeavours, then the nerves slacken, the tears fill the eyes, and the painter turns away from his art, as the lover from a mistress, that scorns him. Alas! how many such have, as the poet says,

> Begun in gladness;
> Whereof has come in the end despondency and madness

not for want of will to proceed, (oh! no,) but for lack of power!

Hence it is that those often do best (up to a certain point of commonplace success) who have least knowledge and least ambition to excel. Their taste keeps pace with their capacity; and they are not deterred by insurmountable difficulties, of which they have no idea. I have known artists (for instance) of considerable merit, and a certain native rough strength and resolution of mind, who have been active and enterprising in their profession, but who never seemed to think of any works but those which they had in hand; they never spoke of a picture, or appeared to have seen one: to them Titian, Raphael, Rubens, Rembrandt, Correggio, were as if they had never been: no tones, mellowed by time to soft perfection, lured them to their luckless doom, no divine forms baffled their vain embrace; no sound of immortality rung in their ears, or drew off their attention from the calls of creditors or of hunger: they walked through collections of the finest works, like the children in the fiery furnace, untouched, unapproached. With these true *terrae filii* the art seemed to begin and end: they thought only of the subject of their next production, the size of their next canvas, the grouping, the getting of the figures in; and conducted their work to its conclusion with as little distraction of mind and as few misgivings as a stagecoach-man conducts a stage, or a carrier delivers a bale of goods, according to its destination. Such persons, if they do not rise above, at least seldom sink below themselves. They do not soar to the 'highest Heaven of invention', nor penetrate the inmost recesses of the heart; but they succeed in all that they attempt, or are capable of, as men of business and industry in their calling. For them the veil of the Temple of Art is not rent asunder, and it is well: one glimpse of the Sanctuary, of the Holy of the Holies, might palsy their hands, and dim their sight for ever after!

I think there are two mistakes, common enough, on this subject; *viz.* that men of genius, or of first-rate capacity, do little, except by intermittent fits, or *per saltum* – and that they do that little in a slight and slovenly manner. There may be instances of this; but they are not the highest, and they are the exceptions, not the rule. On the contrary, the greatest artists have in general been the most prolific or the most elaborate, as the best writers have been frequently the most voluminous as well as indefatigable. We have a great living instance among writers, that the quality of a man's productions is not to be estimated in the inverse ratio of their quantity, I mean in the author of *Waverley*, the fecundity of whose pen is no less admirable than its felicity. Shakespeare is another instance of the same prodigality of genius; his materials being endlessly poured forth with no niggard or fastidious hand, and the mastery of the execution being (in many respects at least) equal to the boldness of the design. As one example among others that I might cite of the attention which he gave to his subject, it is sufficient to observe, that there is scarcely a word in any of his more striking passages that can be altered for the better. If any person, for instance, is trying to recollect a favourite line, and cannot hit upon some particular expression, it is in vain to think of substituting any other so good. That in the original text is not merely the best, but it seems the only right one. I will stop to illustrate this point a little. I was at a loss the other day for the line in *Henry V*:

> *Nice* customs curtesy to great kings.

I could not recollect the word *nice*: I tried a number of others, such as *old*, *grave*, etc. – they would none of them do, but seemed all heavy, lumbering, or from the purpose: the word *nice*, on the contrary, appeared to drop into its place, and be ready to assist in paying the reverence required. Again,

> A jest's *prosperity* lies in the ear
> Of him that hears it.

I thought, in quoting from memory, of 'A jest's *success*', 'A jest's *renown*', etc. I then turned to the volume, and there found the very word that, of all others, expressed the idea. Had Shakespeare searched through the four quarters of the globe, he could not have lighted on another to convey so exactly what he meant – a *casual, hollow, sounding* success! I could multiply such examples, but that I am sure the reader will easily supply them himself; and they show sufficiently that Shakespeare was not (as he is often represented) a loose or clumsy writer. The bold, happy texture of his style, in which every word is prominent, and yet cannot be torn from its place without violence, any more than a limb from the body, is (one should think) the result either of vigilant painstaking or of unerring, intuitive perception, and not the mark of crude conceptions, and 'the random, blindfold blows of Ignorance'.

There cannot be a greater contradiction to the common prejudice that 'Genius is naturally a truant and a vagabond', than the astonishing and (on this hypothesis) unaccountable number of *chef d'oeuvres* left behind them by the old masters. The stream of their invention supplies the taste of successive generations like a river: they furnish a hundred galleries, and preclude competition, not more by the excellence than by the number of their performances. Take Raphael and Rubens alone. There are works of theirs in single collections enough to occupy a long and laborious life, and yet their works are spread through all the collections of Europe. They seem to have cost them no more labour than if they 'had drawn in their breath and puffed it forth again'. But we know that they made drawings, studies, sketches of all the principal of these, with the care and caution of the merest tyros in the art; and they remain equal proofs of their capacity and diligence. The cartoons of Raphael alone might have employed many years, and made a life of illustrious labour, though they look as if they had been struck off at a blow, and are not a tenth part of what he produced in his short but bright career. Titian and Michael Angelo lived longer, but they worked as hard and did as well. Shall we bring in competition with examples like these some trashy caricaturist or idle dauber, who has no sense of the infinite resources of nature or art, nor consequently any power to employ himself upon them for any length of time or to any purpose, to prove that genius and regular industry are incompatible qualities?

In my opinion, the very superiority of the works of the great painters (instead of being a bar to) accounts for their multiplicity. Power is pleasure; and pleasure sweetens pain. A fine poet thus describes the effect of the sight of nature on his mind:

> The sounding cataract
> Haunted me like a passion: the tall rock,
> The mountain, and the deep and gloomy wood,
> Their colours and their forms were then to me
> An appetite, a feeling, and a love,
> That had no need of a remoter charm
> By thought supplied, or any interest
> Unborrowed from the eye.

So the forms of nature, or the human form divine, stood before the great artists of old, nor required any other stimulus to lead the eye to survey, or the hand to embody them, than the pleasure derived from the inspiration of the subject, and 'propulsive force' of the mimic creation. The grandeur of their works was an argument with them, not to stop short, but to proceed. They could have no higher excitement or satisfaction than in the exercise of their art and endless generation of truth and beauty. Success prompts to exertion; and habit facilitates success. It is idle to suppose we can exhaust nature; and the more we employ our own faculties, the more we strengthen them and enrich our stores of observation and invention. The more we do, the more we *can* do. Not indeed if we *get our ideas out of our own heads* – that stock is soon exhausted, and we recur to tiresome, vapid imitations of ourselves. But this is the difference between real and mock talent, between genius and affectation. Nature is not limited, nor does it become effete, like our conceit and vanity. The closer we examine it, the more it refines upon us; it expands as we enlarge and shift our view; it 'grows with our growth, and strengthens with our strength'. The subjects are endless; and our capacity is invigorated as it is called out by occasion and necessity. He who does nothing, renders himself incapable of doing anything; but while we are executing any work, we are preparing and qualifying ourselves to undertake another. The principles are the same in all nature; and we understand them better, as we verify them by experience and practice. It is not as if there was a given number of subjects to work upon, or a set of *innate* or preconceived ideas in our minds which we encroached upon with every new design; the subjects, as I said before, are endless, and we acquire ideas by imparting them. Our expenditure of intellectual wealth makes us rich: we can only be liberal as we have previously accumulated the means. By lying idle, as by standing still, we are confined to the same trite, narrow round of topics: by continuing our efforts, as by moving forwards in a road, we extend our views, and discover continually new tracts of country. Genius, like humanity, rusts for want of use.

Habit also gives promptness; and the soul of dispatch is decision. One man may write a book or paint a picture, while another is deliberating about the plan or the title-page. The great painters were able to do so much, because they knew exactly what they meant to do, and how to set about it. They were thoroughbred workmen, and were not learning their art while they were exercising it. One can do a great deal in a short time if one only knows how. Thus an author may become very voluminous, who only employs an hour or two in a day in study. If he has once obtained, by habit and reflection, a use of his pen with plenty of materials to work upon, the pages vanish before him. The time lost is in beginning, or in stopping after we have begun. If we only go forwards with spirit and confidence, we shall soon arrive at the end of our journey. A practised writer ought never to hesitate for a sentence from the moment he sets pen to paper, or think about the course he is to take. He must trust to his previous knowledge of the subject and to his immediate impulses, and he will get to the close of his task without accidents or loss of time. I can easily understand how the old divines and controversialists produced their folios: I could write folios myself, if I rose early and sat up late at this kind of occupation. But I confess I should be soon tired of it, besides wearying the reader.

In one sense, art is long and life is short. In another sense, this aphorism is not true. The best of us are idle half our time. It is wonderful how much is done in a short space, provided we set about it properly, and give our minds wholly to it. Let anyone devote himself to any art or science ever so strenuously, and he will still have leisure to make considerable progress in half a dozen other acquirements. Leonardo da Vinci was a mathematician, a musician, a poet, and an anatomist, besides being one of the greatest painters of his age. The Prince of Painters was a courtier, a lover, and fond of dress and company. Michael Angelo was a prodigy of versatility of talent – a writer of sonnets (which Wordsworth has thought worth translating) and the admirer of Dante. Salvator was a lutenist and a satirist. Titian was an elegant letter-writer, and a finished gentleman. Sir Joshua Reynolds's *Discourses* are more polished and classical even than any of his pictures. Let a man do all he can in any one branch of study, he must either exhaust himself and doze over it, or vary his pursuit, or else lie idle. All our real labour lies in a nutshell. The mind makes, at some period or other, one Herculean effort, and the rest is mechanical. We have to climb a steep and narrow precipice at first; but after that, the way is broad and easy, where we may drive several accomplishments abreast. Men should have one principal pursuit, which may be both agreeably and advantageously diversified with other lighter ones, as the subordinate parts of a picture may be managed so as to give effect to the centre group. It has been observed by a sensible man,[1] that the having a regular occupation or professional duties to attend to is no excuse for putting forth an inelegant or inaccurate work; for a habit of industry braces and strengthens the mind, and enables it to wield its energies with additional ease and steadier purpose. Were I allowed to instance in myself, if what I write at present is worth nothing, at least it costs me nothing. But it cost me a great deal twenty years ago. I have added little to my stock since then, and taken little from it. I 'unfold the book and volume of the brain', and transcribe the characters I see there as mechanically as anyone might copy the letters in a sampler. I do not say they came there mechanically – I transfer them to the paper mechanically. After eight or ten years' hard study, an author (at least) may go to sleep.

I do not conceive rapidity of execution necessarily implies slovenliness or crudeness. On the contrary, I believe it is often productive both of sharpness and freedom. The eagerness of composition strikes out sparkles of fancy, and runs the thoughts more naturally and closely into one another. There may be less formal method, but there is more life, and spirit, and truth. In the play and agitation of the mind, it runs over, and we dally with the subject, as the glass-blower rapidly shapes the vitreous fluid. A number of new thoughts rise up spontaneously, and they come in the proper places, because they arise from the occasion. They are also sure to partake of the warmth and vividness of that ebullition of mind, from which they spring. *Spiritus precipitandus est*. In these sort of voluntaries in composition, the thoughts are worked up to a state of projection: the grasp of the subject, the presence of mind, the flow of expression must be something akin to *extempore* speaking; or perhaps such bold but finished draughts may be compared to *fresco* paintings, which imply a life of study and great previous preparation, but of which the execution is momentary and irrevocable. I will add a single remark on a point that has been much disputed. Mr Cobbett lays it down that the first word that occurs is always the best. I would venture to differ from so great an authority. Mr Cobbett himself indeed writes as easily and as well as he talks; but he perhaps is hardly a rule for others without his

1   The Revd W. Shepherd, of Gateacre, in the Preface to his *Life of Poggio*.

practice and without his ability. In the hurry of composition three or four words may present themselves, one on the back of the other, and the last may be the best and right one. I grant thus much, that it is in vain to seek for the word we want, or endeavour to get at it second-hand, or as a paraphrase on some other word – it must come of itself, or arise out of an immediate impression or lively intuition of the subject; that is, the proper word must be suggested immediately by the thoughts, but it need not be presented as soon as called for. It is the same in trying to recollect the names of places, persons, etc. We cannot force our memory; they must come of themselves by natural association, as it were; but they may occur to us when we least think of it, owing to some casual circumstance or link of connection, and long after we have given up the search. Proper expressions rise to the surface from the heat and fermentation of the mind, like bubbles on an agitated stream. It is this which produces a clear and sparkling style.

In painting, great execution supplies the place of high finishing. A few vigorous touches, properly and rapidly disposed, will often give more of the appearance and texture (even) of natural objects than the most heavy and laborious details. But this masterly style of execution is very different from coarse daubing. I do not think, however, that the pains or polish an artist bestows upon his works necessarily interferes with their number. He only grows more enamoured of his task, proportionally patient, indefatigable, and devotes more of the day to study. The time we lose is not in overdoing what we are about, but in doing nothing. Rubens had great facility of execution, and seldom went into the details. Yet Raphael, whose oil-pictures were exact and laboured, achieved, according to the length of time he lived, very nearly as much as he. In filling up the parts of his pictures, and giving them the last perfection they were capable of, he filled up his leisure hours, which otherwise would have lain idle on his hands. I have sometimes accounted for the slow progress of certain artists from the unfinished state in which they have left their works at last. These were evidently done by fits and throes – there was no appearance of continuous labour – one figure had been thrown in at a venture, and then another; and in the intervals between these convulsive and random efforts, more time had been wasted than could have been spent in working up each individual figure on the sure principles of art, and by a careful inspection of nature, to the utmost point of practicable perfection.

Some persons are afraid of their own works; and having made one or two successful efforts, attempt nothing ever after. They stand still midway in the road to fame, from being startled at the shadow of their own reputation. This is a needless alarm. If what they have already done possesses real power, this will increase with exercise; if it has not this power, it is not sufficient to ensure them lasting fame. Such delicate pretenders tremble on the brink of *ideal* perfection, like dew-drops on the edge of flowers; and are fascinated, like so many Narcissuses, with the image of themselves, reflected from the public admiration. It is seldom, indeed, that this cautious repose will answer its end. While seeking to sustain our reputation at the height, we are forgotten. Shakespeare gave different advice, and himself acted upon it.

> Perseverance, dear my lord,
> Keeps honour bright. To have done, is to hang
> Quite out of fashion, like a rusty mail,
> In monumental mockery. Take the instant way;
> For honour travels in a strait so narrow,
> Where one but goes abreast. Keep then the path;
> For emulation hath a thousand sons,
> That one by one pursue. If you give way,
> Or hedge aside from the direct forth-right,
> Like to an enter'd tide, they all rush by,
> And leave you hindmost:–
> Or like a gallant horse, fall'n in first rank,
> Lie there for pavement to the abject rear,
> O'er-run and trampled. Then what they do in present,
> Though less than yours in past, must o'ertop yours:
> For time is like a fashionable host,
> That slightly shakes his parting guest by the hand,
> And with his arms outstretch'd as he would fly,
> Grasps in the comer. Welcome ever smiles,
> And farewell goes out sighing. O let not virtue seek
> Remuneration for the thing it was; for beauty, wit,
> High birth, vigour of bone, desert in service,
> Love, friendship, charity, are subjects all
> To envious and calumniating Time.

One touch of nature makes the whole world kin,
That all with one consent praise new-born gauds,
Though they are made and moulded of things past;
And give to dust that is a little gilt
More laud than gilt o'er dusted.
The present eye praises the present object.

Troilus and Cressida

I cannot very well conceive how it is that some writers (even of taste and genius) spend whole years in mere corrections for the press, as it were – in polishing a line or adjusting a comma. They take long to consider, exactly as there is nothing worth the trouble of a moment's thought; and the more they deliberate, the farther they are from deciding: for their fastidiousness increases with the indulgence of it, nor is there any real ground for preference. They are in the situation of *Ned Softly*, in the *Tatler*, who was a whole morning debating whether a line of a poetical epistle should run –

You sing your song with so much art;

or,

Your song you sing with so much art.

These are points that it is impossible ever to come to a determination about; and it is only a proof of a little mind ever to have entertained the question at all.

There is a class of persons whose minds seem to move in an element of littleness; or rather, that are entangled in trifling difficulties, and incapable of extricating themselves from them. There was a remarkable instance of this improgressive, ineffectual, restless activity of temper in a late celebrated and very ingenious landscape-painter. 'Never ending, still beginning', his mind seemed entirely made up of points and fractions, nor could he by any means arrive at a conclusion or a valuable whole. He made it his boast that he never sat with his hands before him, and yet he never did anything. His powers and his time were frittered away in an importunate, uneasy, fidgety attention to little things. The first picture he ever painted (when a mere boy) was a copy of his father's house; and he began it by counting the number of bricks in the front upwards and lengthways, and then made a scale of them on his canvas. This literal style and mode of study stuck to him to the last. He was put under Wilson, whose example (if anything could) might have cured him of this pettiness of conception; but nature prevailed, as it almost always does. To take pains to no purpose, seemed to be his motto, and the delight of his life. He left (when he died, not long ago) heaps of canvases with elaborately finished pencil outlines on them, and with perhaps a little dead-colouring added here and there. In this state they were thrown aside, as if he grew tired of his occupation the instant it gave a promise of turning to account, and his whole object in the pursuit of art was to erect scaffoldings. The same intense interest in the most frivolous things extended to the common concerns of life, to the arranging of his letters, the labelling of his books, and the inventory of his wardrobe. Yet he was a man of sense, who saw the folly and the waste of time in all this, and could warn others against it. The perceiving our own weaknesses enables us to give others excellent advice, but it does not teach us to reform them ourselves. 'Physician, heal thyself!' is the hardest lesson to follow. Nobody knew better than our artist that repose is necessary to great efforts, and that he who is never idle, labours in vain!

Another error is to spend one's life in procrastination and preparations for the future. Persons of this turn of mind stop at the threshold of art, and accumulate the means of improvement, till they obstruct their progress to the end. They are always putting off the evil day, and excuse themselves for doing nothing by commencing some new and indispensable course of study. Their projects are magnificent, but remote, and require years to complete or to put them in execution. Fame is seen in the horizon, and flies before them. Like the recreant boastful knight in Spenser, they turn their backs on their competitors, to make a great career, but never return to the charge. They make themselves masters of anatomy, of drawing, of perspective: they collect prints, casts, medallions, make studies of heads, of hands, of the bones, the muscles; copy pictures; visit Italy, Greece, and return as they went. They fulfil the proverb, 'When you are at Rome, you must do as those at Rome do'. This circuitous, erratic pursuit of art can come to no good. It is only an apology for idleness and vanity. Foreign travel especially makes men pedants, not artists.

What we seek, we must find at home or nowhere. The way to do great things is to set about something, and he who cannot find resources in himself or in his own painting-room, will perform the grand tour, or go through the circle of the arts and sciences, and end just where he began!

The same remarks that have been here urged with respect to an application to the study of art, will, in a great measure (though not in every particular), apply to an attention to business: I mean, that exertion will generally follow success and opportunity in the one, as it does confidence and talent in the other. Give a man a motive to work, and he will work. A lawyer who is regularly feed, seldom neglects to look over his briefs: the more business, the more industry. The stress laid upon early rising is preposterous. If we have anything to do when we get up, we shall not lie in bed, to a certainty. Thomson the poet was found late in bed by Dr Burney, and asked why he had not risen earlier. The Scotchman wisely answered, 'I had no motive, young man!' What indeed had he to do after writing the *Seasons*, but to dream out the rest of his existence, unless it were to write the *Castle of Indolence*![2]

---

2 Schoolboys attend to their tasks as soon as they acquire a relish for study, and apply to that for which they find they have a capacity. If a boy shows no inclination for the Latin tongue, it is a sign he has not a turn for learning languages. Yet he dances well. Give up the thought of making a scholar of him, and bring him up to be a dancing-master!

On the Old Age of Artists

FIRST PUBLISHED *NEW MONTHLY MAGAZINE*, SEPTEMBER 1823

Mr Nollekens died the other day at the age of eighty, and left £240,000 behind him, and the name of one of our best English sculptors. There was a great scramble among the legatees, a codicil to a will with large bequests unsigned, and that last triumph of the dead or dying over those who survive – hopes raised and defeated without a possibility of retaliation, or the smallest use in complaint. The king was at first said to be left residuary legatee. This would have been a fine instance of romantic and gratuitous homage to Majesty, in a man who all his lifetime could never be made to comprehend the abstract idea of the distinction of ranks or even of persons. He would go up to the Duke of York, or Prince of Wales (in spite of warning), take them familiarly by the button like common acquaintance, ask them *how their father did*; and express pleasure at hearing he was well, saying, 'when he was gone, we should never get such another'. He once, when the old king was sitting to him for his bust, fairly stuck a pair of compasses into his nose to measure the distance from the upper lip to the forehead, as if he had been measuring a block of marble. His late Majesty laughed heartily at this, and was amused to find that there was a person in the world, ignorant of that vast interval which separated him from every other man. Nollekens, with all his loyalty, merely liked the man, and cared nothing about the king (which was one of those *mixed modes*, as Mr Locke calls them, of which he had no more idea than if he had been one of the cream-coloured horses) – handled him like so much common clay, and had no other notion of the matter, but that it was his business to make the best bust of him he possibly could, and to set about in the regular way. There was something in this plainness and simplicity that savoured perhaps of the hardness and dryness of his art, and of his own peculiar severity of manner. He conceived that one man's head differed from another's only as it was a better or worse subject for modelling, that a bad bust was not made into a good one by being stuck upon a pedestal, or by any painting or varnishing, and that by whatever name he was called, '*a man's a man for a' that*'. A sculptor's ideas must, I should guess, be somewhat rigid and inflexible, like the materials in which he works. Besides, Nollekens's style was comparatively hard and edgy. He had as much truth and character, but none of the polished graces or transparent softness of Chantry. He had more of the rough, plain, downright honesty of his art. It seemed to be his character. Mr Northcote was once complimenting him on his acknowledged superiority – 'Ay, *you* made the best busts of anybody!' 'I don't know about that', said the other, his eyes (though their orbs were quenched) smiling with a gleam of smothered delight – 'I only know I always tried to make them as like as I could!'

I saw this eminent and singular person one morning in Mr Northcote's painting-room. He had then been for some time blind, and had been obliged to lay aside the exercise of his profession; but he still took a pleasure in designing groups, and in giving directions to others for executing them. He and Northcote made a remarkable pair. He sat down on a low stool (from being rather fatigued), rested with both hands on a stick, as if he clung to the solid and tangible, had an habitual twitch in his limbs and motions, as if catching himself in the act of going too far in chiselling a lip or a dimple in a chin; was *bolt* upright, with features hard and square, but finely cut, a hooked nose, thin lips, an indented forehead; and the defect in his sight completed his resemblance to one of his own masterly busts. He seemed, by time and labour, to 'have *wrought* himself to stone'. Northcote stood by his side – all air and spirit, stooping down to speak to him. The painter was in a loose morning-gown, with his back to the light; his face was like a pale fine piece of colouring; and his eye came out and glanced through the twilight of the past, like an old eagle looking from its eyrie in the clouds. In a moment they had lighted from the top of Mount Cenis in the Vatican –

> As when a vulture on Imaus bred
> Flies tow'rds the springs
> Of Ganges and Hydaspes, Indian streams,

these two fine old men lighted with winged thoughts on the banks of the Tiber, and there bathed and drank of the spirit of their youth. They talked of Titian and Bernini; and Northcote mentioned, that when Roubilliac came back from Rome, after seeing the works of the latter, and went to look at his own in Westminster Abbey, he said – 'By God, they looked like tobacco-pipes'.

They then recalled a number of anecdotes of Day (a fellow-student of theirs), of Barry and Fuseli. Sir Joshua, and Burke, and Johnson were talked of. The names of these great sons of memory were in the room, and they almost seemed to answer to them – Genius and Fame flung a spell into the air,

> And by the force of blear illusion,
> Had drawn me on to my confusion,

had I not been long ere this *siren-proof*! It is delightful, though painful, to hear two veterans in art thus talking over the adventures and studies of their youth, when one feels that they are not quite mortal, that they have one imperishable part about them, and that they are conscious, as they approach the farthest verge of humanity in friendly intercourse and tranquil decay, that they have done something that will live after them. The consolations of religion apart, this is perhaps the only salve that takes out the sting of that sore evil, death; and by lessening the impatience and alarm at his approach, often tempts him to prolong the term of his delay.

It has been remarked that artists, or at least academicians, live long. It is but a short while ago that Northcote, Nollekens, West, Flaxman, Cosway, and Fuseli were all living at the same time, in good health and spirits, without any diminution of faculties, all of them having long past their grand climacteric, and attained to the highest reputation in their several departments. From these striking examples, the diploma of a Royal Academician seems to be a grant of a longer lease of life, among its other advantages. In fact, it is tantamount to the conferring a certain reputation in his profession and a competence on any man, and thus supplies the wants of the body and sets his mind at ease. Artists in general (poor devils!), I am afraid, are not a long-lived race. They break up commonly about forty, their spirits giving way with the disappointment of their hopes of excellence, or the want of encouragement for that which they have attained, their plans disconcerted, and their affairs irretrievable; and in this state of mortification and embarrassment (more or less prolonged and aggravated) they are either starved or else drink themselves to death. But your Academician is quite a different sort of person. He 'bears a charmed life, that must not yield' to duns, or critics, or patrons. He is free of Parnassus, and claims all the immunities of fame in his lifetime. He has but to paint (as the sun has but to shine), to baffle envious maligners. He has but to send his pictures to the exhibition at Somerset House, in order to have them hung up: he has but to dine once a year with the Academy, the nobility, the Cabinet Minister, and the members of the Royal Family, in order not to want a dinner all the rest of the year. Shall hunger come near the man that has feasted with princes – shall a bailiff tap the shoulder on which a Marquis has familiarly leaned, that has been dubbed with knighthood? No, even the fell Serjeant Death stands as it were aloof, and he enjoys a kind of premature immortality in recorded honours and endless labours. Oh what golden hours are his! In the short days of winter he husbands time; the long evenings of summer still find him employed! He paints on, and takes no thought for tomorrow. All is right in that respect. His bills are regularly paid, his drafts are duly honoured. He has exercise for his body, employment for his mind in his profession, and without ever stirring out of his painting-room. He studies as much of other things as he pleases. He goes into the best company, or talks with his sitters – attends at the Academy meetings, and enters into their intrigues and cabals, or stays at home, and enjoys the *otium cum dignitate*. If he is fond of reputation, Fame watches him at work, and weaves a woof, like Iris, over his head – if he is fond of money, Plutus digs a mine under his feet. Whatever he touches becomes gold. He is paid half-price before he begins; and commissions pour in upon commissions. His portraits are like, and

his historical pieces fine; for to question the talents or success of a
Royal Academician is to betray your own want of taste. Or if his
pictures are not quite approved, he is an agreeable man, and con-
verses well. Or he is a person of elegant accomplishments, dresses
well, and is an ornament to a private circle. A man is not an Academician for nothing. 'His life spins round on its soft axle'; and in a round
of satisfied desires and pleasing avocations, without any of the *wear
and tear* of thought or business, there seems no reason why it should
not run smoothly on to its last sand!

Of all the Academicians, the painters, or persons I have ever known,
Mr Northcote is the most to my taste. It may be said of him truly,

> Age cannot wither, nor custom stale
> His infinite variety.

Indeed, it is not possible he should become tedious, since, even if he
repeats the same thing, it appears quite new from his manner, that
breathes new life into it, and from his eye, that is as fresh as the
morning. How you hate anyone who tells the same story or antici-
pates a remark of his – it seems so coarse and vulgar, so dry and
inanimate! There is something like injustice in this preference – but
no! it is a tribute to the spirit that is in the man. Mr Northcote's
manner is completely *extempore*. It is just the reverse of Mr Canning's oratory. All his thoughts come upon him unawares, and for
this reason they surprise and delight you, because they have evidently
the same effect upon his mind. There is the same unconsciousness in
his conversation that has been pointed out in Shakespeare's dialogues;
or you are startled with one observation after another, as when the
mist gradually withdraws from a landscape and unfolds objects one
by one. His figure is small, shadowy, emaciated; but you think only
of his face, which is fine and expressive. His body is out of the question. It is impossible to convey an adequate idea of the *naiveté*, and
unaffected, but delightful ease of the way in which he goes on – now
touching upon a picture – now looking for his snuff-box – now alluding to some book he has been reading – now returning to his
favourite art. He seems just as if he was by himself or in the company
of his own thoughts, and makes you feel quite at home. If it is a
Member of Parliament, or a beautiful woman, or a child, or a young

artist that drops in, it makes no difference; he enters into conversation with them in the same unconstrained manner, as if they were inmates in his family. Sometimes you find him sitting on the floor, like a schoolboy at play, turning over a set of old prints; and I was pleased to hear him say the other day, coming to one of some men putting off in a boat from a shipwreck – '*That* is the grandest and most original thing I ever did!' This was not egotism, but had all the beauty of truth and sincerity. The print was indeed a noble and spirited design. The circumstance from which it was taken happened to Captain Englefield and his crew. He told Northcote the story, sat for his own head, and brought the men from Wapping to sit for theirs; and these he had arranged into a formal composition, till one Jeffrey, a conceited but clever artist of that day, called in upon him, and said, 'Oh! that commonplace thing will never do, it is like West; you should throw them into an action something like this.' Accordingly, the head of the boat was reared up like a seahorse riding the waves, and the elements put into commotion, and when the painter looked at it the last thing as he went out of his room in the dusk of the evening, he said that 'it frightened him'. He retained the expression in the faces of the men nearly as they sat to him. It is very fine, and truly English; and being natural, it was easily made into history. There is a portrait of a young gentleman striving to get into the boat, while the crew are pushing him off with their oars; but at last he prevailed with them by his perseverance and entreaties to take him in. They had only time to throw a bag of biscuits into the boat before the ship went down; which they divided into a biscuit a day for each man, dipping them into water which they collected by holding up their handkerchiefs in the rain and squeezing it into a bottle. They were out sixteen days in the Atlantic, and got ashore at some place in Spain, where the great difficulty was to prevent them from eating too much at once, so as to recover gradually. Captain Englefield observed that he suffered more afterwards than at the time – that he had horrid dreams of falling down precipices for a long while after – that in the boat they told merry stories, and kept up one another's spirits as well as they could, and on some complaint being made of their distressed situation, the young gentleman who had been admitted into their crew remarked, 'Nay, we are not so badly off neither, we are not come to *eating* one another yet!' Thus, whatever is the subject of discourse, the scene is revived in his mind, and every circumstance brought before you without affectation or effort, just as it happened. It might be called *picture-talking*. He has always some pat allusion or anecdote. A young engraver came into his room the other day, with a print which he had put into the crown of his hat, in order not to crumple it, and he said it had been nearly blown away several times in passing along the street. 'You put me in mind', said Northcote, 'of a bird-catcher at Plymouth, who used to put the birds he had caught into his hat to bring them home, and one day meeting my father in the road, he pulled off his hat to make him a low bow, and all the birds flew away!' Sometimes Mr Northcote gets to the top of a ladder to paint a palmtree or to finish a sky in one of his pictures; and in this situation he listens very attentively to anything you tell him. I was once mentioning some strange inconsistencies of our modern poets; and on coming to one that exceeded the rest, he descended the steps of the ladder one by one, laid his pallet and brushes deliberately on the ground, and coming up to me, said – 'You don't say so, it's the very thing I should have supposed of them: yet these are the men that speak against Pope and Dryden'. Never any sarcasms were so fine, so cutting, so careless as his. The grossest things from his lips seem an essence of refinement: the most refined become more so than ever. Hear him talk of Pope's *Epistle to Jervas*, and repeat the lines –

> Yet should the Graces all thy figures place,
> And breathe an air divine on every face;
> Yet should the Muses bid my numbers roll
> Strong as their charms, and gentle as their soul,
> With Zeuxis' Helen thy Bridgewater vie,
> And these be sung till Granville's Myra die:
> Alas! how little from the grave we claim;
> Thou but preserv'st a face, and I a name.

Or let him speak of Boccacio and his story of Isabella and her pot of basil, in which she kept her lover's head and watered it with her tears, 'and how it grew, and it grew, and it grew', and you see his own eyes glisten, and the leaves of the basil-tree tremble to his faltering accents!

Mr Fuseli's conversation is more striking and extravagant, but less pleasing and natural than Mr Northcote's. He deals in paradoxes and caricatures. He talks allegories and personifications, as he paints them. You are sensible of effort without any repose – no careless pleasantry – no traits of character or touches from nature – everything is laboured or overdone. His ideas are gnarled, hard, and distorted, like his features – his theories stalking and straddle-legged, like his gait – his projects aspiring and gigantic, like his gestures – his performance uncouth and dwarfish, like his person. His pictures are also like himself, with eyeballs of stone stuck in rims of tin, and muscles twisted together like ropes or wires. Yet Fuseli is undoubtedly a man of genius, and capable of the most wild and grotesque combinations of fancy. It is a pity that he ever applied himself to painting, which must always be reduced to the test of the senses. He is a little like Dante or Ariosto, perhaps; but no more like Michael Angelo, Raphael, or Correggio, than I am. Nature, he complains, puts him out. Yet he can laugh at artists who 'paint ladies with iron lapdogs', and he describes the great masters of old in words or lines full of truth, and glancing from a pen or tongue of fire. I conceive any person would be more struck with Mr Fuseli at first sight, but would wish to visit Mr Northcote oftener. There is a bold and startling outline in his style of talking, but not the delicate finishing or bland tone that there is in that of the latter. Whatever there is harsh or repulsive about him is, however, in a great degree carried off by his animated foreign accent and broken English, which give character where there is none, and soften its asperities where it is too abrupt and violent.

Compared to either of these artists, West (the late President of the Royal Academy) was a thoroughly mechanical and *commonplace* person – a man 'of no mark or likelihood'. He too was small, thin, but with regular well-formed features, and a precise, sedate, self-satisfied air. This, in part, arose from the conviction in his own mind that he was the greatest painter (and consequently the greatest man) in the world: kings and nobles were common everyday folks, but there was but one West in the many-peopled globe. If there was any one individual with whom he was inclined to share the palm of undivided superiority, it was with Buonaparte. When Mr West had painted a picture, he thought it was perfect. He had no idea of anything in the art but rules, and these he exactly conformed to; so that, according to his theory, what he did was quite right. He conceived of painting as a mechanical or scientific process, and had no more doubt of a face or a group in one of his high ideal compositions being what it ought to be, than a carpenter has that he has drawn a line straight with a ruler and a piece of chalk, or than a mathematician has that the three angles of a triangle are equal to two right ones.

When Mr West walked through his gallery, the result of fifty years' labour, he saw nothing, either on the right or the left, to be added or taken away. The account he gave of his own pictures, which might seem like ostentation or rhodomontade, had a sincere and infantine simplicity in it. When someone spoke of his *St Paul shaking off the serpent from his arm* (at Greenwich Hospital, I believe), he said, 'A little burst of genius, sir!' West was one of those happy mortals who had not an idea of anything beyond himself or his own actual powers and knowledge. I once heard him say in a public room, that he thought he had quite as good an idea of Athens from reading the travelling catalogues of the place, as if he lived there for years. I believe this was strictly true, and that he would have come away with the same slender, literal, unenriched idea of it as he went. Looking at a picture of Rubens, which he had in his possession, he said with great indifference, 'What a pity that this man wanted expression!' This natural self-complacency might be strengthened by collateral circumstances of birth and religion. West, as a native of America, might be supposed to own no superior in the Commonwealth of art: as a Quaker, he smiled with sectarian self-sufficiency at the objections that were made to his theory or practice in painting. He lived long in the firm persuasion of being one of the elect among the sons of Fame, and went to his final rest in the arms of Immortality! Happy error! Enviable old man!

Flaxman is another living and eminent artist, who is distinguished by success in his profession and by a prolonged and active old age. He is diminutive in person, like the others. I know little of him, but that he is an elegant sculptor, and a profound mystic. This last is a character common to many other artists in our days – Loutherbourg, Cosway, Blake, Sharp, Varley, etc. – who seem to relieve the literalness of their professional studies by voluntary excursions into the regions of the preternatural, pass their time between sleeping and waking, and whose ideas are like a stormy night, with the clouds driven rapidly across, and the blue sky and stars gleaming between!

Cosway is the last of these I shall mention. At that name I pause, and must be excused if I consecrate to him a *petit souvenir* in my best manner; for he was Fancy's child. What a fairy palace was his of specimens of art, antiquarianism, and *virtù*, jumbled all together in the richest disorder, dusty, shadowy, obscure, with much left to the imagination (how different from the finical, polished, petty, modernized air of some collections we have seen!) and with copies of the old masters, cracked and damaged; which he touched and retouched with his own hand, and yet swore they were the genuine, the pure originals. All other collectors are fools to him: they go about with painful anxiety to find out the realities: – he *said* he had them – and in a moment made them of the breath of his nostrils and of the fumes of a lively imagination. His was the crucifix that Abelard prayed to – a lock of Eloisa's hair – the dagger with which Felton stabbed the Duke of Buckingham – the first finished sketch of the Jocunda – Titian's large colossal profile of Peter Aretine – a mummy of an Egyptian king – a feather of a phoenix – a piece of Noah's Ark. Were the articles authentic? What matter? – his faith in them was true. He was gifted with a *second sight* in such matters: he believed whatever was incredible. Fancy bore sway in him; and so vivid were his impressions, that they included the substances of things in them. The agreeable and the true with him were one. He believed in Swedenborgianism – he believed in animal magnetism – he had conversed with more than one person of the Trinity – he could talk with his lady at Mantua through some fine vehicle of sense, as we speak to a servant downstairs through a conduit-pipe. Richard Cosway was not the man to flinch from an *ideal* proposition. Once, at an Academy dinner, when some question was made whether the story of Lambert's Leap was true, he started up, and said it was; for he was the person that performed it: he once assured me that the knee-pan of King James I in the ceiling at Whitehall was nine feet across (he had measured it in concert with Mr Cipriani, who was repairing the figures) – he could read in the Book of the Revelations without spectacles, and foretold the return of Buonaparte from Elba – and from St Helena! His wife, the most ladylike of Englishwomen, being asked in Paris what sort of a man her husband was, made answer – '*Toujours riant, toujours gai*'. This was his character. He must have been of French extraction. His soul appeared to possess the life of a bird; and such was the jauntiness of his air and manner, that to see him sit to have his half-boots laced on, you would fancy (by the help of a figure) that, instead of a little withered elderly gentleman, it was Venus attired by the Graces. His miniatures and whole-length drawings were not merely fashionable – they were fashion itself. His imitations of Michael Angelo were not the thing. When more than ninety, he retired from his profession, and used to hold up the palsied hand that had painted lords and ladies for upwards of sixty years, and smiled, with unabated good-humour, at the vanity of human wishes. Take him with all his faults and follies, we scarce 'shall look upon his like again!'

Why should such persons ever die? It seems hard upon them and us! Care fixes no sting in their hearts, and their persons 'present no mark to the foeman'. Death in them seizes upon living shadows. They scarce consume vital air: their gross functions are long at an end – they live but to paint, to talk or think. Is it that the vice of age, the miser's fault, gnaws them? Many of them are not afraid of death, but of coming to want; and having begun in poverty, are haunted with the idea that they shall end in it, and so die – *to save charges*. Otherwise, they might linger on for ever, and 'defy augury!'

— On Envy (A Dialogue) —

HAZLITT   I had a theory about envy at one time, which I have partly given up of late – which was, that there was no such feeling, or that what is usually considered as envy or dislike of real merit is, more properly speaking, jealousy of false pretensions to it. I used to illustrate the argument by saying, that this was the reason we were not envious of the dead, because their merit was established beyond the reach of cavil or contradiction; whereas we are jealous and uneasy at sudden and upstart popularity, which wants the seal of time to confirm it, and which after all may turn out to be false and hollow. There is no danger that the testimony of ages should be reversed, and we add our suffrages to it with confidence, and even with enthusiasm. But we doubt reasonably enough, whether that which was applauded yesterday may not be condemned tomorrow; and are afraid of setting our names to a fraudulent claim to distinction. However satisfied we may be in our own minds, we are not sufficiently borne out by general opinion and sympathy to prevent certain misgivings and scruples on the subject. No one thinks, for instance, of denying the merit of Teniers in his particular style of art, and no one consequently thinks of envying him. The merit of Wilkie, on the contrary, was at first strongly contested, and there were other painters set up in opposition to him, till now that he has become a sort of *classic* in his way, he has ceased to be an object of envy or dislike, because no one doubts his real excellence, as far as it goes. He has no more than justice done him, and the mind never revolts at justice. It only rejects false or superficial claims to admiration, and is incensed to see the world take up with appearances, when they have no solid foundation to support them. We are not envious of Rubens or Raphael, because their fame is a pledge of their genius: but if anyone were to bring forward the highest living names as equal to these, it immediately sets the blood in a ferment, and we try to stifle the sense we have of their merits, not because they are new or modern, but because we are not sure they will ever be old. Could we be certain that posterity would sanction our award, we should grant it without scruple, even to an enemy and a rival.

NORTHCOTE   That which you describe is not envy. Envy is when you hate and would destroy all excellence that you do not yourself possess. So they say that Raphael, after he had copied the figures on one of the antique vases, endeavoured to deface them; and Hoppner, it has been said, used to get pictures of Sir Joshua's into his possession, on purpose to paint them over and spoil them.

H.   I do not believe the first, certainly. Raphael was too great a man, and with too fortunate a temper, to need or to wish to prop himself up on the ruins of others. As to Hoppner, he might perhaps think that there was no good reason for the preference given to Sir Joshua's portraits over his own, that his women of quality were the more airy and fashionable of the two, and might be tempted (once perhaps) in a fit of spleen, of caprice or impatience, to blot what was an eye-sore to himself from its old-fashioned, faded, dingy look, and at the same time dazzled others from the force of tradition and prejudice. Why, he might argue, should that old fellow run away with all the popularity even among those who (as he well knew) in their hearts preferred his own insipid, flaunting style to any other? Though it might be true that Sir Joshua was the greater painter, yet it was not true that Lords and Ladies thought so: he felt that he ought to be *their* favourite, and he might naturally hate what was continually *thrust in his dish*, and (as far as those about him were concerned) unjustly set over his head. Besides, Hoppner had very little of his own to rely on, and might wish, by destroying, to conceal the source from whence he had borrowed almost everything.

N.   Did you never feel envy?

H.   Very little, I think. In truth, I am out of the way of it: for the only pretension of which I am tenacious is that of being a metaphysician; and there is so little attention paid to this subject to pamper one's vanity, and so little fear of losing that little from competition, that there is scarcely any room for envy here. One occupies the niche of eminence in which one places one's self, very quietly and contentedly! If I have ever felt this passion at all, it has been where some very paltry fellow has by trick and management contrived to obtain much more credit than he was entitled to. There was —— ——, to whom I had a perfect antipathy. He was the antithesis of a man of genius; and yet he did better, by mere dint of dullness, than many men of genius. This was intolerable. There was something in the man and in his manner, with which you could not possibly connect the idea of admiration, or of anything that was not merely mechanical –

His look made the still air cold.

He repelled all sympathy and cordiality. What he did (though amounting only to mediocrity) was an insult on the understanding. It seemed that he should be able *to do nothing*; for he was nothing either in himself or in other people's idea of him! Mean actions or gross expressions too often unsettle one's theory of genius. We are unable as well as unwilling to connect the feeling of high intellect with low moral sentiment: the one is a kind of desecration of the other. I have for this reason been sometimes disposed to disparage Turner's fine landscapes, and be glad when he failed in his higher attempts, in order that my conception of the artist and his pictures might be more of a piece. This is not envy or an impatience of extraordinary merit, but an impatience of the incongruities in human nature, and of the drawbacks and stumbling-blocks in the way of our admiration of it. Who is there that admires the author of *Waverley* more than I do? Who is there that despises Sir Walter Scott more? I do not like to think there should be a second instance of the same person's being

The wisest, meanest of mankind

and should be heartily glad if the greatest genius of the age should turn out to be an honest man. The only thing that renders this *misalliance* between first-rate intellect and want of principle endurable is that such an extreme instance of it teaches us that great moral lesson of moderating our expectations of human perfection, and enlarging our indulgence for human infirmity.

N.   You start off with an idea as usual, and torture the plain state of the case into a paradox. There may be some truth in what you suppose; but malice or selfishness is at the bottom of the severity of your criticism, not the love of truth or justice, though you may make it the pretext. You are more angry at Sir Walter Scott's success than at his servility. You would give yourself no trouble about his poverty of spirit, if he had not made a hundred thousand pounds by his writings. The sting lies there, though you may try to conceal it from yourself.

H.   I do not think so. I hate the sight of the Duke of Wellington, for his foolish face, as much as for anything else. I cannot believe that a great general is contained under such a paste-board visor of a man. This, you'll say, is party spite, and rage at his good fortune. I deny it. I always liked Lord Castlereagh for the gallant spirit that shone through his appearance; and his fine bust surmounted and crushed fifty orders that glittered beneath it. Nature seemed to have meant him for something better than he was. But in the other instance, Fortune has evidently played Nature a trick,

> To throw a cruel sunshine on a fool.

N.   The truth is, you were reconciled to Lord Castlereagh's face, and patronised his person, because you felt a sort of advantage over him in point of style. His blunders qualified his success; and you fancied you could take his speeches in pieces, whereas you could not undo the battles that the other had won.

H.   So I have been accused of denying the merits of Pitt, from political dislike and prejudice: but who is there that has praised Burke more than I have? It is a subject I am never weary of, because I feel it.

N.   You mean, because he is dead, and is now little talked of; and you think you show superior discernment and liberality by praising him. If there was a *Burke Club*, you would say nothing about him. You deceive yourself as to your own motives, and weave a wrong theory out of them for human nature. The love of distinction is the ruling passion of the human mind; we grudge whatever draws off attention from ourselves to others; and all our actions are but different contrivances, either by sheer malice or affected liberality, to keep it to ourselves or share it with others. Goldsmith was jealous even of beauty in the other sex. When the people at Amsterdam gathered round the balcony to look at the Miss Hornecks, he grew impatient, and said peevishly, 'There are places where I also am admired'. It may be said – What could their beauty have to do with his reputation? No: it could not tend to lessen it, but it drew admiration from himself to them. So Mr Croker, the other day, when he was at the Academy dinner, made himself conspicuous by displaying the same feeling. He found fault with everything, *damned* all the pictures – landscapes, portraits, busts, nothing pleased him; and not contented with this, he then fell foul of the art itself, which he treated as a piece of idle foolery, and said that Raphael had thrown away his time in doing what was not worth the trouble. This, besides being insincere, was a great breach of good manners, which none but a low-bred man would be guilty of; but he felt his own consequence annoyed; he saw a splendid exhibition of art, a splendid dinner set out, the nobility, the Cabinet Ministers, the branches of the Royal Family invited to it; the most eminent professors were there present; it was a triumph and a celebration of art, a dazzling proof of the height to which it had attained in this country, and of the esteem in which it was held. He felt that he played a very subordinate part in all this; and in order to relieve his own wounded vanity, he was determined (as he thought) to mortify that of others. He wanted to make himself of more importance than anybody else, by trampling on Raphael and on the art itself. It was ridiculous and disgusting, because everyone saw through the motive; so that he defeated his own object.

H.   And he would have avoided this exposure, if, with all his conceit and ill-humour, he had had the smallest taste for the art, or perception of the beauties of Raphael. He has just knowledge enough of drawing to make a whole-length sketch of Buonaparte, verging on caricature, yet not palpably outraging probability; so that it looked like a fat, stupid, *commonplace* man, or a flattering likeness of some legitimate monarch – he had skill, cunning, servility enough to do this with his own hand, and to circulate a print of it with zealous activity, as an indirect means of degrading him in appearance to that low level to which fortune had once raised him in reality. But the man who could do this deliberately, and with satisfaction to his own nature, was not the man to understand Raphael, and might slander him or any other, the greatest of earth's born, without injuring or belying any feeling of admiration or excellence in his own breast; for no such feeling had ever entered there.

N.   Come, this is always the way. Now you are growing personal. Why do you so constantly let your temper get the better of your reason?

H.   Because I hate a hypocrite, a time-server, and a slave. But to return to the question, and say no more about this 'talking potato'[1] – I do not think that, except in circumstances of peculiar aggravation, or of extraordinary ill-temper and moroseness of disposition, anyone who has a thorough feeling of excellence has a delight in gainsaying it. The excellence that we feel, we participate in as if it were our own – it becomes ours by transfusion of mind – it is instilled into our hearts – it mingles with our blood. We are unwilling to allow merit, because we are unable to perceive it. But to be convinced of it, is to be ready to acknowledge and pay homage to it. Illiberality or narrowness of feeling is a narrowness of taste, a want of proper *tact*. A bigotted and exclusive spirit is real blindness to all excellence but our own, or that of some particular school or sect. I think I can give an instance of this in some friends of mine, on whom you will be disposed to have no more mercy than I have on Mr Croker – I mean the *Lake School*. Their system of ostracism is not unnatural: it begins only with the natural limits of their tastes and feelings. Mr Wordsworth, Mr Coleridge, and Mr Southey have no feeling for the excellence of Pope, or Goldsmith, or Gray – they do not enter at all into their merits, and on that account it is that they deny, proscribe, and envy them. *Incredulus odi*, is the explanation here, and in all such cases. I am satisfied that the fine turn of thought in Pope, the gliding verse of Goldsmith, the brilliant diction of Gray have no charms for the author of the *Lyrical Ballads*: he has no faculty in his mind to which these qualities of poetry address themselves. It is not an oppressive, galling sense of them, and a burning

---

1   Mr Croker made his first appearance in this country as a hack writer, and received this surname from the classic lips of Mr Cumberland.

envy to rival them, and shame that he cannot – he would not, if he could. He has no more ambition to write couplets like Pope, than to turn a barrel-organ. He has no pleasure in such poetry, and therefore he has no patience with others that have. The enthusiasm that they feel and express on the subject seems an effect without a cause, and puzzles and provokes the mind accordingly. Mr Wordsworth, in particular, is narrower in his tastes than other people, because he sees everything from a single and original point of view. Whatever does not fall in strictly with this, he accounts no better than a delusion, or a play upon words.

N.   You mistake the matter altogether. The acting principle in their minds is an inveterate selfishness or desire of distinction. They see that a particular kind of excellence has been carried to its height – a height that they have no hope of arriving at – the road is stopped up; they must therefore strike into a different path; and in order to divert the public mind and draw attention to themselves, they affect to decry the old models, and overturn what they cannot rival. They know they cannot write like Pope or Dryden, or would be only imitators if they did; and they consequently strive to gain an original and equal celebrity by singularity and affectation. Their simplicity is not natural to them: it is the *forlorn hope* of impotent and disappointed vanity.

H.   I cannot think that. It may be so in part, but not principally or altogether. Their minds are cast in a peculiar mould, and they cannot produce nor receive any other impressions than those which they do. They are, as to matters of taste, *très bornés.*

N.   You make them out stupider than I thought. I have sometimes spoken disrespectfully of their talents, and so I think, comparatively with those of some of our standard writers. But I certainly should never conceive them so lost to common sense, as not to perceive the beauty, or splendour, or strength of Pope and Dryden. They are dazzled by it, and wilfully shut their eyes to it, and try to throw dust in those of other people. We easily discern and are confounded by excellence, which we are conscious we should in vain attempt to equal. We may see that another is taller than ourselves, and yet we may know that we can never grow to his stature. A dwarf may easily envy a giant.

H.   They would like the comparison to Polyphemus in *Acis and*

Galatea better. They think that little men have run away with the prize of beauty.

N.   No one admires poetry more than I do, or sees more beauties in it; though if I were to try for a thousand years, I should never be able to do anything to please myself.

H.   Perhaps not in the mechanical part; but still you admire and are most struck with those passages in poetry, that accord with the previous train of your own feelings, and give you back the images of your own mind. There is something congenial in taste, at least, between ourselves and those whom we admire. I do not think there is any point of sympathy between Pope and the *Lake School*: on the contrary, I know there is an antipathy between them. When you speak of Titian, you look like him. I can understand how it is that you talk so well on that subject, and that your discourse has an extreme unction about it, a marrowiness like his colouring. But I do not believe that the late Mr West had the least notion of Titian's peculiar excellences – he would think one of his own copies of him as good as the original, and his own historical compositions much better. He would therefore, I conceive, sit and listen to a conversation in praise of him with something like impatience, and think it an interruption to more important discussions on the principles of high art. But if Mr West had ever seen in nature what there is to be found in Titian's copies from it, he would never have thought of such a comparison, and would have bowed his head in deep humility at the very mention of his name. He might not have been able to do like him, and yet might have seen nature with the same eyes.

N.   We do not always admire most what we can do best; but often the contrary. Sir Joshua's admiration of Michael Angelo was perfectly sincere and unaffected; but yet nothing could be more diametrically opposite than the minds of the two men – there was an absolute gulf, between them. It was the consciousness of his own inability to execute such works, that made him more sensible of the difficulty and the merit. It was the same with his fondness for Poussin. He was always exceedingly angry with me for not admiring him enough. But this showed his good sense and modesty. Sir Joshua was always on the *lookout* for whatever might enlarge his notions on the subject of his art, and supply his defects; and did not, like some artists, measure all possible excellence by his own actual deficiencies.

He thus improved and learned something daily. Others have lost their way by setting out with a pragmatical notion of their own self-sufficiency, and have never advanced a single step beyond their first crude conceptions. Fuseli was to blame in this respect. He did not want capacity or enthusiasm, but he had an over-weening opinion of his own peculiar acquirements. Speaking of Vandyke, he said he would not go across the way to see the finest portrait he had ever painted. He asked – 'What is it but a little bit of colour?' Sir Joshua said, on hearing this – 'Aye, he'll live to repent it'. And he has lived to repent it. With that little bit added to his own heap, he would have been a much greater painter, and a happier man.

H.   Yes: but I doubt whether he could have added it in practice. I think the indifference, in the first instance, arises from the want of taste and capacity. If Fuseli had possessed an eye for colour, he would not have despised it in Vandyke. But we reduce others to the limits of our own capacity. We think little of what we cannot do, and envy it where we imagine that it meets with disproportioned admiration from others. A dull, pompous, and obscure writer has been heard to exclaim, 'That *dunce*, Wordsworth!' This was excusable in one who is utterly without feeling for any objects in nature, but those which would make splendid furniture for a drawing room, or any sentiment of the human heart, but that with which a slave looks up to a despot, or a despot looks down upon a slave. This contemptuous expression was an effusion of spleen and impatience at the idea that there should be anyone who preferred Wordsworth's descriptions of a daisy or a linnet's nest to his *auctioneer* poetry about curtains, and palls, and sceptres, and precious stones: but had Wordsworth, in addition to his original sin of simplicity and true genius, been a popular writer, his contempt would have turned into hatred. As it is, he tolerates his *idle nonsense*: there is a link of friendship in mutual political servility; and besides, he has a fellow-feeling with him, as one of those writers of whose merits the world have not been fully sensible. Mr Croley set out with high pretensions, and had some idea of rivalling Lord Byron in a certain lofty, imposing style of versification: but he is probably by this time convinced that mere constitutional *hauteur* as ill supplies the place of elevation of genius, as of the pride of birth; and that the public know how to distinguish between a string of gaudy, painted, turgid phrases, and the vivid creations of fancy, or touching delineations of the human heart.

N.   What did you say the writer's name was?

H.   Croley. He is one of the Royal Society of Authors.

N.   I never heard of him. Is he an imitator of Lord Byron, did you say?

H.   I am afraid neither he nor Lord Byron would have it thought so.

N.   Such imitators do all the mischief, and bring real genius into disrepute. This is in some measure an excuse for those who have endeavoured to disparage Pope and Dryden. We have had a surfeit of imitations of them. Poetry, in the hands of a set of mechanic scribblers, had become such a tame, mawkish thing, that we could endure it no longer, and our impatience of the abuse of a good thing transferred itself to the original source. It was this which enabled Wordsworth and the rest to raise up a new school (or to attempt it) on the ruins of Pope; because a race of writers had succeeded him without one particle of his wit, sense, and delicacy, and the world were tired of their everlasting *sing-song* and *namby-pamby*. People were disgusted at hearing the faults of Pope (the part most easily imitated) cried up as his greatest excellence, and were willing to take refuge from such nauseous cant in any novelty.

H.   What you now observe comes nearly to my account of the matter. *Sir Andrew Wylie* will sicken people of the author of *Waverley*. It was but the other day that someone was proposing that there should be a Society formed for not reading the Scotch novels. But it is not the excellence of that fine writer that we are tired of, or revolt at, but vapid imitations or catchpenny repetitions of himself. Even the quantity of them has an obvious tendency to lead to this effect. It lessens, instead of increasing our admiration: for it seems to be an evidence that there is no difficulty in the task, and leads us to suspect something like trick or deception in their production. We have not been used to look upon works of genius as of the *fungus* tribe. Yet these are so. We had rather doubt our own taste than ascribe such a superiority of genius to another, that it works without consciousness or effort, executes the labour of a life in a few weeks, writes faster than the public can read, and scatters the rich materials of thought and feeling like so much chaff.

N.   Aye, there it is. We had rather do anything than acknowledge the merit of another, if we have any possible excuse or evasion to help it. Depend upon it, you are glad Sir Walter Scott is a Tory – because it gives you an opportunity of qualifying your involuntary admiration of him. You would be sorry indeed if he were what you call an *honest man!* Envy is like a viper coiled up at the bottom of the heart, ready to spring upon and poison whatever approaches it. We live upon the vices, the imperfections, the misfortunes, and disappointments of others, as our natural food. We cannot bear a superior or an equal. Even our pretended cordial admiration is only a subterfuge of our vanity. By raising one, we proportionably lower and mortify others. Our self-love may perhaps be taken by surprise and thrown off its guard by novelty; but it soon recovers itself, and begins to cool in its warmest expressions, and find every possible fault. Ridicule, for this reason, is sure to prevail over truth, because the malice of mankind thrown into the scale gives the casting weight. We have one succession of authors, of painters, of favourites, after another, whom we hail in their turns, because they operate as a diversion to one another, and relieve us of the galling sense of the superiority of any one individual for any length of time. By changing the object of our admiration, we secretly persuade ourselves that there is no such thing as excellence. It is that which we hate above all things. It is the worm that gnaws us, that never dies. The mob shout when a king or a conqueror appears: they would take him and tear him in pieces, but that he is the scapegoat of their pride and vanity, and makes all other men appear like a herd of slaves and cowards. Instead of a thousand equals, we compound for one superior, and allay all heart-burnings and animosities among ourselves, by giving the palm to *the least worthy*. This is the secret of monarchy. Loyalty is not the love of kings, but hatred and jealousy of mankind. A lackey rides behind his lord's coach, and feels no envy of his master. Why? Because he looks down and laughs, in his borrowed finery, at the ragged rabble below. Is it not so in our profession? What Academician eats his dinner in peace, if a rival sits near him; if his own are not the most admired pictures in the room; or, in that case, if there are any others that are at all admired, and divide distinction with him? Is not every artifice used to place the pictures of other artists in the worst light? Do they not go there after their performances are hung up, and try to *paint one another out?* What is the case among players?

Does not a favourite actor threaten to leave the stage, as soon as a new candidate for public favour is taken the least notice of? Would not a manager of a theatre (who has himself pretensions) sooner see it burnt down, than that it should be saved from ruin and lifted into the full tide of public prosperity and favour, by the efforts of one whom he conceives to have supplanted himself in the popular opinion? Do we not see an author, who has had a tragedy damned, sit at the play every night of a new performance for years after, in the hopes of gaining a new companion in defeat? Is it not an indelible offence to a picture-collector and patron of the arts, to hint that another has a fine head in his collection? Will any merchant in the city allow another to be worth a *plum*? What wit will applaud a *bon mot* by a rival? He sits uneasy and out of countenance, till he has made another, which he thinks will make the company forget the first. Do women ever allow beauty in others? Observe the people in a country town, and see how they look at those who are better dressed than themselves; listen to the talk in country places, and mind if it is composed of anything but slanders, gossip, and lies.

H.   But don't you yourself admire Sir Joshua Reynolds?

N.   Why, yes: I think I have no envy myself, and yet I have sometimes caught myself at it. I don't know that I do not admire Sir Joshua merely as a screen against the reputation of bad pictures.

H.   Then, at any rate, what I say is true: we envy the good less than we do the bad.

N.   I do not think so; and am not sure that Sir Joshua himself did not admire Michael Angelo to get rid of the superiority of Titian, Rubens, and Rembrandt, which pressed closer on him, and 'galled his kibe more'.

H.   I should not think that at all unlikely; for I look upon Sir Joshua as rather a spiteful man, and always thought he could have little real feeling for the works of Michael Angelo or Raphael, which he extolled so highly, or he would not have been insensible to their effect the first time he ever beheld them.

N.   He liked Sir Peter Lely better.

Whether Genius is Conscious of its Powers?

COMPOSED AUTUMN 1823

No really great man ever thought himself so. The idea of greatness in the mind answers but ill to our knowledge – or to our ignorance of ourselves. What living prose writer, for instance, would think of comparing himself with Burke? Yet would it not have been equal presumption or egotism in him to fancy himself equal to those who had gone before him – Bolingbroke or Johnson or Sir William Temple? Because his rank in letters is become a settled point with us, we conclude that it must have been quite as self-evident to him, and that he must have been perfectly conscious of his vast superiority to the rest of the world. Alas! not so. No man is truly himself, but in the idea which others entertain of him. The mind, as well as the eye, 'sees not itself, but by reflection from some other thing'. What parity can there be between the effect of habitual composition on the mind of the individual, and the surprise occasioned by first reading a fine passage in an admired author; between what we do with ease, and what we thought it next to impossible ever to be done; between the reverential awe we have for years encouraged, without seeing reason to alter it, for distinguished genius, and the slow, reluctant, unwelcome conviction that after infinite toil and repeated disappointments, and when it is too late and to little purpose, we have ourselves at length accomplished what we at first proposed; between the insignificance of our petty, personal pretensions, and the vastness and splendour which the atmosphere of imagination lends to an illustrious name? He who comes up to his own idea of greatness, must always have had a very low standard of it in his mind. 'What a pity', said someone, 'that Milton had not the pleasure of reading *Paradise Lost!*' He could not read it, as we do, with the weight of impression that a hundred years of admiration have added to it – 'a phoenix gazed by all' – with the sense of the number of editions it has passed through with still increasing reputation, with the tone of solidity, time-proof, which it has received from the breath of cold, envious maligners, with the sound which the voice of Fame has lent to every line of it! The writer of an ephemeral production may be as much dazzled with it as the public: it may sparkle in his own eyes for a moment, and be soon forgotten by everyone else. But no one can anticipate the suffrages of posterity. Every man, in judging of himself, is his own contemporary. He may feel the gale of popularity, but he cannot tell how long it will last. His opinion of himself wants distance, wants time, wants numbers, to set it off and confirm it. He must be indifferent to his own merits, before he can feel a confidence in them. Besides, everyone must be sensible of a thousand weaknesses and deficiencies in himself; whereas Genius only leaves behind it the monuments of its strength. A great name is an abstraction of some one excellence: but whoever fancies himself an abstraction of excellence, so far from being great, may be sure that he is a blockhead, equally ignorant of excellence or defect, of himself or others. Mr Burke, besides being the author of the *Reflections*, and the *Letter to a Noble Lord*, had a wife and son; and had to think as much about them as we do about him. The imagination gains nothing by the minute details of personal knowledge.

On the other hand, it may be said that no man knows so well as the author of any performance what it has cost him, and the length of time and study devoted to it. This is one, among other reasons, why no man can pronounce an opinion upon himself. The happiness of the result bears no proportion to the difficulties overcome or the pains taken. *Materiam superabat opus* is an old and fatal complaint. The definition of genius is that it acts unconsciously; and those who have produced immortal works have done so without knowing how or why. The greatest power operates unseen, and executes its appointed task with as little ostentation as difficulty. Whatever is done best, is done from the natural bent and disposition of the mind. It is only where our incapacity begins, that we begin to feel the obstacles, and to set an undue value on our triumph over them. Correggio, Michael Angelo, Rembrandt, did what they did without premeditation or effort – their works came from their minds as a natural birth – if you had asked them why they adopted this or that style, they would have answered, *because they could not help it*, and because they knew of no other. So Shakespeare says:

> Our poesy is as a gum which issues
> From whence 'tis nourish'd. The fire i' th' flint
> Shows not till it be struck: our gentle flame
> Provokes itself; and, like the current, flies
> Each bound it chafes.

Shakespeare himself was an example of his own rule, and appears to have owed almost everything to chance, scarce anything to industry or design. His poetry flashes from him, like the lightning from the summer cloud, or the stroke from the sunflower. When we look at the admirable comic designs of Hogarth, they seem, from the unfinished state in which they are left, and from the freedom of the pencilling, to have cost him little trouble; whereas the *Sigismunda* is a very laboured and comparatively feeble performance, and he accordingly set great store by it. He also thought highly of his portraits, and boasted that 'he could paint equal to Vandyke, give him his time and let him choose his subject'. This was the very reason why he could not. Vandyke's excellence consisted in this, that he could paint a fine portrait of anyone at sight: let him take ever so much pains or choose ever so bad a subject, he could not help making something of it. His eye, his mind, his hand was cast in the mould of grace and delicacy. Milton again is understood to have preferred *Paradise Regained* to his other works. This, if so, was either because he himself was conscious of having failed in it; or because others thought he had. We are willing to think well of that which we know wants our favourable opinion, and to prop the ricketty bantling. Every step taken, *invitâ Minerva*, costs us something, and is set down to account; whereas we are borne on the full tide of genius and success into the very haven of our desires, almost imperceptibly. The strength of the impulse by which we are carried along prevents the sense of difficulty or resistance: the true inspiration of the Muse is soft and balmy as the air we breathe; and indeed, leaves us little to boast of, for the effect hardly seems to be our own.

There are two persons who always appear to me to have worked under this involuntary, silent impulse more than any others; I mean Rembrandt and Correggio. It is not known that Correggio ever saw a picture of any great master. He lived and died obscurely in an obscure village. We have few of his works, but they are all perfect. What truth, what grace, what angelic sweetness are there! Not one line or tone that is not divinely soft or exquisitely fair; the painter's mind rejecting, by a natural process, all that is discordant, coarse, or unpleasing. The whole is an emanation of pure thought. The work grew under his hand as if of itself, and came out without a flaw, like the diamond from the rock. He knew not what he did; and looked at each modest grace as it stole from the canvas with anxious delight and wonder. Ah gracious God! not he alone; how many more in all time have looked at their works with the same feelings, not knowing but they too may have done something divine, immortal, and finding in that sole doubt ample amends for pining solitude, for want, neglect, and an untimely fate. Oh for one hour of that uneasy rapture, when the mind first thinks it has struck out something that may last for ever; when the germ of excellence bursts from nothing on the startled sight! Take, take away the gaudy triumphs of the world, the long deathless shout of fame, and give back that heartfelt sigh with which the youthful enthusiast first weds immortality as his secret bride! And thou too, Rembrandt, who wert a man of genius, if ever painter was a man of genius, did this dream hang over you as you painted that strange picture of *Jacob's Ladder*? Did your eye strain over those gradual dusky clouds into futurity, or did those white-vested, beaked figures babble to you of fame as they approached? Did you know what you were about, or did you not paint much as it happened? Oh if you had thought once about yourself, or anything but the subject, it would have been all over with 'the glory, the intuition, the amenity', the dream had fled, the spell had been broken. The hills would not have looked like those we see in sleep – that tatterdemalion figure of Jacob, thrown on one side, would not have slept as if the breath was fairly taken out of his body. So much do Rembrandt's pictures savour of the soul and body of reality, that the thoughts seem identical with the objects – if there had been the least question what he should have done, or how he should do it, or how far he had succeeded, it would have spoiled everything. Lumps of light hung upon his pencil and fell upon his canvas like dew-drops: the shadowy veil was drawn over his backgrounds by the dull, obtuse finger of night, making darkness visible by still greater darkness that could only be felt!

Cervantes is another instance of a man of genius, whose work may be said to have sprung from his mind, like Minerva from the head of Jupiter. Don Quixote and Sancho were a kind of twins; and the jests of the latter, as he says, fell from him like drops of rain when he least thought of it. Shakespeare's creations were more multiform, but equally natural and unstudied. Raphael and Milton seem partial exceptions to this rule. Their productions were of the *composite order;* and those of the latter sometimes even amount to centos. Accordingly, we find Milton quoted among those authors, who have left proofs of their entertaining a high opinion of themselves, and of cherishing a strong aspiration after fame. Some of Shakespeare's sonnets have been also cited to the same purpose; but they seem rather to convey wayward and dissatisfied complaints of his untoward fortune than anything like a triumphant and confident reliance on his future renown. He appears to have stood more alone and to have thought less about himself than any living being. One reason for this indifference may have been that as a writer he was tolerably successful in his lifetime, and no doubt produced his works with very great facility.

I hardly know whether to class Claude Lorraine as among those who succeeded most 'through happiness or pains'. It is certain that he imitated no one, and has had no successful imitator. The perfection of his landscapes seems to have been owing to an inherent quality of harmony, to an exquisite sense of delicacy in his mind. His monotony has been complained of, which is apparently produced from a preconceived idea in his mind; and not long ago I heard a person, not more distinguished for the subtlety than the *naïveté* of his sarcasms, remark, 'Oh! I never look at Claude: if one has seen one of his pictures, one has seen them all; they are every one alike: there is the same sky, the same climate, the same time of day, the same tree, and that tree is like a cabbage. To be sure, they say he did pretty well; but when a man is always doing one thing, he ought to do it pretty well.' There is no occasion to write the name under this criticism, and the best answer to it is that it is true – his pictures always are the same, but we never wish them to be otherwise. Perfection is one thing. I confess I think that Claude knew this, and felt that his were the finest landscapes in the world – that ever had been, or would ever be.

I am not in the humour to pursue this argument any farther at present, but to write a digression. If the reader is not already apprised of it, he will please to take notice that I write this at Winterslow. My style there is apt to be redundant and excursive. At other times it may be cramped, dry, abrupt; but here it flows like a river, and overspreads its banks. I have not to seek for thoughts or hunt for images: they come of themselves, I inhale them with the breeze, and the silent groves are vocal with a thousand recollections –

> And visions, as poetic eyes avow,
> Hang on each leaf, and cling to ev'ry bough.

Here I came fifteen years ago, a willing exile; and as I trod the lengthened greensward by the low wood-side, repeated the old line,

> My mind to me a kingdom is!

I found it so then, before, and since; and shall I faint, now that I have poured out the spirit of that mind to the world, and treated many subjects with truth, with freedom, and power, because I have been followed with one cry of abuse ever since *for not being a government tool?* Here I returned a few years after to finish some works I had undertaken, doubtful of the event, but determined to do my best; and wrote that character of Millimant which was once transcribed by fingers fairer than Aurora's, but no notice was taken of it, because I was not a government tool, and must be supposed devoid of taste and elegance by all who aspired to these qualities in their own persons. Here I sketched my account of that old honest Signior Orlando Friscobaldo, which with its fine, racy, acrid tone that old crab-apple, Gifford, would have relished or pretended to relish, had I been a government tool! Here too I have written *Table-Talks* without number, and as yet without a falling-off, till now that they are nearly done, or I should not make this boast. I could swear (were they not mine) the thoughts in many of them are founded as the rock, free as air, the tone like an Italian picture. What then? Had the style been like polished steel, as firm and as bright, it would have availed me nothing, for I am not a government tool! I had endeavoured to guide the taste of the English people to the best old English writers; but I had said that English kings did not reign by right divine, and that his present majesty was descended from an elector of Hanover in a right line; and no loyal subject would after this look into Webster or Deckar because I had pointed them out. I had done something (more than anyone except Schlegel) to vindicate the *Characters of Shakespear's Plays* from the stigma of French criticism: but our Anti-Jacobin and Anti-Gallican writers soon found out that I had said and written that Frenchmen, Englishmen, men were not slaves by birth-right. This was enough to *damn* the work. Such has been the head and front of my offending. While my friend Leigh Hunt was writing the *Descent of Liberty*, and strewing the march of the Allied Sovereigns with flowers, I sat by the waters of Babylon and hung my harp upon the willows. I knew all along there was but one alternative – the cause of kings or of mankind. This I foresaw, this I feared; the world see it now, when it is too late. Therefore I lamented, and would take no comfort when the Mighty fell, because we, all men, fell with him, like lightning from heaven, to grovel in the grave of Liberty, in the sty of Legitimacy! There is but one question in the hearts of monarchs, whether mankind are their property or not. There was but this one question in mine. I had made an abstract, metaphysical principle of this question. I was not the dupe of the voice of the charmers. By my hatred of tyrants I knew what their hatred of the free-born spirit of man must be, of the semblance, of the very name of Liberty and Humanity. And while others bowed their heads to the image of the BEAST, I spit upon it and buffetted it, and made mouths at it, and pointed at it, and drew aside the veil that then half concealed it, but has been since thrown off, and named it by its right name; and it is not to be supposed that my having penetrated their mystery would go unrequited by those whose darling and whose delight the idol, half-brute, half-demon, was, and who were ashamed to acknowledge the image and superscription as their own! Two half-friends of mine, who would not make a whole one between them, agreed the other day that the indiscriminate, incessant abuse of what I write was mere prejudice and party-spirit, and that what I do in periodicals and without a name does well, pays well, and is 'cried out upon in the top of the compass'. It is this indeed that has saved my shallow skiff from quite foundering on Tory spite and rancour; for when people have been reading and approving an article in a miscellaneous journal, it does not do to say when they discover the author afterwards (whatever might have been the case before) it is written by a blockhead; and even Mr Jerdan recommends the volume of *Characteristics* as an excellent little work, because it has no cabalistic name in the title-page, and swears 'there is a first-rate article of forty pages in the last number of the Edinburgh from Jeffrey's own hand', though when he learns against his will that it is mine, he devotes three successive numbers of the *Literary Gazette* to abuse 'that *strange* article in the last number of the Edinburgh Review'. Others who had not this advantage have fallen a sacrifice to the obloquy attached to the suspicion of doubting, or of being acquainted with anyone who is known to doubt, the divinity of kings. Poor Keats paid the forfeit of this *lezè majesté* with his health and life. What, though his verses were like the breath of spring, and many of his thoughts like flowers – would this, with the circle of critics that beset a throne, lessen the crime of their having been praised in *The Examiner?* The lively and most agreeable editor of that paper has in like manner been driven from his country and his friends who delighted in him, for no other reason than having written *The Story of Rimini*, and asserted ten years ago, 'that the most accomplished prince in Europe was an Adonis of fifty!'

> Return, Alpheus, the dread voice is past,
> That shrunk thy streams; return, Sicilian Muse!

I look out of my window and see that a shower has just fallen: the fields look green after it, and a rosy cloud hangs over the brow of the hill; a lily expands its petals in the moisture, dressed in its lovely green and white; a shepherd-boy has just brought some pieces of turf with daisies and grass for his young mistress to make a bed for her skyark, not doomed to dip his wings in the dappled dawn – my cloudy thoughts draw off, the storm of angry politics has blown over

– Mr Blackwood, I am yours – Mr Croker, my service to you – Mr T. Moore, I am alive and well – really, it is wonderful how little the worse I am for fifteen years' wear and tear, how I come upon my legs again on the ground of truth and nature, and 'look abroad into universality', forgetting that there is any such person as myself in the world!

I have let this passage stand (however critical) because it may serve as a practical illustration to show what authors really think of themselves when put upon the defensive (I confess, the subject has nothing to do with the title at the head of the essay!) and as a warning to those who may reckon upon their fair portion of popularity as the reward of the exercise of an independent spirit and such talents as they possess. It sometimes seems at first sight as if the low scurrility and jargon of abuse by which it is attempted to overlay all common sense and decency by a tissue of lies and nicknames, everlastingly repeated and applied indiscriminately to all those who are not of the regular government party, was peculiar to the present time, and the anomalous growth of modern criticism; but if we look back, we shall find the same system acted upon, as often as power, prejudice, dullness, and spite found their account in playing the game into one another's hands – in decrying popular efforts, and in giving currency to every species of base metal that had their own conventional stamp upon it. The names of Pope and Dryden were assailed with daily and unsparing abuse – the epithet A.P.E. was levelled at the sacred head of the former – and if even men like these, having to deal with the consciousness of their own infirmities and the insolence and spurns of wanton enmity, must have found it hard to possess their souls in patience, any living writer amidst such contradictory evidence can scarcely expect to retain much calm, steady conviction of his own merits, or build himself a secure reversion in immortality.

However one may in a fit of spleen and impatience turn round and assert one's claims in the face of low-bred, hireling malice, I will here repeat what I set out with saying, that there never yet was a man of sense and proper spirit, who would not decline rather than court a comparison with any of those names, whose reputation he really emulates – who would not be sorry to suppose that any of the great heirs of memory had as many foibles as he knows himself to possess – and who would not shrink from including himself or being included by others in the same praise, that was offered to long-established and universally acknowledged merit, as a kind of profanation. Those who are ready to fancy themselves Raphaels and Homers are very inferior men indeed – they have not even an idea of the mighty names that 'they take in vain'. They are as deficient in pride as in modesty, and have not so much as served an apprenticeship to a true and honourable ambition. They mistake a momentary popularity for lasting renown, and a sanguine temperament for the inspirations of genius. The love of fame is too high and delicate a feeling in the mind to be mixed up with realities – it is a solitary abstraction, the secret sigh of the soul–

> It is all one as we should love
> A bright particular star, and think to wed it.

A name 'fast-anchored in the deep abyss of time' is like a star twinkling in the firmament, cold, silent, distant, but eternal and sublime; and our transmitting one to posterity is as if we should contemplate our translation to the skies. If we are not contented with this feeling on the subject, we shall never sit in Cassiopeia's chair, nor will our names, studding Ariadne's crown or streaming with Berenice's locks, ever make

> the face of heaven so bright,
> That birds shall sing, and think it were not night.

Those who are in love only with noise and show, instead of devoting themselves to a life of study, had better hire a booth at Bartlemy Fair, or march at the head of a recruiting regiment with drums beating and colours flying!

It has been urged, that however little we may be disposed to indulge the reflection at other times or out of mere self-complacency, yet the mind cannot help being conscious of the effort required for any great work while it is about it, of

> The high endeavour and the glad success.

I grant that there is a sense of power in such cases, with the exception before stated; but then this very effort and state of excitement engrosses the mind at the time, and leaves it listless and exhausted afterwards. The energy we exert, or the high state of enjoyment we feel, puts us out of conceit with ourselves at other times: compared to what we are in the act of composition, we seem dull, common-place people, generally speaking; and what we have been able to perform is rather matter of wonder than of self-congratulation to us. The stimulus of writing is like the stimulus of intoxication, with which we can hardly sympathize in our sober moments, when we are no longer under the inspiration of the demon, or when the virtue is gone out of us. While we are engaged in any work, we are thinking of the subject, and cannot stop to admire ourselves; and when it is done, we look at it with comparative indifference. I will venture to say, that no one but a pedant ever read his own works regularly through. They are not *his* – they are become mere words, wastepaper, and have none of the glow, the creative enthusiasm, the vehemence, and natural spirit with which he wrote them. When we have once committed our thoughts to paper, written them fairly out, and seen that they are right in the printing, if we are in our right wits, we have done with them forever. I sometimes try to read an article I have written in some magazine or review (for when they are bound up in a volume, I dread the very sight of them) but stop after a sentence or two, and never recur to the task. I know pretty well what I have to say on the subject, and do not want to go to school to myself. It is the worst instance of the *bis repetita crambe* in the world. I do not think that even painters have much delight in looking at their works after they are done. While they are in progress, there is a great degree of satisfaction in considering what has been done, or what is still to do – but this is hope, is reverie, and ceases with the completion of our efforts. I should not imagine Raphael or Correggio would have much pleasure in looking at their former works, though they might recollect the pleasure they had had in painting them; they might spy defects in them (for the idea of unattainable perfection still keeps pace with our actual approaches to it), and fancy that they were not worthy of immortality. The greatest portrait-painter the world ever saw used to write under his pictures, '*Titianus faciebat*', signifying that they were imperfect; and in his letter to Charles V accompanying one of his most admired works, he only spoke of the time he had been about it. Annibal Caracci boasted that he could do like Titian and Correggio, and, like most boasters, was wrong. (*See his spirited Letter to his cousin Ludovico, on seeing the pictures at Parma.*)

The greatest pleasure in life is that of reading, while we are young. I have had as much of this pleasure as perhaps anyone. As I grow older, it fades; or else, the stronger stimulus of writing takes off the edge of it. At present, I have neither time nor inclination for it: yet I should like to devote a year's entire leisure to a course of the English novelists; and perhaps clap on that old sly knave, Sir Walter, to the end of the list. It is astonishing how I used formerly to relish the style of certain authors, at a time when I myself despaired of ever writing a single line. Probably this was the reason. It is not in mental as in natural ascent – intellectual objects seem higher when we survey them from below, than when we look down from any given elevation above the common level. My three favourite writers about the time I speak of were Burke, Junius, and Rousseau. I was never weary of admiring and wondering at the felicities of the style, the turns of expression, the refinements of thought and sentiment: I laid the book down to find out the secret of so much strength and beauty, and took it up again in despair, to read on and admire. So I passed whole days, months, and I may add, years; and have only this to say now, that as my life began, so I could wish that it may end. The last time I tasted this luxury in its full perfection was one day after a sultry day's walk in summer between Farnham and Alton. I was fairly tired out; I walked into an inn-yard (I think at the latter place); I was shown by the waiter to what looked at first like common outhouses at the other end of it, but they turned out to be a suite of rooms, probably a hundred years old – the one I entered opened into an old-fashioned garden, embellished with beds of larkspur and a leaden Mercury; it was wainscoted, and there was a grave-looking, dark-coloured portrait of Charles II hanging up over the tiled chimney-piece. I had *Love for Love* in my pocket, and began to read; coffee was brought in in a silver coffee-pot; the cream, the bread and butter, everything was excellent, and the fla-vour of Congreve's style prevailed over all. I prolonged the enter-tainment till a late hour, and relished this divine comedy better even than when I used to see it played by Miss Mellon, as *Miss Prue*; Bob Palmer, as *Tattle*; and Bannister; as honest *Ben*. This circumstance happened just five years ago, and it seems like yester-day. If I count my life so by lustres, it will soon glide away; yet I shall not have to repine, if, while it lasts, it is enriched with a few such recollections!

On the Pleasure of Hating

COMPOSED NOVEMBER – DECEMBER 1823

There is a spider crawling along the matted floor of the room where I sit (not the one which has been so well allegorized in the admirable *Lines to a Spider*, but another of the same edifying breed) – he runs with heedless, hurried haste, he hobbles awkwardly towards me, he stops – he sees the giant shadow before him, and, at a loss whether to retreat or proceed, meditates his huge foe – but as I do not start up and seize upon the straggling caitiff, as he would upon a hapless fly within his toils, he takes heart, and ventures on, with mingled cunning, impudence, and fear. As he passes me, I lift up the matting to assist his escape, am glad to get rid of the unwelcome intruder, and shudder at the recollection after he is gone. A child, a woman, a clown, or a moralist a century ago, would have crushed the little reptile to death – my philosophy has got beyond that – I bear the creature no ill-will, but still I hate the very sight of it. The spirit of malevolence survives the practical exertion of it. We learn to curb our will and keep our overt actions within the bounds of humanity, long before we can subdue our sentiments and imaginations to the same mild tone. We give up the external demonstration, the *brute* violence, but cannot part with the essence or principle of hostility. We do not tread upon the poor little animal in question (that seems barbarous and pitiful!) but we regard it with a sort of mystic horror and superstitious loathing. It will ask another hundred years of fine writing and hard thinking to cure us of the prejudice, and make us feel towards this ill-omened tribe with something of 'the milk of human kindness', instead of their own shyness and venom.

Nature seems (the more we look into it) made up of antipathies: without something to hate, we should lose the very spring of thought and action. Life would turn to a stagnant pool, were it not ruffled by the jarring interests, the unruly passions of men. The white streak in our own fortunes is brightened (or just rendered visible) by making all around it as dark as possible; so the rainbow paints its form upon the cloud. Is it pride? Is it envy? Is it the force of contrast? Is it weakness or malice? But so it is, that there is a secret affinity, a *hankering* after evil in the human mind, and that it takes a perverse, but a fortunate delight in mischief, since it is a never-failing source of satisfaction. Pure good soon grows insipid, wants variety and spirit. Pain is a bitter-sweet, which never surfeits. Love turns, with a little indulgence, to indifference or disgust: hatred alone is immortal. Do we not see this principle at work everywhere? Animals torment and worry one another without mercy: children kill flies for sport: everyone reads the accidents and offences in a newspaper, as the cream of the jest: a whole town runs to be present at a fire, and the spectator by no means exults to see it extinguished. It is better to have it so, but it diminishes the interest; and our feelings take part with our passions, rather than with our understandings. Men assemble in crowds, with eager enthusiasm, to witness a tragedy: but if there were an execution going forward in the next street, as Mr Burke observes, the theatre would be left empty. A strange cur in a village, an idiot, a crazy woman, are set upon and baited by the whole community. Public nuisances are in the nature of public benefits. How long did the Pope, the Bourbons, and the Inquisition keep the people of England in breath, and supply them with nicknames to vent their spleen upon! Had they done us any harm of late? No: but we have always a quantity of superfluous bile upon the stomach, and we wanted an object to let it out upon. How loath were we to give up our pious belief in ghosts and witches, because we liked to persecute the one, and frighten ourselves to death with the other! It is not the quality so much as the quantity of excitement that we are anxious about: we cannot bear a state of indifference and *ennui*: the mind seems to abhor a *vacuum* as much as ever matter was supposed to do. Even when the spirit of the age (that is, the progress of intellectual refinement, warring with our natural infirmities) no longer allows us to carry our vindictive and headstrong humours into effect, we try to revive them in description, and keep up the old bugbears, the phantoms of our terror and our hate, in imagination. We burn Guy Faux in effigy, and the hooting and buffeting and maltreating that poor tattered figure of rags and straw makes a festival in every village in England once a year. Protestants and Papists do not now burn one another at the stake: but we subscribe to new editions of Fox's *Book of Martyrs*; and the secret of the success of the *Scotch novels* is much the same – they carry us back to the feuds, the heart-burnings, the havoc, the dismay, the wrongs and the revenge of a barbarous age and people – to the rooted prejudices and deadly animosities of sects and parties in politics and religion, and of contending chiefs and clans in war and intrigue. We feel the full force of the spirit of hatred with all of them in turn. As we read, we throw aside the trammels of civilization, the flimsy veil of humanity. 'Off, you lendings!' The wild beast resumes its sway within us, we feel like hunting-animals, and as the hound starts in his sleep and rushes on the chase in fancy, the heart rouses itself in its native lair, and utters a wild cry of joy, at being restored once more to freedom and lawless, unrestrained impulses. Everyone has his full swing, or goes to the Devil his own way. Here are no Jeremy Bentham panopticons, none of Mr Owen's impassable parallelograms (Rob Roy would have spurned and poured a thousand curses on them), no long calculations of self-interest – the will takes its instant way to its object; as the mountain-torrent flings itself over the precipice, the greatest possible good of each individual consists in doing all the mischief he can to his neighbour: that is charming, and finds a sure and sympathetic chord in every breast! So Mr Irving, the celebrated preacher, has rekindled the old, original, almost exploded hellfire in the aisles of the Caledonian Chapel, as they introduce the real water of the New River at Sadler's Wells, to the delight and astonishment of his fair audience. *'Tis pretty, though a plague*, to sit and peep into the pit of Tophet, to play at *snapdragon* with flames and brimstone (it gives a smart electrical shock, a lively fillip to delicate constitutions), and to see Mr Irving, like a huge Titan, looking as grim and swarthy as if he had to forge tortures for all the damned! What a strange being man is! Not content with doing all he can to vex and hurt his fellows here, 'upon this bank and shoal of time', where one would think there were heartaches, pain, disappointment, anguish, tears, sighs, and groans enough, the bigoted maniac takes him to the top of the high peak of school divinity to hurl him down the yawning gulf of penal fire; his speculative malice asks eternity to wreak its infinite spite in, and calls on the Almighty to execute its relentless doom! The cannibals burn their enemies and eat them, in good fellowship with one another: meek Christian divines cast those who differ from them but a hair's breadth, body and soul, into hellfire, for the glory of God and the good of his creatures! It is well that the power of such persons is not co-ordinate with their wills: indeed, it is from the sense of their weakness and inability to control the opinions of others, that they thus 'outdo termagant', and endeavour to frighten them into conformity by big words and monstrous denunciations.

The pleasure of hating, like a poisonous mineral, eats into the heart of religion, and turns it to rankling spleen and bigotry; it makes patriotism an excuse for carrying fire, pestilence, and famine into other lands: it leaves to virtue nothing but the spirit of censoriousness, and a narrow, jealous, inquisitorial watchfulness over the actions and motives of others. What have the different sects, creeds, doctrines in religion been but so many pretexts set up for men to wrangle, to quarrel, to tear one another in pieces about, like a target as a mark to shoot at? Does anyone suppose that the love of country in an Englishman implies any friendly feeling or disposition to serve another, bearing the same name? No, it means only hatred to the French, or the inhabitants of any other country that we happen to be at war with for the time. Does the love of virtue denote any wish to discover or amend our own faults? No, but it atones for an obstinate adherence to our own vices by the most virulent intolerance to human frailties. This principle is of a most universal application. It extends to good as well as evil: if it makes us hate folly, it makes us no less dissatisfied with distinguished merit. If it inclines us to resent the wrongs of others, it impels us to be as impatient of their prosperity. We revenge injuries: we repay benefits with ingratitude. Even our strongest partialities and likings soon take this turn. 'That which was luscious as

locusts, anon becomes bitter as coloquintida'; and love and friendship melt in their own fires. We hate old friends: we hate old books:
we hate old opinions; and at last we come to hate ourselves.

I have observed that few of those, whom I have formerly known
most intimate, continue on the same friendly footing, or combine
the steadiness with the warmth of attachment. I have been acquainted with two or three knots of inseparable companions, who
saw each other 'six days in the week', that have broken up and
dispersed. I have quarrelled with almost all my old friends (they
might say this is owing to my bad temper), but they have also
quarrelled with one another. What is become of 'that set of whist-
players', celebrated by Elia in his set of whist-players, celebrated
by Elia in his notable *Epistle to Robert Southey, Esq.* (and now I
think of it – that I myself have celebrated in this very volume) 'that
for so many years called Admiral Burney friend?' They are scattered, like last year's snow. Some of them are dead – or gone to live
at a distance – or pass one another in the street like strangers; or if
they stop to speak, do it as coolly and try to *cut* one another as
soon as possible. Some of us have grown rich – others poor. Some
have got places under Government – others a *niche* in the *Quarterly Review*. Some of us have dearly earned a name in the world;
whilst others remain in their original privacy. We despise the one;
and envy and are glad to mortify the other. Times are changed; we
cannot revive our old feelings; and we avoid the sight and are uneasy in the presence of those, who remind us of our infirmity, and
put us upon an effort at seeming cordiality, which embarrasses
ourselves and does not impose upon our *quondam* associates. Old
friendships are like meats served up repeatedly, cold, comfortless,
and distasteful. The stomach turns against them. Either constant
intercourse and familiarity breed weariness and contempt; or if we
meet again after an interval of absence, we appear no longer the
same. One is too wise, another too foolish for us; and we wonder
we did not find this out before. We are disconcerted and kept in a
state of continual alarm by the wit of one, or tired to death of the
dullness of another. The *good things* of the first (besides leaving
stings behind them) by repetition grow stale, and lose their startling effect; and the insipidity of the last becomes intolerable. The
most amusing or instructive companion is at best like a favourite

volume, that we wish after a time to *lay upon the shelf*; but as our friends are not willing to be laid there, this produces a misunderstanding and ill-blood between us. Or if the zeal and integrity of friendship is not abated, or its career interrupted by any obstacle arising out of its own nature, we look out for other subjects of complaint and sources of dissatisfaction. We begin to criticize each other's dress, looks, and general character. 'Such a one is a pleasant fellow, but it is a pity he sits so late!' Another fails to keep his appointments, and that is a sore that never heals. We get acquainted with some fashionable young men or with a mistress, and wish to introduce our friend; but he is awkward and a sloven, the interview does not answer, and this throws cold water on our intercourse. Or he makes himself obnoxious to opinion – and we shrink from our own convictions on the subject as an excuse for not defending him. All or any of these causes mount up in time to a ground of coolness or irritation – and at last they break out into open violence as the only amends we can make ourselves for suppressing them so long, or the readiest means of banishing recollections of former kindness, so little compatible with our present feelings. We may try to tamper with the wounds or patch up the carcase of departed friendship, but the one will hardly bear the handling, and the other is not worth the trouble of embalming! The only way to be reconciled to old friends is to part with them for good: at a distance we may chance to be thrown back (in a waking dream) upon old times and old feelings: or at any rate, we should not think of renewing our intimacy, till we have fairly *spit our spite*, or said, thought, and felt all the ill we can of each other. Or if we can pick a quarrel with someone else, and make him the scapegoat, this is an excellent contrivance to heal a broken bone. I think I must be friends with Lamb again, since he has written that magnanimous *Letter to Southey*, and told him a piece of his mind! I don't know what it is that attaches me to Haydon, so much, except that he and I, whenever we meet, sit in judgement on another set of old friends, and 'carve them as a dish fit for the gods'. There was Leigh Hunt, John Scott, Mrs Novello, whose dark raven locks make a picturesque background to our discourse, Barnes, who is grown fat, and is, they say, married, Rickman; these had all separated long ago, and their foibles are the common link that holds us together. We do not affect to condole or whine over their follies; we enjoy, we laugh at them till we are ready to burst our sides, '*sans* intermission, for hours by the dial'. We serve up a course of anecdotes, *traits*, master-strokes of character, and cut and hack at them till we are weary. Perhaps some of them are even with us. For my own part, as I once said, I like a friend the better for having faults that one can talk about. 'Then', said Mrs Montagu, 'you will never cease to be a philanthropist!' Those in question were some of the choice-spirits of the age, not 'fellows of no mark or likelihood'; and we so far did them justice: but it is well they did not hear what we sometimes said of them. I care little what anyone says of me, particularly behind my back, and in the way of critical and analytical discussion – it is looks of dislike and scorn, that I answer with the worst venom of my pen. The expression of the face wounds me more than the expressions of the tongue. If I have in one instance mistaken this expression, or resorted to this remedy where I ought not, I am sorry for it. But the face was too fine over which it mantled, and I am too old to have misunderstood it! . . . I sometimes go up to Hume's; and as often as I do, resolve never to go again. I do not find the old homely welcome. The ghost of friendship meets me at the door, and sits with me all dinner-time. They have got a set of fine notions and new acquaintance. Allusions to past occurrences are thought trivial, nor is it always safe to touch upon more general subjects. Hume does not begin as he formerly did every five minutes, 'Fawcett used to say', etc. That topic is something worn. The girls are grown up, and have a thousand accomplishments. I perceive there is a jealousy on both sides. They think I give myself airs, and I fancy the same of them. Every time I am asked, 'If I do not think Mr Washington Irvine a very fine writer?' I shall not go again till I receive an invitation for Christmas Day in company with Mr Liston. The only intimacy I never found to flinch or fade was a purely intellectual one. There was none of the cant of candour in it, none of the whine of mawkish sensibility. Our mutual acquaintance were considered merely as subjects of conversation and knowledge, not at all of affection. We regarded them no more in our experiments than 'mice in an air-pump': or like malefactors, they were regularly cut down and given over to the dissecting-knife. We spared neither friend nor foe. We sacrificed human infirmities at the shrine of truth. The skeletons of character might be seen, after the juice was extracted, dangling in the air like flies in cobwebs: or they were kept for future inspection in some refined acid. The demonstration was as beautiful as it was new. There is no surfeiting on gall: nothing keeps so well as a decoction of spleen. We grow tired of everything but turning others into ridicule, and congratulating ourselves on their defects.

We take a dislike to our favourite books, after a time, for the same reason. We cannot read the same works for ever. Our honeymoon, even though we wed the Muse, must come to an end; and is followed by indifference, if not by disgust. There are some works, those indeed that produce the most striking effect at first by novelty and boldness of outline, that will not bear reading twice: others of a less extravagant character, and that excite and repay attention by a greater nicety of details, have hardly interest enough to keep alive our continued enthusiasm. The popularity of the most successful writers operates to wean us from them, by the cant and fuss that is made about them, by hearing their names everlastingly repeated, and by the number of ignorant and indiscriminate admirers they draw after them: – we as little like to have to drag others from their unmerited obscurity, lest we should be exposed to the charge of affection and singularity of taste. There is nothing to be said respecting an author that all the world have made up their minds about: it is a thankless as well as hopeless task to recommend one that nobody has ever heard of. To cry up Shakespeare as the god of our idolatry, seems like a vulgar, national prejudice: to take down a volume of Chaucer, or Spenser, or Beaumont and Fletcher, or Ford, or Marlowe, has very much the look of pedantry and egotism. I confess it makes me hate the very name of Fame and Genius when works like these are 'gone into the wastes of time', while each successive generation of fools is busily employed in reading the trash of the day, and women of fashion gravely join with their waiting-maids in discussing the preference between *Paradise Lost* and Mr Moore's *Loves of the Angels*. I was pleased the other day on going into a shop to ask, 'If they had any of the *Scotch novels?*' to be told – 'That they had just sent out the last, *Sir Andrew Wylie!*' Mr Galt will also be pleased with this answer! The reputation of some books is raw and *unaired*: that of others is worm-eaten and mouldy. Why fix our affections on that which we cannot bring ourselves to have faith in, or which others have long ceased to trouble themselves about? I am half afraid to look into *Tom Jones*, lest it should not answer my expectations at this time of day; and if it did not, I should certainly be disposed to fling it into the fire, and never look into another novel while I lived. But surely, it may be said, there are some works, that, like nature, can never grow old; and that must always touch the imagination and passions alike! Or there are passages that seem as if we might brood over them all our lives, and not exhaust the sentiments of love and admiration they excite: they become favourites, and we are fond of them to a sort of dotage. Here is one:

> Sitting in my window
> Printing my thoughts in lawn, I saw a God,
> I thought (but it was you), enter our gates;
> My blood flew out and back again, as fast
> As I had puffed it forth and sucked it in
> Like breath; then was I called away in haste
> To entertain you: never was a man
> Thrust from a sheepcote to a sceptre, raised
> So high in thoughts as I; you left a kiss
> Upon these lips then, which I mean to keep
> From you for ever. I did hear you talk
> Far above singing!

A passage like this indeed leaves a taste on the palate like nectar, and we seem in reading it to sit with the gods at their golden tables: but if we repeat it often in ordinary moods, it loses its flavour, becomes vapid, 'the wine of *poetry* is drank, and but the lees remain'. Or, on the other hand, if we call in the aid of extraordinary circumstances to set it off to advantage, as the reciting it to a friend, or after having our feelings excited by a long walk in some romantic situation, or while we

> play with Amaryllis in the shade,
> Or with the tangles of Neaera's hair –

we afterwards miss the accompanying circumstances, and instead of transferring the recollection of them to the favourable side, regret what we have lost, and strive in vain to bring back 'the irrevocable hour' – wondering in some instances how we survive it, and at the melancholy blank that is left behind! The pleasure rises to its height in some moment of calm solitude or intoxicating sympathy, declines ever after, and from the comparison and a conscious falling-off, leaves rather a sense of satiety and irksomeness behind it. . . . 'Is it the same in pictures?' I confess it is, with all but those from Titian's hand. I don't know why, but an air breathes from his landscapes, pure, refreshing as if it came from other years; there is a look in his faces that never passes away. I saw one the other day. Amidst the heartless desolation and glittering finery of Fonthill, there is a portfolio of the Dresden Gallery. It opens, and a young female head looks from it; a child, yet woman grown; with an air of rustic innocence and the graces of a princess, her eyes like those of doves, the lips about to open, a smile of pleasure dimpling the whole face, the jewels sparkling in her crisped hair, her youthful shape compressed in a rich antique dress, as the bursting leaves contain the April buds! Why do I not call up this image of gentle sweetness, and place it as a perpetual barrier between mischance and me? It is because pleasure asks a greater effort of the mind to support it than pain; and we turn, after a little idle dalliance, from what we love to what we hate!

As to my old opinions, I am heartily sick of them. I have reason, for they have deceived me sadly. I was taught to think, and I was willing to believe, that genius was not a bawd – that virtue was not a mask – that liberty was not a name – that love had its seat in the human heart. Now I would care little if these words were struck out of the dictionary, or if I had never heard them. They are become to my ears a mockery and a dream. Instead of patriots and friends of freedom, I see nothing but the tyrant and the slave, the people linked with kings to rivet on the chains of despotism and superstition. I see folly join with knavery, and together make up public spirit and public opinions. I see the insolent Tory, the blind reformer, the coward Whig! If mankind had wished for what is right, they might have had it long ago. The theory is plain enough; but they are prone to mischief, 'to every good work reprobate'. I have seen all that had been done by the mighty yearnings of the spirit and intellect of men, 'of whom the world was not worthy', and that promised a proud opening to truth and good through the vista of future years, undone by one man, with just glimmering of understanding enough to feel that he was a king, but not to comprehend how he could be king of a free people! I have seen this triumph celebrated by poets, the friends of my youth and the friends of man, but who were carried away by the infuriate tide that, setting in from a throne, bore down every distinction of right reason before it; and I have seen all those who did not join in applauding this insult and outrage on humanity proscribed, hunted down (they and their friends made a byword of), so that it has become an understood thing that no one can live by his talents or knowledge who is not ready to prostitute those talents and that knowledge to betray his species, and prey upon his fellow-man. 'This was some time a mystery: but the time gives evidence of it.' The echoes of liberty had awakened once more in Spain, and the morning of human hope dawned again: but that dawn has been overcast by the foul breath of bigotry, and those reviving sounds stifled by fresh cries from the time-rent towers of the Inquisition – man yielding (as it is fit he should) first to brute force, but more to the innate perversity and dastard spirit of his own nature, which leaves no room for farther hope or disappointment. And England, that arch-reformer, that heroic deliverer, that mouther about liberty and tool of power, stands gaping by, not feeling the blight and mildew coming over it, nor its very bones crack and turn to a paste under the grasp and circling folds of this new monster, Legitimacy!

In private life do we not see hypocrisy, servility, selfishness, folly, and impudence succeed, while modesty shrinks from the encounter, and merit is trodden under foot? How often is 'the rose plucked from the forehead of a virtuous love to plant a blister there!' What chance is there of the success of real passion? What certainty of its continuance? Seeing all this as I do, and unravelling the web of human life into its various threads of meanness, spite, cowardice, want of feeling, and want of understanding, of indifference towards others and ignorance of ourselves – seeing custom prevail over all excellence, itself giving way to infamy – mistaken as I have been in my public and private hopes, calculating others from myself, and calculating wrong; always disappointed where I placed most reliance; the dupe of friendship, and the fool of love; have I not reason to hate and to despise myself? Indeed I do; and chiefly for not having hated and despised the world enough.[1]

1   The only exception to the general drift of this essay (and that is an exception in theory – I know of none in practice) is, that in reading we always take the right side, and make the case properly our own. Our imaginations are sufficiently excited, we have nothing to do with the matter but as a pure creation of the mind, and we therefore yield to the natural, unwarped impression of good and evil. Our own passions, interests, and prejudices out of the question, or in an abstracted point of view, we judge fairly and conscientiously; for conscience is nothing but the abstract idea of right and wrong. But no sooner have we to act or suffer, than the spirit of contradiction or some other demon comes into play, and there is an end of common sense and reason. Even the very strength of the speculative faculty, or the desire to square things with an *ideal* standard of perfection (whether we can or no) leads perhaps to half the absurdities and miseries of mankind. We are hunting after what we cannot find, and quarrelling with the good within our reach. Among the thousands that have read *The Heart of Midlothian* there assuredly never was a single person who did not wish Jeanie Deans success. Even Gentle George was sorry for what he had done, when it was over, though he would have played the same prank the next day: and the *unknown* author, in his immediate character of contributor to *Blackwood* and *The Sentinel*, is about as respectable a personage as Daddy Ratton himself. On the stage, everyone takes part with Othello against Iago. Do boys at school, in reading Homer, generally side with the Greeks or Trojans?

On Egotism

COMPOSED *c.* MAY 1821

It is mentioned in *The Life of Salvator Rosa*, that on the occasion of an altar-piece of his being exhibited at Rome, in the triumph of the moment, he compared himself to Michael Angelo, and spoke against Raphael, calling him *hard, dry,* etc. Both these were fatal symptoms for the ultimate success of the work: the picture was in fact afterwards severely censured, so as to cause him much uneasiness; and he passed a great part of his life in quarrelling with the world for admiring his landscapes, which were truly excellent, and for not admiring his historical pieces, which were full of defects. Salvator wanted self-knowledge, and that respect for others, which is both a cause and consequence of it. Like many more, he mistook the violent and irritable workings of self-will (in a wrong direction) for the impulse of genius, and his insensibility to the vast superiority of others for a proof of his equality with them.

In the first place, nothing augurs worse for anyone's pretensions to the highest rank of excellence than his making free with those of others. He who boldly and unreservedly places himself on a level with the *mighty dead*, shows a want of sentiment – the only thing that can ensure immortality to his own works. When we forestall the judgement of posterity, it is because we are not confident of it. A mind that brings all others into a line with its own naked or assumed merits, that sees all objects in the foreground as it were, that does not regard the lofty monuments of genius through the atmosphere of fame, is coarse, crude, and repulsive as a picture without aerial perspective. Time, like distance, spreads a haze and a glory round all things. Not to perceive this, is to want a sense, is to be without imagination. Yet there are those who strut in their own self-opinion, and deck themselves out in the plumes of fancied self-importance as if they were crowned with laurel by Apollo's own hand. There was nothing in common between Salvator and Michael Angelo: if there had, the consciousness of the power with which he had to contend would have over-awed and struck him dumb; so that the very familiarity of his approaches proved (as much as anything else) the immense distance placed between them. Painters alone seem to have a trick of putting themselves on an equal footing with the greatest of their predecessors, of advancing, on the sole strength of their vanity and presumption, to the highest seats in the Temple of Fame, of talking of themselves and Raphael and Michael Angelo in the same breath! What should we think of a poet who should publish to the world, or give a broad hint in private, that he conceived himself fully on a par with Homer or Milton or Shakespeare? It would be too much for a friend to say so of him. But artists suffer their friends to puff them in the true 'King Cambyses' vein' without blushing. Is it that they are often men without a liberal education, who have no notion of anything that does not come under their immediate observation, and who accordingly prefer the living to the dead, and themselves to all the rest of the world? Or that there is something in the nature of the profession itself, fixing the view on a particular point of time, and not linking the present either with the past or future?

Again, Salvator's disregard for Raphael, instead of inspiring him with anything like 'vain and self-conceit', ought to have taught him the greatest diffidence in himself. Instead of anticipating a triumph over Raphael from this circumstance, he might have foreseen in it the sure source of his mortification and defeat. The public looked to find in *his* pictures what he did not see in Raphael, and were necessarily disappointed. He could hardly be expected to produce that which when produced and set before him, he did not feel or understand. The genius for a particular thing does not imply taste in general or for other things, but it assuredly presupposes a taste or feeling for that particular thing. Salvator was so much offended with the *dryness, hardness,* etc. of Raphael, only because he was not struck, that is, did not sympathize with the divine mind within. If he had, he would have bowed as at a shrine, in spite of the homeliness or finicalness of the covering. Let no man build himself a spurious self-esteem on his contempt or indifference for acknowledged excellence. He will in the end pay dear for a momentary delusion: for the world will sooner or later discover those deficiencies in him, which render him insensible to all merits but his own.

Of all modes of acquiring distinction and, as it were, 'getting the start of the majestic world', the most absurd as well as disgusting is that of setting aside the claims of others in the lump, and holding out our own particular excellence or pursuit as the only one worth attending to. We thus set ourselves up as the standard of perfection, and treat everything else that diverges from that standard as beneath our notice. At this rate, a contempt for anything and a superiority to it are synonymous. It is a cheap and a short way of showing that we possess all excellence within ourselves, to deny the use or merit of all those qualifications that do not belong to us. According to such a mode of computation, it would appear that our value is to be esti-mated not by the number of acquirements that we *do* possess, but of those in which we are deficient and to which we are insensible – so that we can at any time supply the place of wisdom and skill by a due proportion of ignorance, affectation, and conceit. If so, the dullest fellow, with impudence enough to despise what he does not under-stand, will always be the brightest genius and the greatest man. If stupidity is to be a substitute for taste, knowledge, and genius, any-one may dogmatize and play the critic on this ground. We may easily make a monopoly of talent, if the torpedo-touch of our callous and wilful indifference is to neutralize all other pretensions. We have only to deny the advantages of others to make them our own: illiberality will carve out the way to pre-eminence much better than toil or study or quickness of parts; and by narrowing our views and divest-ing ourselves at last of common feeling and humanity, we may arro-gate every valuable accomplishment to ourselves, and exalt ourselves vastly above our fellow-mortals! That is, in other words, we have only to shut our eyes, in order to blot the sun out of heaven, and to annihilate whatever gives light or heat to the world, if it does not emanate from one single source, by spreading the cloud of our own envy, spleen, malice, want of comprehension, and prejudice over it. Yet how many are there who act upon this theory in good earnest, grow more bigoted to it every day, and not only become the dupes of it themselves, but by dint of gravity, by bullying and brow-beating, succeed in making converts of others!

A man is a political economist. Good: but this is no reason he should think there is nothing else in the world, or that everything else is good for nothing. Let us suppose that this is the most important subject, and that being his favourite study, he is the best judge of that point, still it is not the only one – why then treat every other question or pursuit with disdain as insignificant and mean, or endeavour to put others who have devoted their whole time to it out of conceit with that on which they depend for their amusement or (perhaps) subsistence? I see neither the wit, wisdom, nor good nature of this mode of proceeding. Let him fill his library with books on this one subject, yet other persons are not bound to follow the example, and exclude every other topic from theirs – let him write, let him talk, let him think on nothing else, but let him not impose the same pedantic humour as a duty or a mark of taste on others – let him ride the high horse, and drag his heavy load of mechanical knowledge along the iron railway of the master-science, but let him not move out of it to taunt or jostle those who are jogging quietly along upon their several *hobbies*, who 'owe him no allegiance', and care not one jot for his opinion. Yet we could forgive such a person, if he made it his boast that he had read *Don Quixote* twice through in the original Spanish, and preferred *Lycidas* to all Milton's smaller poems! What would Mr Mill say to anyone who should profess a contempt for political economy? He would answer very bluntly and very properly, 'Then you know nothing about it'. It is a pity that so sensible a man and close a reasoner should think of putting down other lighter and more elegant pursuits by professing a contempt or indifference for them, which springs from precisely the same source, and is of just the same value. But so it is that there seems to be a tacit presumption of folly in whatever gives pleasure; while an air of gravity and wisdom hovers round the painful and pedantic!

A man comes into a room, and on his first entering, declares without preface or ceremony his contempt for poetry. Are we therefore to conclude him a greater genius than Homer? No: but by this cavalier opinion he assumes a certain natural ascendancy over those who admire poetry. To *look down* upon anything seemingly implies a greater elevation and enlargement of view than to *look up* to it. The present Lord Chancellor took upon him to declare in open court that he would not go across the street to hear Madame Catalani sing. What did this prove? His want of an ear for music, not his capacity for anything higher. So far as it went, it only showed him to be inferior to those thousands of persons who go with eager expectation to hear her, and come away with astonishment and rapture. A man might as well tell you he is deaf, and expect you to look at him with more respect. The want of any external sense or organ is an acknowledged defect and infirmity: the want of an internal sense or faculty is equally so, though our self-love contrives to give a different turn to it. We mortify others by *throwing cold water* on that in which they have an advantage over us, or stagger their opinion of an excellence which is not of self-evident or absolute utility, and lessen its supposed value, by limiting the universality of a taste for it. Lord Eldon's protest on this occasion was the more extraordinary, as he is not only a good natured but a successful man. These little spiteful allusions are most apt to proceed from disappointed vanity, and an apprehension that justice is not done to ourselves. By being at the top of a profession, we have leisure to look beyond it. Those who really excel and are allowed to excel in anything have no excuse for trying to gain a reputation by undermining the pretensions of others; they stand on their own ground: and do not need the aid of invidious comparisons. Besides, the consciousness of excellence produces a fondness for, a faith in it. I should half suspect that anyone could not be a great lawyer, who denied that Madame Catalani was a great singer. The Chancellor must dislike her decisive tone, the rapidity of her movements! The late Chancellor (Erskine) was a man of (at least) a different stamp. In the exuberance and buoyancy of his animal spirits, he scattered the graces and ornaments of life over the dust and cobwebs of the law. What is there that is now left of him – what is there to redeem his foibles, or to recall the flush of early enthusiasm in his favour, or kindle one spark of sympathy in the breast, but his romantic admiration of Mrs Siddons? There are those who, if you praise Walton's *Complete Angler*, sneer at it as a childish or old-womanish performance: some laugh at the amusement of fishing as silly, others carp at it as cruel; and Dr Johnson said that 'a fishing-rod was a stick with a hook at one end, and a fool at the other'. I would rather take the word of one who had stood for days, up to his knees in water, and in the coldest weather, intent on this employ, who returned to it again with unabated relish, and who spent his whole life in the same manner without being weary of it at last. There is something in this more than Dr Johnson's definition accounts for. A *fool* takes no interest in anything; or if he does, it is better to be a fool, than a wise man, whose only pleasure is to disparage the pursuits and occupations of others, and out of ignorance or prejudice to condemn them, merely because they are not *his*.

Whatever interests, is interesting. I know of no way of estimating the real value of objects in all their bearings and consequences, but I can tell at once their intellectual value by the degree of passion or sentiment the very idea and mention of them excites in the mind. To judge of things by reason or the calculations of positive utility is a slow, cold, uncertain, and barren process – their power of appealing to and affecting the imagination as subjects of thought and feeling is best measured by the habitual impression they leave upon the mind, and it is with this only we have to do in expressing our delight or admiration of them, or in setting a just mental value upon them. They ought to excite all the emotion which they do excite; for this is the instinctive and unerring result of the constant experience we have had of their power of affecting us, and of the associations that cling unconsciously to them. Fancy, feeling may be very inadequate tests of truth; but truth itself operates chiefly on the human mind through them. It is in vain to tell me that what excites the heartfelt sigh of youth, the tears of delight in age, and fills up the busy interval between with pleasing and lofty thoughts, is frivolous, or a waste of time, or of no use. You only by that give me a mean opinion of your ideas of utility. The labour of years, the triumph of aspiring genius and consummate skill, is not to be put down by a cynical frown, by a supercilious smile, by an ignorant sarcasm. Things barely of use are subjects of professional skill and scientific enquiry: they must also be beautiful and pleasing to attract common attention, and be naturally and universally interesting. A pair of shoes is good to wear: a pair of sandals is a more picturesque object; and a statue or a poem are certainly good to think and talk about, which are part of the business of life. To think and speak of them with contempt is therefore a wilful and studied solecism. Pictures are good things to go and see.

This is what people do; they do not expect to eat or make a dinner of them; but we sometimes want to fill up the time before dinner. The progress of civilization and refinement is from instrumental to final causes; from supplying the wants of the body to providing luxuries for the mind. To stop at the *mechanical*, and refuse to proceed to the *fine arts*, or churlishly to reject all ornamental studies and elegant accomplishments as mean and trivial, because they only afford employment to the imagination, create food for thought, furnish the mind, sustain the soul in health and enjoyment, is a rude and barbarous theory –

> Et propter vitam vivendi perdere causas.

Before we absolutely condemn anything, we ought to be able to show something better, not merely in itself, but in the same class. To know the best in each class infers a higher degree of taste; to reject the class is only a negation of taste; for different classes do not interfere with one another, nor can anyone's *ipse dixit* be taken on so wide a question as abstract excellence. Nothing is truly and altogether despicable that excites angry contempt or warm opposition, since this always implies that someone else is of a different opinion, and takes an equal interest in it.

When I speak of what is interesting, however, I mean not only to a particular profession, but in general to others. Indeed, it is the very popularity and obvious interest attached to certain studies and pursuits, that excites the envy and hostile regard of graver and more recondite professions. Man is perhaps not naturally an egotist, or at least he is satisfied with his own particular line of excellence and the value that he supposes inseparable from it, till he comes into the world and finds it of so little account in the eyes of the vulgar; and he then turns round and vents his chagrin and disappointment on those more attractive, but (as he conceives) superficial studies, which cost less labour and patience to understand them, and are of so much less use to society. The injustice done to ourselves makes us unjust to others. The man of science and the hard student (from this cause, as well as from a certain unbending hardness of mind) come at last to regard whatever is generally pleasing and striking as worthless and light, and to proportion their contempt to the admiration of others;

while the artist, the poet, and the votary of pleasure and popularity treat the more solid and useful branches of human knowledge as disagreeable and dull. This is often carried to too great a length. It is enough that 'wisdom is justified of her children': the philosopher ought to smile, instead of being angry at the folly of mankind (if such it is), and those who find both pleasure and profit in adorning and polishing the airy 'capitals' of science and of art, ought not to grudge those who toil underground at the foundation, the praise that is due to their patience and self-denial. There is a variety of tastes and capacities that requires all the variety of men's talents to administer to it. The less excellent must be provided for as well as the more excellent. Those who are only capable of amusement ought to be amused. If all men were forced to be great philosophers and lasting benefactors of their species, how few of us could ever do anything at all! But nature acts more impartially, though not improvidently. Wherever she bestows a *turn* for anything on the individual, she implants a corresponding taste for it in others. We have only to 'throw our bread upon the waters, and after many days we shall find it again'. Let us do our best, and we need not be ashamed of the smallness of our talent, or afraid of the calumnies and contempt of envious maligners. When Goldsmith was talking one day to Sir Joshua of writing a fable in which little fishes were to be introduced, Dr Johnson rolled about uneasily in his seat and began to laugh, on which Goldsmith said rather angrily – 'Why do you laugh? If you were to write a fable for little fishes, you would make them speak like great whales!' The reproof was just. Johnson was in truth conscious of Goldsmith's superior inventiveness, and of the lighter graces of his pen, but he wished to reduce everything to his own pompous and oracular style. There are not only *books for children*, but books for all ages and for both sexes. After we grow up to years of discretion, we do not all become equally wise at once. Our own tastes change: the tastes of other individuals are still more different. It was said the other day, that 'Thomson's *Seasons* would be read while there was a boarding-school girl in the world'. If a thousand volumes were written against Hervey's *Meditations*, the *Meditations* would be read when the criticisms were forgotten. To the illiterate and vain, affectation and verbiage will always pass for fine writing, while the world stands. No woman ever liked Burke, or disliked

Goldsmith. It is idle to set up an universal standard. There is a large
class who, in spite of themselves, prefer Westall or Angelica Kauffman
to Raphael; nor is it fit they should do otherwise. We may come to
something like a fixed and exclusive standard of taste, if we confine
ourselves to what will please the best judges, meaning thereby persons of the most refined and cultivated minds, and by persons of the
most refined and cultivated minds, generally meaning *ourselves!*[1]

To return to the original question. I can conceive of nothing so
little or ridiculous as pride. It is a mixture of insensibility and ill-
nature, in which it is hard to say which has the largest share. If a man
knows or excels in, or has ever studied any two things, I will venture
to affirm he will be proud of neither. It is perhaps excusable for a
person who is ignorant of all but one thing, to think *that* the sole
excellence, and to be full of himself as the possessor. The way to cure
him of this folly is to give him something else to be proud of. Vanity
is a building that falls to the ground as you widen its foundation, or
strengthen the props that should support it. The greater a man is,
the less he necessarily thinks of himself, for his knowledge enlarges
with his attainments. In himself he feels that he is nothing, a point, a
speck in the universe, except as his mind reflects that universe, and as
he enters into the infinite variety of truth, beauty, and power contained in it. Let anyone be brought up among books, and taught to
think words the only things, and he may conceive highly of himself
from the proficiency he has made in language and in letters. Let him
then be compelled to attempt some other pursuit – painting, for
instance – and be made to feel the difficulties, the refinements of
which it is capable, and the number of things of which he was utterly
ignorant before, and there will be an end of his pedantry and his
pride together. Nothing but the want of comprehension of view or
generosity of spirit can make anyone fix on his own particular ac-
quirement as the limit of all excellence. No one is (generally speaking) great in more than one thing – if he extends his pursuits, he
dissipates his strength – yet in that one thing how small is the inter-

1   The books that we like in youth we return to in age, if there is nature and simplicity in them. At what age should *Robinson Crusoe* be laid aside? I do not think that
Don Quixote is a book for children; or at least, they understand it better as they
grow up.

val between him and the next in merit and reputation to himself! But he thinks nothing of, or scorns or loathes the name of his rival, so that all that the other possesses in common goes for nothing, and the fraction of a difference between them constitutes (in his opinion) the sum and substance of all that is excellent in the universe! Let a man be wise, and then let us ask, will his wisdom make him proud? Let him excel all others in the graces of the mind, has he also those of the body? He has the advantage of fortune, but has he also that of birth, or if he has both, has he health, strength, beauty in a supreme degree? Or have not others the same, or does he think all these nothing because he does not possess them? The proud man fancies that there is no one worth regarding but himself: he might as well fancy there is no other being but himself. The one is not a greater stretch of madness than the other. To make pride justifiable, there ought to be but one proud man in the world, for if any one individual has a right to be so, nobody else has. So far from thinking ourselves superior to all the rest of the species, we cannot be sure that we are above the meanest and most despised individual of it: for he may have some virtue, some excellence, some source of happiness or usefulness within himself, which may redeem all other disadvantages: or even if he is without any such hidden worth, this is not a subject of exultation, but of regret, to anyone tinctured with the smallest humanity, and he who is totally devoid of the latter, cannot have much reason to be proud of anything else. Arkwright, who invented the spinning-jenny, for many years kept a paltry barber's shop in a provincial town: yet at that time that wonderful machinery was working in his brain, which has added more to the wealth and resources of this country than all the pride of ancestry or insolence of upstart nobility for the last hundred years. We should be cautious whom we despise. If we do not know them, we can have no right to pronounce a hasty sentence: if we do, they may espy some few defects in us. *No man is a hero to his valet-de-chambre.* What is it then that makes the difference? The dress and pride. But he is the most of a hero who is least distinguished by the one, and most free from the other. If we enter into conversation upon equal terms with the lowest of the people, unrestrained by circumstance, unawed by interest, we shall find in ourselves but little superiority over them. If we know what they do not, they know what we do not. In general, those who do things for others, know more

about them than those for whom they are done. A groom knows
more about horses than his master. He rides them too: but the one
rides behind, the other before! Hence the number of forms and cer-
emonies that have been invented to keep the magic circle of fancied
self-importance inviolate. The late King sought but one interview
with Dr Johnson: his present Majesty is never tired of the company
of Mr Croker.

The collision of truth or genius naturally gives a shock to the pride
of exalted rank: the great and mighty usually seek out the dregs of
mankind, buffoons and flatterers, for their pampered self-love to repose on. Pride soon tires of everything but its shadow, servility: but
how poor a triumph is that which exists only by excluding all rivalry,
however remote. He who invites competition (the only test of merit),
who challenges fair comparisons, and weighs different claims, is alone
possessed of manly ambition; but will not long continue vain or proud.
Pride is 'a cell of ignorance; travelling abed'. If we look at all out of
ourselves, we must see how far short we are of what we would be
thought. The man of genius is poor;[2] the rich man is not a lord: the
lord wants to be a king: the king is uneasy to be a tyrant or a god. Yet
he alone, who could claim this last character upon earth, gave his life
a ransom for others! The dwarf in the romance, who saw the shadows of the fairest and the mightiest among the sons of men pass
before him, that he might assume the shape he liked best, had only
his choice of wealth, or beauty, or valour, or power. But could he
have clutched them all, and melted them into one essence of pride,

---

2   I do not speak of poverty as an absolute evil; though when accompanied with
    luxurious habits and vanity, it is a great one. Even hardships and privations have
    their use, and give strength and endurance. Labour renders ease delightful –
    hunger is the best sauce. The peasant, who at noon rests from his weary task
    under a hawthorn hedge, and eats his slice of coarse bread and cheese or rusty
    bacon, enjoys more real luxury than the prince with pampered, listless appetite
    under a canopy of state. Why then does the mind of man pity the former, and
    envy the latter? It is because the imagination changes places with others in situa-
    tion only, not in feeling; and in fancying ourselves the peasant, we revolt at his
    homely fare, from not being possessed of his gross taste or keen appetite, while in
    thinking of the prince, we suppose ourselves to sit down to his delicate viands
    and sumptuous board, with a relish unabated by long habit and vicious excess. I
    am not sure whether Mandeville has not given the same answer to this hackneyed
    question.

the triumph would not have been lasting. Could vanity take all pomp and power to itself, could it, like the rainbow, span the earth, and seem to prop the heavens, after all it would be but the wonder of the ignorant, the pageant of a moment. The fool who dreams that he is great should first forget that he is a man, and before he thinks of being proud, should pray to be mad! The only great man in modern times, that is, the only man who rose in deeds and fame to the level of antiquity, who might turn his gaze upon himself, and wonder at his height, for on him all eyes were fixed as his majestic stature towered above thrones and monuments of renown, died the other day in exile, and in lingering agony; and we still see fellows strutting about the streets, and fancying they are something!

Personal vanity is incompatible with the great and the *ideal*. He who has not seen, or thought, or read of something finer than himself, has seen, or read, or thought little; and he who has, will not be always looking in the glass of his own vanity. Hence poets, artists, and men of genius in general, are seldom coxcombs, but often slovens; for they find something out of themselves better worth studying than their own persons. They have an imaginary standard in their minds, with which ordinary features (even their own) will not bear a comparison, and they turn their thoughts another way. If a man had a face like one of Raphael's or Titian's heads, he might be proud of it, but not else; and, even then, he would be stared at as a *nondescript* by 'the universal English nation'. Few persons who have seen the Antinous or the Theseus will be much charmed with their own beauty or symmetry; nor will those who understand the *costume* of the antique, or Vandyke's dresses, spend much time in decking themselves out in all the deformity of the prevailing fashion. A coxcomb is his own lay-figure, for want of any better models to employ his time and imagination upon.

There is an inverted sort of pride, the reverse of that egotism that has been above described, and which, because it cannot be everything, is dissatisfied with everything. A person who is liable to this infirmity 'thinks nothing done, while anything remains to be done'. The sanguine egotist prides himself on what he can do or possesses, the morbid egotist despises himself for what he wants, and is ever going out of his way to attempt hopeless and impossible tasks. The effect in either case is not at all owing to reason, but to temperament. The one is as easily depressed by what mortifies his latent ambition, as the other is elated by what flatters his immediate vanity. There are persons whom no success, no advantages, no applause can satisfy, for they dwell only on failure and defeat. They constantly 'forget the things that are behind, and press forward to the things that are before'. The greatest and most decided acquisitions would not indemnify them for the smallest deficiency. They go beyond the old motto – *Aut Caesar, aut nihil* – they not only want to be at the head of whatever they undertake, but if they succeed in that, they immediately want to be at the head of something else, no matter how gross or trivial. The charm that rivets their affections is not the importance or reputation annexed to the new pursuit, but its novelty or difficulty. That must be a wonderful accomplishment indeed, which baffles their skill – nothing is with them of any value but as it gives scope to their restless activity of mind, their craving after an uneasy and importunate state of excitement. To them the pursuit is everything, the possession nothing. I have known persons of this stamp, who, with every reason to be satisfied with their success in life, and with the opinion entertained of them by others, despised themselves because they could not do something which they were not bound to do, and which, if they could have done it, would not have added one jot to their respectability, either in their own eyes or those of anyone else, the very insignificance of the attainment irritating their impatience, for it is the humour of such dispositions to argue, 'If they cannot succeed in what is trifling and contemptible, how should they succeed in anything else?' If they could make the circuit of the arts and sciences, and master them all, they would take to some mechanical exercise, and if they failed, be as discontented as ever. All that they can do vanishes out of sight the moment it is within their grasp, and 'nothing is but what is not'. A poet of this description is ambitious of the thews and muscles of a prize fighter, and thinks himself nothing without them. A prose writer would be a fine tennis player, and is thrown into despair because he is not one, without considering that it requires a whole life devoted to the game to excel in it; and that, even if he could dispense with this apprenticeship, he would still be just as much bound to excel in rope-dancing, or horsemanship, or playing at cup and ball like the Indian jugglers, all which is impossible. This feeling is a strange mixture of modesty and pride. We think nothing of what we are, because we cannot be everything with a wish. Goldsmith was even jealous of beauty in the other sex, and the same character is attributed to Wharton by Pope:

> Though listening senates hung on all he spoke,
> The club must hail him master of the joke.

Players are for going into the church – officers in the army turn players. For myself, do what I might, I should think myself a poor creature unless I could beat a boy of ten years old at chuck-farthing, or an elderly gentlewoman at piquet!

The extreme of fastidious discontent and repining is as bad as that of overweening presumption. We ought to be satisfied if we have succeeded in any one thing, or with having done our best. Anything more is for health and amusement, and should be resorted to as a source of pleasure, not of fretful impatience, and endless, petty, self-imposed mortification. Perhaps the jealous, uneasy temperament is most favourable to continued exertion and improvement, if it does not lead us to fritter away attention on too many pursuits. By looking out of ourselves, we gain knowledge: by being little satisfied with what we have done, we are less apt to sink into indolence and security. To conclude with a piece of egotism: I never begin one of these *essays* with a consciousness of having written a line before; and having got to the end of the volume, hope never to look into it again.

Hot and Cold

COMPOSED LATE 1825

*Hot, cold, moist, and dry, four champions fierce, Strive here for
mastery.* Milton

'The Protestants are much cleaner than the Catholics', said a shopkeeper of Vevey to me. 'They are so', I replied, 'but why should
they?' A prejudice appeared to him a matter-of-fact, and he did not
think it necessary to assign reasons for a matter-of-fact. That is not
my way. He had not bottomed his proposition on proofs, nor rightly
defined it.

Nearly the same remark, as to the extreme cleanliness of the people in this part of the country, had occurred to me as soon as I got to
Brigg, where however the inhabitants are Catholics. So the original
statement requires some qualification as to the mode of enunciation.
I had no sooner arrived in this village, which is situated just under
the Simplon, and where you are surrounded with *glaciers* and *goi-
tres,* than the genius of the place struck me on looking out at the
pump under my window the next morning, where the 'neat-handed
Phyllises' were washing their greens in the water, that not a caterpil-
lar could crawl on them, and scouring their pails and tubs that not a
stain should be left in them. The raw, clammy feeling of the air was
in unison with the scene. I had not seen such a thing in Italy. They
have there no delight in splashing and dabbling in fresh streams and
fountains – they have a dread of ablutions and absterions, almost
amounting to *hydrophobia.* Heat has an antipathy in nature to cold.
The sanguine Italian is chilled and shudders at the touch of cold
water, while the Helvetian boor, whose humours creep through his
veins like the dank mists along the sides of his frozen mountains, is

'native and endued unto that element'. Here everything is purified
and filtered: there it is baked and burnt up, and sticks together in a
most amicable union of filth and laziness. There is a little mystery
and a little contradiction in the case – let us try if we cannot get rid of
both by means of caution and daring together. It is not that the
difference of latitude between one side of the Alps and the other can
signify much: but the phlegmatic blood of their German ancestors is
poured down the valleys of the Swiss like water, and *iced* in its progress;
whereas that of the Italians, besides its vigorous origin, is enriched
and ripened by basking in more genial plains. A single Milanese mar-
ket-girl (to go no farther south) appeared to me to have more blood
in her body, more fire in her eye (as if the sun had made a burning
lens of it), more spirit and probably more mischief about her than all
the nice, *tidy*, good-looking, hard-working girls I have seen in Switzerland. To turn this physiognomical observation to a metaphysical
account, I should say then that northern people are clean and southern people dirty as a general rule, because where the principle of life
is more cold, weak, and impoverished, there is a greater shyness and
aversion to come in contact with external matter (with which it does
not so easily amalgamate), a greater fastidiousness and delicacy in
choosing its sensations, a greater desire to know surrounding objects and to keep them clear of each other, than where this principle
being more warm and active, it may be supposed to absorb outward
impressions in itself, to melt them into its own essence, to impart its
own vital impulses to them, and in fine, instead of shrinking from
everything, to be shocked at nothing. The southern temperament is
(so to speak) more sociable with matter, more gross, impure, indifferent, from relying on its own strength; while that opposed to it,
from being less able to react on external applications, is obliged to
be more cautious and particular as to the kind of excitement to which
it renders itself liable. Hence the timidity, reserve, and occasional
hypocrisy of northern manners; the boldness, freedom, levity, and
frequent licentiousness of southern ones. It would be too much to
say, that if there is anything of which a genuine Italian has a horror,
it is of cleanliness; or that if there is anything which seems ridiculous
to a thoroughbred Italian woman, it is modesty: but certainly the
degree to which nicety is carried by some people is a *bore* to an
Italian imagination, as the excess of delicacy which is pretended or

practised by some women is quite incomprehensible to the females
of the South. It is wrong, however, to make the greater confidence
or forwardness of manners an absolute test of morals: the love of
virtue is a different thing from the fear or even hatred of vice. The
squeamishness and prudery in the one case have a more plausible
appearance; but it does not follow that there may not be more native
goodness and even habitual refinement in the other, though accompanied with stronger nerves and a less morbid imagination. But to
return to the first question.[1] I can readily understand how a Swiss
peasant should stand a whole morning at a pump, washing cabbages,
cauliflowers, salads, and getting rid half a dozen times over of the
sand, dirt, and insects they contain, because I myself should not only
be *gravelled* by meeting with the one at table, but should be in horrors at the other. A Frenchman or an Italian would be thrown into
convulsions of laughter at this superfluous delicacy, and would think
his repeat enriched or none the worse for such additions. The reluc-
tance to prey on life, or on what once had it, seems to arise from a
sense of incongruity, from the repugnance between life and death –
from the cold, clammy feeling which belongs to the one, and which
is enhanced by the contrast to its former warm, lively state, and by
the circumstance of its being taken into the mouth, and devoured as
food. Hence the desire to get rid of the idea of the living animal even
in ordinary cases by all the disguises of cookery, of boiled and roast,
and by the artifice of changing the name of the animal into something different when it becomes food.[2] Hence sportsmen are not
devourers of game, and hence the aversion to kill the animals we

1 Women abroad (generally speaking) are more like men in the tone of their conversation and habits of thinking, so that from the same premises you cannot draw
   the same conclusions as in England.
2 This circumstance is noticed in *Ivanhoe*, though a different turn is given to it by
   the philosopher of Rotherwood.
      'Nay, I can tell you more', said Wamba in the same tone, 'there is old Alder-
   man Ox continues to hold his Saxon epithet, while he is under the charge of serfs
   and bondsmen such as thou; but becomes Beef, a fiery French gallant, when he
   arrives before the worshipful jaws that are destined to consume him. Mynheer
   Calf too becomes Monsieur de Veau in like manner: he is Saxon when he requires
   tendance, and takes a Norman name when he becomes matter of enjoyment.'
   Vol. 1, ch. I.

eat.[3] There is a contradiction between the animate and the inanimate, which is felt as matter of peculiar annoyance by the more cold
and congealed temperament which cannot so well pass from one to
the other; but this objection is easily swallowed by the inhabitant of
gayer and more luxurious regions, who is so full of life himself that
he can at once impart it to all that comes in his way, or never troubles
himself about the difference. So the Neapolitan bandit takes the life
of his victim with little remorse, because he has enough and to spare
in himself: his pulse still beats warm and vigorous, while the blood of
a more humane native of the frozen north would run cold with horror at the sight of the stiffened corse, and this makes him pause before he stops in another the gushing source, of which he has such
feeble supplies in himself. The wild Arab of the desert can hardly
entertain the idea of death, neither dreading it for himself nor re-
gretting it for others. The Italians, Spaniards, and people of the south
swarm alive without being sick or sorry at the circumstance: they
hunt the accustomed prey in each other's tangled locks openly in the
streets and on the highways, without manifesting shame or repugnance: combs are an invention of our northern climes. Now I can
comprehend this, when I look at the dirty, dingy, greasy, sunburnt
complexion of an Italian peasant or beggar, whose body seems alive
all over with a sort of tingling, oily sensation, so that from any given
particle of his shining skin to the beast 'whose name signifies love'
the transition is but small. This populousness is not unaccountable
where all teems with life, where all is glowing and in motion, and
every pore thrills with an exuberance of feeling. Not so in the dearth
of life and spirit, in the drossy, dry, material texture, the clear complexions and fair hair of the Saxon races, where the puncture of an
insect's sting is a solution of their personal identity, and the idea of
life attached to and courting an intimacy with them in spite of themselves, naturally produces all the revulsions of the most violent antipathy and nearly drives them out of their wits. How well the smooth
ivory comb and auburn hair agree – while the Greek *dandy*, on entering a room, applies his hand to brush a cloud of busy stragglers

---

3   Hence the peculiar horror of cannibalism from the stronger sympathy with our
    own sensations, and the greater violence that is done to it by the sacrilegious use
    of what once possessed human life and feeling.

from his hair like powder, and gives himself no more concern about them than about the motes dancing in the sunbeams! The dirt of the Italians is as it were baked into them, and so ingrained as to become a part of themselves, and occasion no discontinuity of their being.

I can forgive the dirt and sweat of a gypsy under a hedge, when I consider that the earth is his mother, the sun is his father. He hunts vermin for food: he is himself hunted like vermin for prey. His existence is not one of choice, but of necessity. The hungry Arab devours the raw shoulder of a horse. This again I can conceive. His feverish blood seethes it, and the virulence of his own breath carries off the disagreeableness of the smell. I do not see that the horse should be reckoned among unclean animals, according to any notions I have of the matter. The dividing of the hoof or the contrary, I should think, has not anything to do with the question. I can understand the distinction between beasts of prey and the herbivorous and domestic animals, but the horse is tame. The natural distinction between clean and unclean animals (which has been sometimes made into a religious one) I take to depend on two circumstances, *viz.* the claws and bristly hide, which generally, though not always, go together. One would not wish to be torn in pieces instead of making a comfortable meal, 'to be supped upon' where we thought of supping. With respect to the wolf, the tiger, and other animals of the same species, it seems a question which of us should devour the other: this baulks our appetite by distracting our attention, and we have so little relish for being eaten ourselves, or for the fangs and teeth of these shocking animals, that it gives us a distaste for their whole bodies. The horror we conceive at preying upon them arises in part from the fear we had of being preyed upon by them. No such apprehension crosses the mind with respect to the deer, the sheep, the hare – 'here all is conscience and tender heart'. These gentle creatures (whom we compliment as useful) offer no resistance to the knife, and there is therefore nothing shocking or repulsive in the idea of devoting them to it. There is no confusion of ideas, but a beautiful simplicity and uniformity in our relation to each other, we as the slayers, they as the slain. A perfect understanding subsists on the subject. The hair of animals of prey is also strong and bristly, and forms an obstacle to our epicurean designs. The calf or fawn is sleek and smooth: the bristles on a dog's or a cat's back are like 'the quills upon the fretful

porcupine', a very impracticable repast to the imagination, that stick
in the throat and turn the stomach. Who has not read and been
edified by the account of the supper in *Gil Blas*? Besides, there is also
in all probability the practical consideration urged by Voltaire's traveller, who being asked 'which he preferred – black mutton or white?'
replied, 'Either, provided it was tender'. The greater rankness in the
flesh is however accompanied by a corresponding irritability of surface, a tenaciousness, a pruriency, a soreness to attack, and not that
fine, round, pampered passiveness to impressions which cuts up into
handsome joints and entire pieces without any fidgety process, and
with an obvious view to solid, wholesome nourishment. Swine's flesh,
the abomination of the Jewish law, certainly comes under the objection here stated; and the bear with its shaggy fur is only smuggled
into the Christian larder as half-brother to the wild boar, and because from its lazy, lumpish character and appearance, it seems matter of indifference whether it eats or is eaten. The horse, with sleek
round haunches, is fair game, except from custom; and I think I
could survive having swallowed part of an ass's foal without being
utterly loathsome to myself.[4] Mites in a rotten cheese are endurable,
from being so small and dry that they are scarce distinguishable from
the atoms of the cheese itself, 'so drossy and divisible are they': but
the Lord deliver me from their more thriving next-door neighbours!
Animals that are made use of as food should either be so small as to
be imperceptible, or else we should dig into the quarry of life, hew
away the masses, and not leave the form standing to reproach us
with our gluttony and cruelty. I hate to see a rabbit trussed, or a hare

4   Thomas Cooper of Manchester, the able logician and political partisan, tried the
    experiment some years ago, when he invited a number of gentlemen and officers
    quartered in the town to dine with him on an ass's foal instead of a calf's head,
    on the anniversary of the 30th of January. The circumstance got wind, and gave
    great offence. Mr Cooper had to attend a county-meeting soon after at Boulton-
    le-Moors, and one of the country magistrates coming to the inn for the same
    purpose, and when he asked 'If anyone was in the room?' receiving for answer –
    'No one but Mr Cooper of Manchester' – ordered out his horse and immediately
    rode home again. Some verses made on the occasion by Mr Scarlett and Mr
    Shepherd of Gateacre explained the story thus –

        The reason how this came to pass is
        The Justice had heard that Cooper ate asses!

brought to table in the form which it occupied while living: they seem to me apparitions of the burrowers in the earth or the rovers in the wood, sent to scare away appetite. One reason why toads and serpents are disgusting, is from the way in which they run against or suddenly cling to the skin: the encountering them causes a solution of continuity, and we shudder to feel a life which is not ours in contact with us. It is this disjointed or imperfect sympathy which in the recoil produces the greatest antipathy. Sterne asks why a sword, which takes away life, may be named without offence, though other things, which contribute to perpetuate it, cannot? Because the idea in the one case is merely painful, and there is no mixture of the agreeable to lead the imagination on to a point from which it must make a precipitate retreat. The morally indecent arises from the doubtful conflict between temptation and duty: the physically revolting is the product of alternate attraction and repulsion, of partial adhesion, or of something that is foreign to us sticking closer to our persons than we could wish. The nastiest tastes and smells are not the most pungent and painful, but a compound of sweet and bitter, of the agreeable and disagreeable; where the sense, having been relaxed and rendered effeminate as it were by the first, is unable to contend with the last, faints and sinks under it, and has no way of relieving itself but by violently throwing off the load that oppresses it. Hence loathing and sickness. But these hardly ever arise without something contradictory or *impure* in the objects, or unless the mind, having been invited and prepared to be gratified at first, this expectation is turned to disappointment and disgust. Mere pains, mere pleasures do not have this effect, save from an excess of the first causing insensibility and then a faintness ensues, or of the last, causing what is called a surfeit. Seasickness has some analogy to this. It comes on with that unsettled motion of the ship, which takes away the ordinary footing or firm hold we have of things, and by relaxing our perceptions, unbraces the whole nervous system. The giddiness and swimming of the head on looking down a precipice, when we are ready with every breath of imagination to topple down into the abyss, has its source in the same uncertain and rapid whirl of the fancy through possible extremes. Thus we find that for cases of fainting, seasickness, etc. a glass of brandy is recommended as 'the sovereign'st thing on earth', because by grappling with the coats of the stomach and bringing our

sensations to a *focus*, it does away that nauseous fluctuation and sus-
pense of feeling which is the root of the mischief. I do not know
whether I make myself intelligible, for the utmost I can pretend is to
suggest some very subtle and remote analogies: but if I have at all
succeeded in opening up the train of argument I intend, it will at
least be possible to conceive how the sanguine Italian is less nice in
his intercourse with material objects, less startled at incongruities,
less liable to take offence, than the more literal and conscientious
German, because the more headstrong current of his own sensations
fills up the gaps and 'makes the odds all even'. He does not care to
have his cabbages and salads washed ten times over, or his beds cleared
of vermin: he can lend or borrow satisfaction from all objects indif-
ferently. The air over his head is full of life, of the hum of insects; the
grass under his feet rings and is loud with the cry of the grasshopper;
innumerable green lizards dart from the rocks and sport before him:
what signifies it if any living creature approaches nearer his own person, where all is one vital glow? The Indian even twines the forked
serpent round his hand unharmed, copper-coloured like it, his veins
as heated; and the Brahmin cherishes life and disregards his own
person as an act of his religion – the religion of fire and of the sun!
Yet how shall we reconcile to this theory the constant ablutions (five
times a day) of the Eastern nations, and the squalid customs of some
northern people, the dirtiness of the Russians and of the Scotch?
Superstition may perhaps account for the one, and poverty and bar-
barism for the other.[5]

Laziness has a great deal to do in the question, and this again is
owing to a state of feeling sufficient to itself, and rich in enjoyment
without the help of action. Clothilde (the finest and darkest of the
Gensano girls) fixes herself at her door about noon (when her day's
work is done): her smile reflects back the brightness of the sun, she
darts upon a little girl with a child in her arms, nearly overturns

---

5 What a plague Moses had with his Jews to make them 'reform and live cleanly!'
   To this day (according to a learned traveller) the Jews, wherever scattered, have
   an aversion to agriculture and almost to its products; and a Jewish girl will refuse
   to accept a flower – if you offer her a piece of money, of jewellery or embroidery,
   she knows well enough what to make of the proffered courtesy. See *Hacquet's
   Travels in Carpathia*, etc.

both, devours it with kisses, and then resumes her position at the
door, with her hands behind her back and her shoes down at heel.
This slatternliness and negligence is the more remarkable in so fine
a girl, and one whose ordinary costume is a gorgeous picture, but it
is a part of the character; her dress would never have been so rich, if
she could take more pains about it – they have no nervous or fidgety feeling whether a thing is coming off or not: all their sensations,
as it were, sit loose upon them. Their clothes are no part of themselves – they even fling their limbs about as if they scarcely be-
longed to them; the heat in summer requires the utmost freedom
and airiness (which becomes a habit), and they have nothing tight-
bound or strait-laced about their minds or bodies. The same girl in
winter (for 'dull, cold winter *does* inhabit here' also) would have a
scaldaletto (an earthen pan with coals in it) dangling at her wrists
for four months together, without any sense of encumbrance or
distraction, or any other feeling but of the heat it communicated to
her hands. She does not mind its chilling the rest of her body or
disfiguring her hands, making her fingers look like 'long purples' –
these children of nature 'take the good the Gods provide them',
and trouble themselves little about consequences or appearances.
Their self-will is much stronger than their vanity – they have as little
curiosity about others as concern for their good opinion. Two Italian peasants talking by the roadside will not so much as turn their
heads to look at an English carriage that is passing. They have no
interest except in what is personal, sensual. Hence they have as little tenaciousness on the score of property as in the acquisition of
ideas. They want neither. Their good spirits are food, clothing, and
books to them. They are fond of comfort too, but their notion of it
differs from ours – ours consists in accumulating the means of enjoyment, theirs in being free to enjoy, in the dear *far niente*. What
need have they to encumber themselves with furniture or wealth or
business, when all they require (for the most part) is air, a bunch of
grapes, bread, and stone walls? The Italians, generally speaking,
have nothing, do nothing, want nothing – to the surprise of foreigners, who ask how they live? The men are too lazy to be thieves,
the women to be something else. The dependence of the Swiss and
English on their comforts, that is, on all 'appliances and means to
boot', as helps to enjoyment or hindrances to annoyance, makes

them not only eager to procure different objects of accommodation and luxury, but makes them take such pains in their preservation and embellishment, and *pet* them so when acquired. 'A man', says Yorick, 'finds an apple, spits upon it, and calls it his.' The more anyone finds himself clinging to material objects for existence or gratification, the more he will take a personal interest in them, and the more will he clean, repair, polish, scrub, scour, and tug at them without end, as if it were his own soul that he was keeping clear from spot or blemish. A Swiss dairy-maid scours the very heart out of a wooden pail; a scullion washes the taste as well as the worms out of a dish of broccoli. The wenches are in like manner neat and clean in their own persons, but insipid. The most coarse and ordinary furniture in Switzerland has more pains bestowed upon it to keep it in order, than the finest works of art in Italy. There the pictures are suffered to moulder on the walls; and the Claudes in the Doria Palace at Rome are black with age and dirt. We set more store by them in England, where we have scarce any other sunshine! At the common inns on this side the Simplon, the very sheets have a character for whiteness to lose: the rods and testers of the beds are like a peeled wand. On the opposite side you are thankful when you are not shown into an apartment resembling a three-stalled stable, with horse-cloths for coverlids to hide the dirt, and beds of horsehair or withered leaves as harbourage for vermin. The more, the merrier; the dirtier, the warmer; live and let live, seem maxims inculcated by the climate. Wherever things are not kept carefully apart from foreign admixtures and contamination, the distinctions of property itself will not, I conceive, be held exceedingly sacred. This feeling is strong as the passions are weak. A people that are remarkable for cleanliness, will be so for industry, for honesty, for avarice, and vice versa. The Italians cheat, steal, rob (when they think it worth their while to do so) with licensed impunity: the Swiss, who feel the value of property, and labour incessantly to acquire it, are afraid to lose it. At Brigg I first heard the cry of watchmen at night, which I had not heard for many months. I was reminded of the traveller who after wandering in remote countries saw a gallows near at hand, and knew by this circumstance that he approached the confines of civilization. The police in Italy is both secret and severe, but it is directed chiefly to political and not to civil matters. Patriot sighs are heaved unheard in the dungeons of St Angelo: the Neapolitan bandit breathes the free air of his native mountains!

It may by this time be conjectured why Catholics are less cleanly than Protestants, because in fact they are less scrupulous, and swallow whatever is set before them in matters of faith as well as other things. Protestants, as such, are captious and scrutinizing, try to pick holes and find fault – have a dry, meagre, penurious imagination. Catholics are buoyed up over doubts and difficulties by a greater redundance of fancy, and make religion subservient to a sense of enjoyment. The one are for detecting and weeding out all corruptions and abuses in doctrine or worship: the others enrich theirs with the dust and cobwebs of antiquity, and think their ritual none the worse for the tarnish of age. Those of the Catholic Communion are willing to take it for granted that everything is right; the professors of the Reformed religion have a pleasure in believing that everything is wrong, in order that they may have to set it right. In morals, again, Protestants are more precise than their Catholic brethren. The creed of the latter absolves them of half their duties, of all those that are a clog on their inclinations, atones for all slips, and patches up all deficiencies. But though this may make them less censorious and sour, I am not sure that it renders them less in earnest in the part they do perform. When more is left to freedom of choice, perhaps the service that is voluntary will be purer and more effectual. That which is not so may as well be done by proxy; or if it does not come from the heart, may be suffered to exhale merely from the lips. If less is owing in this case to a dread of vice and fear of shame, more will proceed from a love of virtue, free from the least sinister construction. It is asserted that Italian women are more gross; I can believe it, and that they are at the same time more refined than others. Their religion is in the same manner more sensual: but is it not to the full as visionary and imaginative as any? I have heard Italian women say things that others would not – it does not therefore follow that they would do them: partly because the knowledge of vice that makes it familiar renders it indifferent; and because the same masculine tone of thinking that enables them to confront vice, may raise them above it into a higher sphere of sentiment. If their senses are more inflammable, their passions (and their love of virtue and of religion among the rest) may glow with proportionable ardour. Indeed the truest virtue is that which is least susceptible of contamination from its opposite. I may admire a Raphael, and yet not swoon at sight of a daub. Why should there not be the same taste in morals as in pictures or poems? Granting that vice has more votaries here, at least it has fewer mercenary ones, and this is no trifling advantage. As to manners, the Catholics must be allowed to carry it over all the world. The better sort not only say nothing to give you pain; they say nothing of others that it would give them pain to hear repeated. Scandal and tittle-tattle are long banished from good society. After all, to be wise is to be humane. What would our English *bluestockings* say to this? The fault and the excellence of Italian society is, that the shocking or disagreeable is not supposed to have an existence in the nature of things.[6]

6   The dirt and comparative want of conveniences among Catholics is often attributed to the number of their saints' days and festivals, which divert them from labour, and give them an idle and disorderly turn of mind.

On the Difference — Between Writing and — Speaking

FIRST PUBLISHED *LONDON MAGAZINE*, JULY 1820

'Some minds are proportioned to that which may be dispatched at once, or within a short return of time: others to that which begins afar off, and is to be won with length of pursuit.' Lord Bacon

It is a common observation, that few persons can be found who speak and write equally well. Not only is it obvious that the two faculties do not always go together in the same proportions: but they are not unusually in direct opposition to each other. We find that the greatest authors often make the worst company in the world; and again, some of the liveliest fellows imaginable in conversation, or extempore speaking, seem to lose all their vivacity and spirit the moment they set pen to paper. For this a greater degree of quickness or slowness of parts, education, habit, temper, turn of mind, and a variety of collateral and predisposing causes are necessary to account. The subject is at least curious, and worthy of an attempt to explain it. I shall endeavour to illustrate the difference by familiar examples rather than by analytical reasonings. The philosopher of old was not unwise, who defined motion by getting up and walking.

The great leading distinction between writing and speaking is, that more time is allowed for the one than the other: and hence different faculties are required for, and different objects attained by, each. He is properly the best speaker who can collect together the greatest number of apposite ideas at a moment's warning: he is properly the best writer who can give utterance to the greatest quantity of valuable knowledge in the course of his whole life. The chief requisite for the one, then, appears to be quickness and facility of perception – for the other, patience of soul, and a power increasing with the difficulties it has to master. He cannot be denied to be an expert speaker, a lively companion, who is never at a loss for something to say on every occasion or subject that offers: he, by the same rule, will make a respectable writer, who, by dint of study, can find out anything good to say upon any one point that has not been touched upon before, or who, by asking for time, can give the most complete and comprehensive view of any question. The one must be done offhand, at a single blow: the other can only be done by a repetition of blows, by having time to think and do better. In speaking, less is required of you, if you only do it at once, with grace and spirit: in writing, you stipulate for all that you are capable of, but you have the choice of your own time and subject. You do not expect from the manufacturer the same dispatch in executing an order that you do from the shopkeeper or warehouseman. The difference of *quicker* and *slower*, however, is not all: that is merely a difference of comparison in doing the same thing. But the writer and speaker have to do things essentially different. Besides habit, and greater or less facility, there is also a certain reach of capacity, a certain depth or shallowness, grossness or refinement of intellect, which marks out the distinction between those whose chief ambition is to shine by producing an immediate effect, or who are thrown back, by a natural bias, on the severe researches of thought and study.

We see persons of that standard or texture of mind that they can do nothing, but on the spur of the occasion: if they have time to deliberate, they are lost. There are others who have no resource, who cannot advance a step by any efforts or assistance, beyond a successful arrangement of commonplaces: but these they have always at command, at everybody's service. There is Finnerty; meet him where you will in the street, he has his topic ready to discharge in the same breath with the customary forms of salutation; he is hand and glove with it; on it goes and off, and he manages it like Wart his caliver.

> Hear him but reason in divinity,
> And, all-admiring, with an inward wish
> You would desire that he were made a prelate.
> Let him but talk of any state-affair,
> You'd say it had been all in all his study.
> Turn him to any cause of policy,
> The Gordian knot of it he will unloose,
> Familiar as his garter. When he speaks,
> The air, a charter'd libertine, stands still –

but, ere you have time to answer him, he is off like a shot, to repeat the same rounded, fluent observations to others – a perfect master of the sentences, a walking polemic wound up for the day, a smartly bound political pocket-book! Set the same person to write a common paragraph, and he cannot get through it for very weariness: ask him a question, ever so little out of the common road, and he stares you in the face. What does all this bustle, animation, plausibility, and command of words amount to? A lively flow of animal spirits, a good deal of confidence, a communicative turn, and a tolerably tenacious memory with respect to floating opinions and current phrases. Beyond the routine of the daily newspapers and coffee-house criticism, such persons do not venture to think at all: or if they did, it would be so much the worse for them, for they would only be perplexed in the attempt, and would perform their part in the mechanism of society with so much the less alacrity and easy volubility.

The most dashing orator I ever heard is the flattest writer I ever read. In speaking, he was like a volcano vomiting out *lava*; in writing, he is like a volcano burnt out. Nothing but the dry cinders, the hard shell remains. The tongues of flame, with which, in haranguing a mixed assembly, he used to illuminate his subject, and almost scorched up the panting air, do not appear painted on the margin of his works. He was the model of a flashy, powerful demagogue – a madman blessed, with a fit audience. He was possessed, infuriated with the patriotic *mania*; he seemed to rend and tear the rotten carcase of corruption with the remorseless, indecent rage of a wild beast: he mourned over the bleeding body of his country, like another Antony over the dead body of Caesar, as if he would 'move the very stones of Rome to rise and mutiny': he pointed to the 'Persian abodes, the glittering temples' of oppression and luxury, with prophetic exultation; and, like another Helen, had almost fired another Troy! The lightning of national indignation flashed from his eye; the workings of the popular mind were seen labouring in his bosom: it writhed and swelled with its rank 'fraught of aspics' tongues', and the poison frothed over at his lips. Thus qualified, he 'wielded at will the fierce democracy, and fulmin'd over' an area of souls, of no mean circumference. He who might be said to have 'roared you in the ears of the groundlings an 'twere any lion, aggravates his voice' on paper, 'like any sucking-dove'. It is not merely that the same individual cannot sit down quietly in his closet, and produce the same, or a correspondent effect – that what he delivers over to the compositor is tame, and trite, and tedious – that he cannot by any means, as it were, 'create a soul under the ribs of death' – but sit down yourself, and read one of these very popular and electrical effusions (for they have been published) and you would not believe it to be the same! The thunder-and-lightning mixture of the orator turns out a mere drab-coloured suit in the person of the prose writer. We wonder at the change, and think there must be some mistake, some legerdemain trick played off upon us, by which what before appeared so fine now appears to be so worthless. The deception took place *before*; now it is removed. 'Bottom! thou art translated!' might be placed as a motto under most collections of printed speeches that I have had the good fortune to meet with, whether originally addressed to the people, the senate, or the bar. Burke's and Windham's form an exception: Mr Coleridge's *Conciones ad Populum* do not, any more than Mr Thelwall's *Tribune*. What we read is the same: what we hear and see is different – 'the self-same words, but *not* to the self-same tune'. The orator's vehemence of gesture, the loudness of the voice, the speaking eye, the conscious attitude, the inexplicable dumb show and noise – all 'those brave sublunary things that made his raptures clear' – are no longer there, and without these he is nothing; his 'fire and air' turn to puddle and ditch-water, and the god of eloquence and of our idolatry sinks into a common mortal, or an image of lead, with a few labels, nicknames, and party watchwords stuck in his mouth. The truth is, that these always made up the stock of his intellectual wealth; but a certain exaggeration and extravagance of *manner* covered the nakedness, and swelled out the emptiness of the *matter*: the sympathy of angry multitudes with an impassioned theatrical declaimer supplied the place of argument or wit; while the physical animation and ardour of the speaker evaporated in 'sound and fury, signifying nothing', and leaving no trace behind it. A popular speaker (such as I have been here describing) is like a vulgar actor off the stage – take away his cue, and he has nothing to say for himself. Or he is so accustomed to the intoxication of popular applause, that without that stimulus he has no motive or power of exertion left – neither imagination, understanding, liveliness, common sense, words or ideas – he is fairly cleared out; and in the intervals of sober reason, is the dullest and most imbecile of all mortals.

An orator can hardly get beyond *commonplaces:* if he does, he gets beyond his hearers. The most successful speakers, even in the House of Commons, have not been the best scholars or the finest writers – neither those who took the most profound views of their subject, nor who adorned it with the most original fancy, or the richest combinations of language. Those speeches that in general told best at the time, are not now readable. What were the materials of which they were chiefly composed? An imposing detail of passing events, a formal display of official documents, an appeal to established maxims, an echo of popular clamour, some worn-out metaphor newly vamped-up – some hackneyed argument used for the hundredth, nay thousandth time, to fall in with the interests, the passions, or prejudices of listening and devoted admirers – some truth or falsehood, repeated as the Shibboleth of party time out of mind, which gathers strength from sympathy as it spreads, because it is understood or assented to by the million, and finds, in the increased action of the minds of numbers, the weight and force of an instinct. A COMMON-PLACE does not leave the mind 'sceptical, puzzled, and undecided in the moment of action' – 'it gives a body to opinion, and a permanence to fugitive belief'. It operates mechanically, and opens an instantaneous and infallible communication between the hearer and speaker. A set of cant phrases, arranged in sounding sentences, and pronounced 'with good emphasis and discretion', keep the gross and irritable humours of an audience in constant fermentation; and levy no tax on the understanding. To give a reason for anything is to breed a doubt of it, which doubt you may not remove in the sequel; either because your reason may not be a good one, or because the person to whom it is addressed may not be able to comprehend it, or because *others* may not be able to comprehend it. He who offers to go into the grounds of an acknowledged axiom, risks the unanimity of the company 'by most admired disorder', as he who digs to the foundation of a building to show its solidity, risks its falling. But a commonplace is enshrined in its own unquestioned evidence, and constitutes its own immortal basis. Nature, it has been said, abhors a *vacuum*; and the House of Commons, it might be said, hates everything but a commonplace! Mr Burke did not often shock the prejudices of the House: he endeavoured to *account for them*, to 'lay the flattering unction' of philosophy 'to their souls'. They could not endure him. Yet he did not attempt this by dry argument alone: he called to his aid the flowers of poetical fiction, and strewed the most dazzling colours of language over the Standing Orders of the House. It was a double offence to them – an aggravation of the encroachments of his genius. They would rather 'hear a cat mew or an axletree grate', than hear a man talk philosophy by the hour –

> Not harsh and crabbed, as dull fools suppose,
> But musical as is Apollo's lute,
> And a perpetual feast of nectar'd sweets,
> Where no crude surfeit reigns.

He was emphatically called the *dinner-bell*. They went out by shoals when he began to speak. They coughed and shuffled him down. While he was uttering some of the finest observations (to speak in compass) that ever were delivered in that House, they walked out, not as the beasts came out of the ark, by twos and by threes, but in droves and companies of tens, of dozens, and scores! Oh! it is 'the heaviest stone which melancholy can throw at a man', when you are in the middle of a delicate speculation to see 'a robusteous, periwig-pated fellow' deliberately take up his hat and walk out. But what effect could Burke's finest observations be expected to have on the House of Commons in their corporate capacity? On the supposition that they were original, refined, comprehensive, his auditors had never heard, and assuredly they had never thought of them before: how then should they know that they were good or bad, till they had time to consider better of it, or till they were told what to think? In the meantime, their effect would be to stop the question: they were blanks in the debate: they could at best only be laid aside and left *ad referendum*. What would it signify if four or five persons, at the utmost, felt their full force and fascinating power the instant they were delivered? They would be utterly unintelligible to nine-tenths of the persons present, and their impression upon any particular individual, more knowing than the rest, would be involuntarily paralysed by the torpedo touch of the elbow of a country-gentleman or city-orator. There is a reaction in insensibility as well as in enthusiasm; and men in society judge not by their own convictions, but by sympathy with others. In reading, we may go over the page again, whenever anything new or questionable 'gives us pause': besides, we are by ourselves, and it is *a word to the wise*. We are not afraid of understanding too much, and being called upon to unriddle. In hearing we are (saving the mark!) in the company of fools; and time presses. Was the debate to be suspended while Mr Fox or Mr Windham took this or that Honourable Member aside, to explain to them *that fine observation* of Mr Burke's, and to watch over the new birth of their understandings, the dawn of this new light! If we were to wait till Noble Lords and Honourable Gentlemen were inspired with a relish for abstruse thinking, and a taste for the loftier flights of fancy, the business of this great nation would shortly be at a stand. No: it is too much to ask that our good things should be duly appreciated by the first person we meet, or in the next minute after their disclosure; if the world are a little, a very little, the wiser or better for them a century hence, it is full as much as can be modestly expected! The impression of anything delivered in a large assembly must be comparatively null and void, unless you not only understand and feel its value yourself, but are conscious that it is felt and understood by the meanest capacity present. Till that is the case, the speaker is in your power, not you in his. The eloquence that is effectual and irresistible must stir the inert mass of prejudice, and pierce the opaquest shadows of ignorance. Corporate bodies move slow in the progress of intellect, for this reason, that they must keep back, like convoys, for the heaviest sailing vessels under their charge. The sinews of the wisest councils are, after all, impudence and interest: the most enlightened bodies are often but slaves of the weakest intellects they reckon among them, and the best-intentioned are but tools of the greatest hypocrites and knaves. To conclude what I had to say on the character of Mr Burke's parliamentary style, I will just give an instance of what I mean in affirming that it was too recondite for his hearers; and it shall be even in so obvious a thing as a quotation. Speaking of the newfangled French Constitution, and in particular of the King (Louis XVI) as the chief power in form and appearance only, he repeated the famous lines in Milton describing Death, and concluded with peculiar emphasis,

> What *seem'd* its head,
> The *likeness* of a kingly crown had on.

The person who heard him make the speech said that, if ever a poet's language had been finely applied by an orator to express his thoughts and make out his purpose, it was in this instance. The passage, I believe, is not in his reported speeches; and I should think, in all likelihood, it 'fell still-born' from his lips; while one of Mr Canning's well-thumbed quotations out of Virgil would electrify the Treasury Benches, and be echoed by all the politicians of his own standing, and the tyros of his own school, from Lord Liverpool in the Upper down to Mr William Ward in the Lower House.

Mr Burke was an author before he was a Member of Parliament: he ascended to that practical eminence from 'the platform' of his literary pursuits. He walked out of his study into the House. But he never became a thoroughbred debater. He was not 'native to that element', nor was he ever 'subdued to the quality' of that motley crew of knights, citizens, and burgesses. The late Lord Chatham was made for, and by it. He seemed to vault into his seat there, like Hotspur, with the exclamation in his mouth – 'that roan shall be my throne'. Or he sprang out of the genius of the House of Commons, like Pallas from the head of Jupiter, completely armed. He assumed an ascendancy there from the very port and stature of his mind – from his aspiring and fiery temperament. He vanquished, because he could not yield. He controlled the purposes of others, because he was strong in his own obdurate self-will. He convinced his followers, by never doubting himself. He did not argue, but assert; he took what he chose for granted, instead of making a question of it. He was not a dealer in *moot points*. He seized on some stronghold in the argument, and held it fast with a convulsive grasp

– or wrested the weapons out of his adversaries' hands by main force. He entered the lists like a gladiator. He made political controversy a combat of personal skill and courage. He was not for wasting time in long-winded discussions with his opponents, but tried to disarm them by a word, by a glance of his eye, so that they should not dare to contradict or confront him again. He did not wheedle, or palliate, or circumvent, or make a studied appeal to the reason or the passions – he *dictated* his opinions to the House of Commons. 'He spoke as one having authority, and not as the scribes.' But if he did not produce such an effect either by reason or imagination, how did he produce it? The principle by which he exerted his influence over others (and it is a principle of which some speakers that I might mention seem not to have an idea, even in possibility) was sympathy. He himself evidently had a strong possession of his subject, a thorough conviction, an intense interest; and this communicated itself from his *manner*, from the tones of his voice, from his commanding attitudes, and eager gestures, instinctively and unavoidably to his hearers. His will was surcharged with electrical matter like a Voltaic battery; and all who stood within its reach felt the full force of the shock. Zeal will do more than knowledge. To say the truth, there is little knowledge – no ingenuity, no parade of individual details, not much attempt at general argument, neither with nor fancy in his speeches – but there are a few plain truths told home: whatever he says, he does not mince the matter, but clenches it in the most unequivocal manner, and with the fullest sense of its importance, in clear, short, pithy, old English sentences. The most obvious things, as he puts them, read like axioms – so that he appears, as it were, the genius of common sense personified; and in turning to his speeches you fancy that you have met with (at least) one honest statesman! Lord Chatham commenced his career in the intrigues of a camp and the bustle of a mess-room, where he probably learnt that the way to govern others, is to make your will your warrant, and your word a law. If he had spent the early part of his life, like Mr Burke, in writing a treatise on the *Sublime and Beautiful,* and in dreaming over the abstract nature and causes of things, he would never have taken the lead he did in the British senate.

Both Mr Fox and Mr Pitt (though as opposite to each other as possible) were essentially speakers, not authors, in their mode of oratory. Beyond the moment, beyond the occasion, beyond the immediate power shown, astonishing as that was, there was little remarkable or worth preserving in their speeches. There is no thought in them that implies a habit of deep and refined reflection (more than we are accustomed ordinarily to find in people of education); there is no knowledge that does not lie within the reach of obvious and mechanical search; and as to the powers of language, the chief miracle is, that a source of words so apt, forcible, and well-arranged, so copious and unfailing, should have been found constantly open to express their ideas without any previous preparation. Considered as written style, they are not far out of the common course of things; and perhaps it is assuming too much, and making the wonder greater than it is, with a very natural love of indulging our admiration of extraordinary persons, when we conceive that parliamentary speeches are in general delivered without any previous preparation. They do not, it is true, allow of preparation at the moment, but they have the preparation of the preceding night, and of the night before that, and of nights, weeks, months, and years of the same endless drudgery and routine, in going over the same subjects, argued (with some paltry difference) on the same grounds. *Practice makes perfect.* He who has got a speech by heart on any particular occasion, cannot be much gravelled for lack of matter on any similar occasion in future. Not only are the topics the same; the very same phrases – whole batches of them – are served up as the Order of the Day; the same parliamentary bead-roll of grave impertinence is twanged off, in full cadence, by the Honourable Member or his Learned and Honourable Friend; and the well-known, voluminous, calculable periods roll over the drowsy ears of the auditors, almost before they are delivered from the vapid tongue that utters them! It may appear, at first sight, that here are a number of persons got together, picked out from the whole nation, who can speak at all times upon all subjects in the most exemplary manner; but the fact is, they only repeat the same things over and over and over on the same subjects – and they obtain credit for general capacity and ready wit, like Chaucer's Monk, who, by having three words of Latin always in his mouth, passed for a great scholar.

A few termes coude he, two or three,
That he had learned out of som decree;
No wonder is, he herd it all the day.

Try them on any other subject *out of doors*, and see how soon the
extempore wit and wisdom 'will halt for it'. See how few of those
who have distinguished themselves *in* the House of Commons have
done anything *out of it*, how few that have, shine *there*! Read over
the collections of old debates, twenty, forty, eighty, a hundred years
ago; they are the same *mutatis mutandis*, as those of yesterday. You
wonder to see how little has been added; you grieve that so little has
been lost. Even in their own favourite topics, how much are they to
seek! They still talk gravely of the sinking fund in St Stephen's Chapel,
which has been for some time exploded as a juggle by Mr Place of
Charing Cross; and a few of the principles of Adam Smith, which
everyone else had been acquainted with long since, are just now
beginning to dawn on the collective understanding of the two Houses
of Parliament. Instead of an exuberance of sumptuous matter, you
have the same meagre standing dishes for every day in the year. You
must serve an apprenticeship to a want of originality, to a suspension
of thought and feeling. You are in a go-cart of prejudices, in a regularly constructed machine of pretexts and precedents; you are not
only to wear the livery of other men's thoughts, but there is a House
of Commons jargon which must be used for everything. A man of
simplicity and independence of mind cannot easily reconcile himself
to all this formality and mummery; yet woe to him that shall attempt
to discard it! You can no more move against the stream of custom,
than you can make head against a crowd of people; the mob of lords
and gentlemen will not let you speak or think but as they do. You are
hemmed in, stifled, pinioned, pressed to death – and if you make
one false step, are 'trampled under the hoofs of a swinish multitude!'
Talk of mobs! Is there any body of people that has this character in a
more consummate degree than the House of Commons? Is there
any set of men that determines more by acclamation, and less by
deliberation and individual conviction? That is moved more *en masse*,
in its aggregate capacity, as brute force and physical number? That
judges with more Midas ears, blind and sordid, without discrimination of right and wrong? The greatest test of courage I can conceive,

is to speak truth in the House of Commons. I have heard Sir Francis Burdett say things there which I could not enough admire; and which he could not have ventured upon saying, if, besides his honesty, he had not been a man of fortune, of family, of character – aye, and a very good-looking man into the bargain! Dr Johnson had a wish to try his hand in the House of Commons. An elephant might as well have been introduced there, in all the forms: Sir William Curtis makes a better figure. Either he or the Speaker (Onslow) must have re-signed. The orbit of his intellect was not the one in which the intel-lect of the house moved by ancient privilege. *His* commonplaces were not *their* commonplaces. Even Horne Tooke failed, with all his *tact*, his self-possession, his ready talent, and his long practice at the hustings. He had weapons of his own with which he wished to make play, and did not lay his hand upon the established levers for wield-ing the House of Commons. A succession of dry, sharp-pointed say-ings, which come in excellently well in the pauses or quick turns of conversation, do not make a speech. A series of drops is not a stream. Besides, he had been in the practice of rallying his guests and tam-pering with his subject; and this ironical tone did not suit his new situation. He had been used to 'give his own little Senate laws', and when he found the resistance of the great one more than he could manage, he shrunk back from the attempt, disheartened and power-less. It is nothing that a man can talk (the better, the worse it is for him) unless he can talk in trammels; he must be drilled into the regi-ment; he must not run out of the course! The worst thing a man can do is to set up for a wit there – or rather (I should say) for a humorist – to say odd out-of-the-way things, to ape a character, to play the clown or the wag in the House. This is the very forlorn hope of a parliamentary ambition. They may tolerate it till they know what you are at, but no longer. It may succeed once or twice, but the third time you will be sure to break your neck. They know nothing of you, or your whims, nor have they time to look at a puppet-show. 'They look only at the stop-watch, my Lord!' We have seen a very lively sally of this sort which failed lately. The House of Commons is the last place where a man will draw admiration by making a jest of his own character. But if he has a mind to make a jest of humanity, of liberty, and of common sense and decency, he will succeed well enough!

The only person who ever 'hit the House between wind and water' in this way, who made sport for the Members, and kept his own dignity (in our time at least), was Mr Windham. He carried on the traffic in parliamentary conundrums and enigmas with great *éclat* for more than one season. He mixed up a vein of characteristic eccentricity with a succession of far-fetched and curious speculations, very pleasantly. Extremes meet; and Mr Windham overcame the obstinate attachment of his hearers to fixed opinions by the force of paradoxes. He startled his bedrid audience effectually. A paradox was a treat to them, on the score of novelty at least; 'the sight of one', according to the Scotch proverb, 'was good for sore eyes'. So Mr Windham humoured them in the thing for once. He took all sorts of commonly received doctrines and notions (with an understood reserve) – reversed them, and set up a fanciful theory of his own instead. The changes were like those in a pantomime. Ask the first old woman you met her opinion on any subject, and you could get at the statesman's; for his would be just the contrary. He would be wiser than the old woman at any rate. If a thing had been thought cruel, he would prove that it was humane; if barbarous, manly; if wise, foolish; if sense, nonsense. His creed was the antithesis of common sense, loyalty excepted. Economy he could turn into ridicule, 'as a saving of cheese-parings and candle-ends'; and total failure was with him 'negative success'. He had no occasion, in thus setting up for original thinking, to enquire into the truth or falsehood of any proposition, but to ascertain whether it was currently believed in, and then to contradict it point-blank. He made the vulgar prejudices of others 'servile ministers' to his own solecisms. It was not easy always to say whether he was in jest or earnest – but he contrived to hitch his extravagances into the midst of some grave debate; the House had their laugh for nothing; the question got into shape again, and Mr Windham was allowed to have been more *brilliant* than ever.[1]

---

1   It must be granted, however, that there was something *piquant* and provoking in his manner of 'making the worse appear the better reason'. In keeping off the ill odour of a bad cause, he applied hartshorn and burnt feathers to the offended sense; and did not, like Mr Canning, treat us with the faded flowers of his oratory, like the faint smell of a perfumer's shop, or try to make Government 'love-locks' of dead men's hair!

Mr Windham was, I have heard, a silent man in company. Indeed his whole style was an artificial and studied imitation, or capricious caricature of Burke's bold, natural, discursive manner. This did not imply much spontaneous power or fertility of invention; he was an intellectual posture-master, rather than a man of real elasticity and vigour of mind. Mr Pitt was also, I believe, somewhat taciturn and reserved. There was nothing clearly in the subject-matter of his speeches to connect with the ordinary topics of discourse, or with any given aspect of human life. One would expect him to be quite as much in the clouds as the automaton chess-player, or the last new opera-singer. Mr Fox said little in private, and complained that in writing he had no style. So (to compare great things with small) Jack Davies, the unrivalled racket-player, never said anything at all in company, and was what is understood by a modest man. When the racket was out of his hand, his occupation, his delight, his glory (that which he excelled all mankind in), was gone! So when Mr Fox had no longer to keep up the ball of debate, with the floor of St Stephen's for a stage, and the world for spectators of the game, it is hardly to be wondered at that he felt a little at a loss – without his usual train of subjects, the same crowd of associations, the same spirit of competition, or stimulus to extraordinary exertion. The excitement of leading in the House of Commons (which, in addition to the immediate attention and applause that follows, is a sort of whispering gallery to all Europe) must act upon the brain like brandy or laudanum upon the stomach; and must, in most cases, produce the same debilitating effects afterwards. A man's faculties must be quite exhausted, his virtue gone out of him. That anyone accustomed all his life to the tributary roar of applause from the great council of the nation, should think of dieting himself with the prospect of posthumous fame as an author, is like offering a confirmed dram-drinker a glass of fair water for his morning's draught. Charles Fox is not to be blamed for having written an indifferent history of James II but for having written a history at all. It was not his business to write a history – his business was *not to have made any more Coalitions*! But he found writing so dull, he thought it better to be a colleague of Lord Grenville! He did not want style (to say so is nonsense, because the style of his speeches was just and fine) – he wanted a sounding-board in the ear of posterity to try his periods upon. If he had gone to the House of Commons in the morning, and tried to make a speech fasting, when there was nobody to hear him, he might have been equally disconcerted at his want of style. The habit of speaking is the habit of being heard, and of wanting to be heard; the habit of writing is the habit of thinking aloud, but without the help of an echo. The orator sees his subject in the eager looks of his auditors; and feels doubly conscious, doubly impressed with it in the glow of their sympathy; the author can only look for encouragement in a blank piece of paper. The orator feels the impulse of popular enthusiasm,

> like proud seas under him:

the only Pegasus the writer has to boast, is the hobby-horse of his own thoughts and fancies. How is he to get on then? From the lash of necessity. We accordingly see persons of rank and fortune continually volunteer into the service of oratory – and the State; but we have few authors who are not paid by the sheet! I myself have heard Charles Fox engaged in familiar conversation. It was in the Louvre. He was describing the pictures to two persons that were with him. He spoke rapidly, but very unaffectedly. I remember his saying – 'All those blues and greens and reds are the Guercinos; you may know them by the colours'. He set Opie right as to Domenichino's St Jerome. 'You will find', he said, 'though you may not be struck with it at first, that there is a great deal of truth and good sense in that picture'. There was a person at one time a good deal with Mr Fox, who, when the opinion of the latter was asked on any subject, very frequently interposed to give the answer. This sort of tantalizing interruption was ingeniously enough compared by someone to walking up Ludgate Hill, and having the spire of St Martin's constantly getting in your way, when you wish to see the dome of St Paul's! Burke, it is said, conversed as he spoke in public, and as he wrote. He was communicative, diffuse, magnificent. 'What is the use', said Mr Fox to a friend, 'of Sheridan's trying to swell himself out in this manner, like the frog in the fable?' – alluding to his speech on Warren Hastings's trial. 'It is very well for Burke to express himself in that figurative way. It is natural to him; he talks so to his wife, to his servants, to his children; but as for Sheridan, he either never opens his mouth at all, or if he does, it is to utter some joke. It is out of the question for him to affect these *Orientalisms*.' Burke once came into Sir Joshua Reynolds's painting-room, when one of his pupils was sitting for one of the sons of Count Ugolino; this gentleman was personally introduced to him – 'Ah! then', said Burke, 'I find that Mr Northcote has not only a head that would do for Titian to paint, but is himself a painter'. At another time, he came in when Goldsmith was there, and poured forth such a torrent of violent personal abuse against the King, that they got to high words, and Goldsmith threatened to leave the room if he did not desist. Goldsmith bore testimony to his powers of conversation. Speaking of Johnson, he said, 'Does he wind into a subject like a serpent, as Burke does?' With respect to his facility in composition, there are contradictory accounts. It has been stated by some, that he wrote out a plain sketch first, like a sort of dead colouring, and added the ornaments and tropes afterwards. I have been assured by a person who had the best means of knowing, that the *Letter to a Noble Lord* (the most rapid, impetuous, glancing, and sportive of all his works) was printed off, and the proof sent to him: and that it was returned to the printing office with so many alterations and passages interlined, that the compositors refused to correct it as it was – took the whole matter in pieces, and reset the copy. This looks like elaboration and afterthought. It was also one of Burke's latest compositions.[2] A regularly bred speaker would have made up his mind beforehand; but Burke's mind being, as originally constituted and by its first bias, that of an author, never became set. It was in further search and progress. It had an internal spring left. It was not tied down to the printer's forme. It could still project itself into new beauties, and explore strange regions from the unwearied impulse of its own delight or curiosity. Perhaps among the passages interlined, in this case, were the description of the Duke of Bedford, as 'the Leviathan among all the creatures of the crown' –

---

2 Tom Paine, while he was busy about any of his works, used to walk out, compose a sentence or paragraph in his head, come home and write it down, and never altered it afterwards. He then added another, and so on, till the whole was completed.

the *catalogue raisonnée* of the Abbé Sieyes's pigeonholes – or the comparison of the English Monarchy to 'the proud keep of Windsor, with its double belt of kindred and coeval towers'. Were these to be given up? If he had had to make his defence of his pension in the House of Lords, they would not have been ready in time, it appears; and, besides, would have been too difficult of execution on the spot: a speaker must not set his heart on such forbidden fruit. But Mr Burke was an author, and the press did not 'shut the gates of *genius* on mankind'. A set of oratorical flourishes, indeed, is soon exhausted, and is generally all that the extempore speaker can safely aspire to. Not so with the resources of art or nature, which are inexhaustible, and which the writer has time to seek out, to embody, and to fit into shape and use, if he has the strength, the courage, and patience to do so.

There is then a certain range of thought and expression beyond the regular rhetorical routine, on which the author, to vindicate his title, must trench somewhat freely. The proof that this is understood to be so, is, that what is called an oratorical style is exploded from all good writing; that we immediately lay down an article, even in a common newspaper, in which such phrases occur as 'the Angel of Reform', 'the drooping Genius of Albion'; and that a very brilliant speech at a loyal dinner-party makes a very flimsy, insipid pamphlet. The orator has to get up for a certain occasion a striking compilation of partial topics, which, 'to leave no rubs or botches in the work', must be pretty familiar, as well as palatable to his hearers; and in doing this, he may avail himself of all the resources of an artificial memory. The writer must be original, or he is nothing. He is not to take up with ready-made goods; for he has time allowed him to create his own materials, to make novel combinations of thought and fancy, to contend with unforeseen difficulties of style and execution, while we look on, and admire the growing work in secret and at leisure. There is a degree of finishing as well as of solid strength in writing, which is not to be got at every day, and we can wait for perfection. The author owes a debt to truth and nature which he cannot satisfy at sight, but he has pawned his head on redeeming it. It is not a string of claptraps to answer a temporary or party-purpose – violent, vulgar, and illiberal – but general and lasting truth that we require at his hands. We go to him as pupils, not as partisans. We have a right to expect from him profounder views of things; finer observations; more ingenious illustrations; happier and bolder expressions. He is to give the choice and picked results of a whole life of study; what he has struck out in his most felicitous moods, has treasured up with most pride, has laboured to bring to light with most anxiety and confidence of success. He may turn a period in his head fifty different ways, so that it comes out smooth and round at last. He may have caught a glimpse of a simile, and it may have vanished again: let him be on the watch for it, as the idle boy watches for the lurking-place of the adder. We can wait. He is not satisfied with a reason he has offered for something; let him wait till he finds a better reason. There is some word, some phrase, some idiom that expresses a particular idea better than any other, but he cannot for the life of him recollect it: let him wait till he does. Is it strange that among twenty thousand words in the English language, the one of all others that he most needs should have escaped him? There are more things in nature than there are words in the English language, and he must not expect to lay rash hands on them all at once.

> Learn to *write* slow: all other graces
> Will follow in their proper places.

You allow a writer a year to think of a subject; he should not put you off with a truism at last. You allow him a year more to find out words for his thoughts; he should not give us an echo of all the fine things that have been said a hundred times.[3] All authors, however, are not so squeamish; but take up with words and ideas as they find them delivered down to them. Happy are they who write Latin verses! Who copy the style of Dr Johnson! Who hold up the phrase of ancient Pistol! They do not trouble themselves with those hair-breadth distinctions of thought or meaning that puzzle nicer heads – let us leave them to their repose! A person in habits of composition often hesitates in conversation for a particular word: it is because he is in search of the best word, and *that* he cannot hit

---

3   Just as a poet ought not to cheat us with lame metre and defective rhymes, which might be excusable in an improvisatori versifier.

upon. In writing he would stop till it came.[4] It is not true, however, that the scholar could avail himself of a more ordinary word if he chose, or readily acquire a command of ordinary language; for his associations are habitually intense, not vague and shallow; and words occur to him only as *tallies* to certain modifications of feeling. They are links in the chain of thought. His imagination is fastidious, and rejects all those that are 'of no mark or likelihood'. Certain words are in his mind indissolubly wedded to certain things; and none are admitted at the *levée* of his thoughts, but those of which the banns have been solemnized with scrupulous propriety. Again, the student finds a stimulus to literary exertion, not in the immediate *éclat* of his undertaking, but in the difficulty of his subject, and the progressive nature of his task. He is not wound up to a sudden and extraordinary effort of presence of mind; but is forever awake to the silent influxes of things, and his life is one long labour. Are there no sweeteners of his toil? No reflections, in the absence of popular applause or social indulgence, to cheer him on his way? Let the reader judge. *His* pleasure is the counterpart of, and borrowed from, the same source as the writer's. A man does not read out of vanity, nor in company, but to amuse his own thoughts. If the reader, from disinterested and merely intellectual motives, relishes an author's 'fancies and good nights', the last may be supposed to have relished them no less. If he laughs at a joke, the inventor chuckled over it to the full as much. If he is delighted with a phrase, he may be sure the writer jumped at it; if he is pleased to cull a straggling flower from the page, he may believe that it was plucked with no less fondness from the face of nature. Does he fasten, with gathering brow and looks intent, on some difficult speculation? He may be convinced that the writer thought it a fine thing to split his brain in solving so curious a problem, and to publish his discovery to the world. There is some satisfaction in the contemplation of power; there is also a little pride in the conscious possession of it. With what pleasure do we read books! If authors could but feel this, or remember what they

---

4   That is essentially a bad style which seems as if the person writing it never stopped for breath, nor gave himself a moment's pause, but strove to make up by redundancy and fluency for want of choice and correctness of expression.

themselves once felt, they would need no other temptation to persevere.

To conclude this account with what perhaps I ought to have set out with, a definition of the character of an author. There are persons who in society, in public intercourse, feel no excitement,

> Dull as the lake that slumbers in the storm,

but who, when left alone, can lash themselves into a foam. They are never less alone than when alone. Mount them on a dinner-table, and they have nothing to say; shut them up in a room by themselves, and they are inspired. They are 'made fierce with dark keeping'. In revenge for being tongue-tied, a torrent of words flows from their pens, and the storm which was so long collecting comes down apace. It never rains but it pours. Is not this strange, unaccountable? Not at all so. They have a real interest, a real knowledge of the subject, and they cannot summon up all that interest, or bring all that knowledge to bear, while they have anything else to attend to. Till they can do justice to the feeling they have, they can do nothing. For this they look into their own minds, not in the faces of a gaping multitude. What they would say (if they could) does not lie at the orifices of the mouth ready for delivery, but is wrapped in the folds of the heart and registered in the chambers of the brain. In the sacred cause of truth that stirs them, they would put their whole strength, their whole being into requisition; and as it implies a greater effort to drag their words and ideas from their lurking-places, so there is no end when they are once set in motion. The whole of a man's thoughts and feelings cannot lie on the surface, made up for use; but the whole must be a greater quantity, a mightier power, if they could be got at, layer under layer, and brought into play by the levers of imagination and reflection. Such a person then sees farther and feels deeper than most others. He plucks up an argument by the roots, he tears out the very heart of his subject. He has more pride in conquering the difficulties of a question, than vanity in courting the favour of an audience. He wishes to satisfy himself before he pretends to enlighten the public. He takes an interest in things in the abstract more than by common consent. Nature is his mistress, truth his idol. The contemplation of a pure idea is the ruling passion of his breast. The intervention of other people's notions, the being the immediate object of their censure or their praise, puts him out. What will tell, what will produce an effect, he cares little about; and therefore he produces the greatest. The *personal* is to him an impertinence; so he conceals himself and writes. Solitude 'becomes his glittering bride, and airy thoughts his children'. Such a one is a true author; and not a member of any Debating Club, or Dilettanti Society whatever![5]

5   I have omitted to dwell on some other differences of body and mind that often prevent the same person from shining in both capacities of speaker and writer. There are natural impediments to public speaking, such as the want of a strong voice and steady nerves. A high authority of the present day (Mr Canning) has thought this a matter of so much importance, that he goes so far as even to let it affect the constitution of Parliament, and conceives that gentlemen who have not bold foreheads and brazen lungs, but modest pretensions and patriotic views, should be allowed to creep into the great assembly of the nation through the avenue of close boroughs, and not be called upon 'to face the storms of the hustings'. In this point of view, Stentor was a man of genius, and a noisy jack-pudding may cut a considerable figure in the 'Political House that Jack built'. I fancy Mr C. Wynne is the only person in the kingdom who has fully made up his mind that a total defect of voice is the most necessary qualification for a Speaker of the House of Commons!

On a Portrait of an
—— English Lady, by ——
Vandyke

COMPOSED WINTER 1824–5

The portrait I speak of is in the Louvre, where it is numbered 416, and the only account of it in the *Catalogue* is that of a *Lady and her daughter*. It is companion to another whole-length by the same artist, No. 417, of a *Gentleman and a little girl*. Both are evidently English.

The face of the lady has nothing very remarkable in it, but that it may be said to be the very perfection of the English female face. It is not particularly beautiful, but there is a sweetness in it, and a goodness conjoined, which is inexpressibly delightful. The smooth ivory forehead is a little ruffled, as if some slight cause of uneasiness, like a cloud, had just passed over it. The eyes are raised with a look of timid attention; the mouth is compressed with modest sensibility; the complexion is delicate and clear; and over the whole figure (which is seated) there reign the utmost propriety and decorum. The habitual gentleness of the character seems to have been dashed with some anxious thought or momentary disquiet, and, like the shrinking flower, in whose leaves the lucid drop yet trembles, looks out and smiles at the storm that is overblown. A mother's tenderness, a mother's fear, appears to flutter on the surface, and on the extreme verge of the expression, and not to have quite subsided into thoughtless indifference or mild composure. There is a reflection of the same expression in the little child at her knee, who turns her head round with a certain appearance of constraint and innocent wonder; and perhaps it is the difficulty of getting her to sit (or to sit still) that has caused the transient contraction of her mother's brow – that lovely, unstained mirror of pure affection, too fair, too delicate, too soft and feminine for the breath of serious misfortune ever to come near, or not to crush it. It is a face, in short, of the greatest purity and sensibility, sweetness and simplicity, or such as Chaucer might have described

> Where all is conscience and tender heart.

I have said that it is an English face; and I may add (without being invidious) that it is not a French one. I will not say that they have no face to equal this; of that I am not a judge; but I am sure they have no face equal to this, in the qualities by which it is distinguished. They may have faces as amiable, but then the possessors of them will be conscious of it. There may be equal elegance, but not the same ease; there may be even greater intelligence, but without the innocence; more vivacity, but then it will run into petulance or coquetry; in short, there may be every other good quality but a total absence of all pretension to or wish to make a display of it, but the same unaffected modesty and simplicity. In French faces (and I have seen some that were charming both for the features and expression) there is a varnish of insincerity, a something theatrical or meretricious; but here, every particle is pure to the 'last recesses of the mind'. The face (such as it is, and it has a considerable share both of beauty and meaning) is without the smallest alloy of affectation. There is no false glitter in the eyes to make them look brighter; no little wrinkles about the corners of the eyelids, the effect of self-conceit; no pursing up of the mouth, no significant leer, no primness, no extravagance, no assumed levity or gravity. You have the genuine text of nature without gloss or comment. There is no heightening of conscious charms to produce greater effect, no studying of airs and graces in the glass of vanity. You have not the remotest hint of the milliner, the dancing-master, the dealer in paints and patches. You have before you a real English lady of the seventeenth century, who looks like one, because she cannot look otherwise; whose expression of sweetness, intelligence, or concern is just what is natural to her, and what the occasion requires; whose entire demeanour is the emanation of her habitual sentiments and disposition, and who is as free from guile or affectation as the little child by her side. I repeat that this is not the distinguishing character of the French physiognomy, which, at its best, is often spoiled by a consciousness of what it is, and a restless desire to be something more.

Goodness of disposition, with a clear complexion and handsome features, is the chief ingredient in English beauty. There is a great difference in this respect between Vandyke's portraits of women and Titian's, of which we may find examples in the Louvre. The picture, which goes by the name of his *Mistress*, is one of the most celebrated of the latter. The neck of this picture is like a broad crystal mirror; and the hair which she holds so carelessly in her hand is like meshes of beaten gold. The eyes which roll in their ample sockets, like two shining orbs, and which are turned away from the spectator, only dart their glances the more powerfully into the soul; and the whole picture is a paragon of frank cordial grace, and transparent brilliancy of colouring. Her tight bodice compresses her full but finely proportioned waist; while the tucker in part conceals and almost clasps the snowy bosom. But you never think of anything beyond the personal attractions, and a certain sparkling intelligence. She is not marble, but a fine piece of animated clay. There is none of that retired and shrinking character, that modesty of demeanour, that sensitive delicacy, that starts even at the shadow of evil – that are so evidently to be traced in the portrait by Vandyke. Still there is no positive vice, no meanness, no hypocrisy, but an unconstrained elastic spirit of self-enjoyment, more bent on the end than scrupulous about the means; with firmly braced nerves, and a tincture of vulgarity. She is not like an English lady, nor like a lady at all; but she is a very fine servant-girl, conscious of her advantages, and willing to make the most of them. In fact, Titian's *Mistress* answers exactly, I conceive, to the idea conveyed by the English word, *sweetheart*. The Marchioness of Guasto is a fairer comparison. She is by the supposition a lady, but still an Italian one. There is a honeyed richness about the texture of the skin, and her air is languid from a sense of pleasure. Her dress, though modest, has the marks of studied coquetry about it; it touches the very limits which it dares not pass; and her eyes which are bashful and downcast, do not seem to droop under the fear of observation, but to retire from the gaze of kindled admiration,

> As if they thrill'd
> Frail hearts, yet quenched not!

One might say, with Othello, of the hand with which she holds the globe that is offered to her acceptance:

> This hand of yours requires
> A sequester from liberty, fasting and pray'r,
> Much castigation, exercise devout;
> For here's a young and *melting* devil here,
> That commonly rebels.

The hands of Vandyke's portrait have the purity and coldness of marble. The colour of the face is such as might be breathed upon it by the refreshing breeze; that of the Marchioness of Guasto's is like the glow it might imbibe from a golden sunset. The expression in the English lady springs from her duties and her affections; that of the Italian Countess inclines more to her ease and pleasures. The Marchioness of Guasto was one of three sisters, to whom, it is said, the inhabitants of Pisa proposed to pay divine honours, in the manner that beauty was worshipped by the fabulous enthusiasts of old. Her husband seems to have participated in the common infatuation, from the fanciful homage that is paid to her in this allegorical composition; and if she was at all intoxicated by the incense offered to her vanity, the painter must be allowed to have 'qualified' the expression of it 'very craftily'.

I pass on to another female face and figure, that of the Virgin, in the beautiful picture of the *Presentation in the Temple*, by Guido. The expression here is *ideal*, and has a reference to visionary objects and feelings. It is marked by an abstraction from outward impressions, a downcast look, an elevated brow, an absorption of purpose, a stillness and resignation, that become the person and the scene in which she is engaged. The colour is pale or gone; so that purified from every grossness, dead to worldly passions, she almost seems like a statue kneeling. With knees bent, and hands uplifted, her motionless figure appears supported by a soul within, all whose thoughts, from the low ground of humility, tend heavenward. We find none of the triumphant buoyancy of health and spirit as in the *Titian's Mistress,* nor the luxurious softness of the portrait of the Marchioness of Guasto, nor the flexible, tremulous sensibility, nor the anxious attention to passing circumstances, nor the familiar look of the lady by Vandyke; on the contrary, there is a complete unity and concentration of expression, the whole is wrought up and moulded into one intense feeling, but that feeling fixed on objects remote, refined, and ethereal as the form of the fair supplicant. A still greater contrast to this internal, or as it were, *introverted* expression, is to be found in the group of female heads by the same artist, Guido, in his picture of the *Flight of Paris and Helen.* They are the three last heads on the left-hand side of the picture. They are thrown into every variety of attitude, as if to take the heart by surprise at every avenue. A tender warmth is suffused over their faces; their head-dresses are airy and fanciful, their complexion sparkling and glossy; their features seem to catch pleasure from every surrounding object, and to reflect it back again. Vanity, beauty, gaiety glance from their conscious looks and wreathed smiles, like the changing colours from the ring-dove's neck. To sharpen the effect and point the moral, they are accompanied by a little negro boy, who holds up the train of elegance, fashion, and voluptuous grace!

Guido was the 'genteelest' of painters; he was a poetical Vandyke. The latter could give, with inimitable and perfect skill, the airs and graces of people of fashion under their daily and habitual aspects, or as he might see them in a looking-glass. The former saw them in his 'mind's eye', and could transform them into supposed characters and imaginary situations. Still the elements were the same. Vandyke gave them with the *mannerism* of habit and the individual details; Guido, as they were rounded into grace and smoothness by the breath of fancy, and borne along by the tide of sentiment. Guido did not want the *ideal* faculty, though he wanted strength and variety. There is an effeminacy about his pictures, for he gave only the different modifications of beauty. It was the Goddess that inspired him, the Siren that seduced him; and whether as saint or sinner, was equally welcome to him. His creations are as frail as they are fair. They all turn on a passion for beauty, and without this support, are nothing.

He could paint beauty combined with pleasure or sweetness, or grief, or devotion; but unless it were the groundwork aud the primary condition of his performance, he became insipid, ridiculous, and extravagant. There is one thing to be said in his favour; he knew his own powers or followed his own inclinations; and the delicacy of his *tact* in general prevented him from attempting subjects uncongenial with it. He 'trod the primrose path of dalliance' with equal prudence and modesty. That he is a little monotonous and tame is all that can be said against him; and he seldom went out of his way to expose his deficiencies in a glaring point of view. He came round to subjects of beauty at last, or gave them that turn. A story is told of his having painted a very lovely head of a girl, and being asked from whom he had taken it, he replied, 'From his old man!' This is not unlikely. He is the only great painter (except Correggio) who appears constantly to have subjected what he saw to an imaginary standard. His Magdalens are more beautiful than sorrowful; in his Madonnas there is more of sweetness and modesty than of elevation. He makes but little difference between his heroes and his heroines; his angels are women, and his women angels! If it be said that he repeated himself too often, and has painted too many Magdalens and Madonnas, I can only say in answer, 'Would he had painted twice as many!' If Guido wanted compass and variety in his art, it signifies little, since what he wanted is abundantly supplied by others. He had softness, delicacy and *ideal* grace in a supreme degree, and his fame rests on these as the cloud on the rock. It is to the highest point of excellence in any art or department that we look back with gratitude and admiration, as it is the highest mountain-peak that we catch in the distance, and lose sight of only when it turns to air.

I know of no other difference between Raphael and Guido, than that the one was twice the man the other was. Raphael was a bolder genius, and invented according to nature: Guido only made draughts after his own disposition and character. There is a common cant of criticism which makes Titian merely a colourist. What he really wanted was invention: he had expression in the highest degree. I declare I have seen heads of his with more meaning in them than any of Raphael's. But he fell short of Raphael in this, that (except in one or two instances) he could not heighten and adapt the expression that he saw to different and more striking circumstances. He gave more of what he saw than any other painter that ever lived, and in the imitative part of his art had a more universal genius than Raphael had in composition and invention. Beyond the actual and habitual look of nature, however, 'the demon that he served' deserted him, or became a very tame one. Vandyke gave more of the general air and manners of fashionable life than of individual character; and the subjects that he treated are neither remarkable for intellect nor passion. They are people of polished manners, and placid constitutions; and many of the very best of them are 'stupidly good'. Titian's portraits, on the other hand, frequently present a much more formidable than inviting appearance. You would hardly trust yourself in a room with them. You do not bestow a cold, leisurely approbation on them, but look to see what they may be thinking of you, not without some apprehension for the result. They have not the clear smooth skins or the even pulse that Vandyke's seem to possess. They are, for the most part, fierce, wary, voluptuous, subtle, haughty. Raphael painted Italian faces as well as Titian. But he threw into them a character of intellect rather than of temperament. In Titian the irritability takes the lead, sharpens and gives direction to the understanding. There seems to be a personal controversy between the spectator and the individual whose portrait he contemplates, which shall be master of the other. I may refer to two portraits in the Louvre, the one by Raphael, the other by Titian (Nos 1153 and 1210), in illustration of these remarks. I do not know two finer or more characteristic specimens of these masters, each in its way. The one is of a student dressed in black, absorbed in thought, intent on some problem, with the hands crossed and leaning on a table for support, as it were to give freer scope to the labour of the brain, and though the eyes are directed towards you, it is with evident absence of mind. Not so the other portrait, No. 1210. All its faculties are collected to see what it can make of you, as if you had intruded upon it with some hostile design, it takes a defensive attitude, and shows as much vigilance as dignity. It draws itself up, as if to say, 'Well, what do you think of me?' and exercises a discretionary power over you. It has 'an eye to threaten and command', not to be lost in idle thought, or in ruminating over some abstruse, speculative proposition. It is this intense personal character which, I think, gives the superiority to Titian's portraits over all others, and stamps them with a living and permanent interest. Of other pictures you tire, if you have them constantly before you; of his, never. For other pictures have either an abstracted look and you dismiss them, when you have made up your mind on the subject as a matter of criticism; or an heroic look, and you cannot be always straining your enthusiasm; or an insipid look, and you sicken of it. But whenever you turn to look at Titian's portraits, they appear to be looking at you; there seems to be some question pending between you, as though an intimate friend or inveterate foe were in the room with you; they exert a kind of fascinating power; and there is that exact resemblance of individual nature which is always new and always interesting, because you cannot carry away a mental abstraction of it, and you must recur to the object to revive it in its full force and integrity. I would as soon have Raphael's or most other pictures hanging up in a collection, that I might pay an occasional visit to them: Titian's are the only ones that I should wish to have hanging in the same room with me for company!

Titian in his portraits appears to have understood the principle of historical design better than anybody. Every part tells, and has a bearing on the whole. There is no one who has such simplicity and repose – no violence, no affectation, no attempt at forcing an effect; insomuch that by the uninitiated he is often condemned as unmeaning and insipid. A turn of the eye, a compression of the lip decides the point. He just draws the face out of its most ordinary state, and gives it the direction he would have it take; but then every part takes the same direction, and the effect of this united impression (which is absolutely momentary and all but habitual) is wonderful. It is that which makes his portraits the most natural and the most striking in the world. It may be compared to the effect of a number of small lodestones, that by acting together lift the greatest weights. Titian seized upon the lines of character in the most original and connected point of view. Thus in his celebrated portrait of Hippolito de Medici, there is a keen, sharpened expression that strikes you, like a blow from the spear that he holds in his hand. The look goes through you; yet it has no frown, no startling gesticulation, no affected penetration. It is quiet, simple, but it almost withers you. The whole face and each separate feature is cast in the same acute or wedgelike form. The forehead is high and narrow, the eyebrows raised and coming to a point in the middle, the nose straight and peaked, the mouth contracted and drawn up at the corners, the chin acute, and the two sides of the face slanting to a point. The number of acute angles which the lines of the face form, are, in fact, a net entangling the attention and subduing the will. The effect is felt at once, though it asks time and consideration to understand the cause. It is a face which you would beware of rousing into anger or hostility, as you would beware of setting in motion some complicated and dangerous machinery. The possessor of it, you may be sure, is no trifler. Such, indeed, was the character of the man. This is to paint true portrait and true history. So if our artist painted a mild and thoughtful expression, all the lines of the countenance were softened and relaxed. If the mouth was going to speak, the whole face was going to speak. It was the same in colour. The gradations are infinite, and yet so blended as to be imperceptible. No two tints are the same, though they produce the greatest harmony and simplicity of tone, like flesh itself. 'If', said a person, pointing to the shaded side of a portrait of Titian, 'you could turn this round to the light, you would find it would be of the same colour as the other side!' In short, there is manifest in his portraits a greater tenaciousness and identity of impression than in those of any other painter. Form, colour, feeling, character, seemed to adhere to his eye, and to become part of himself; and his pictures, on this account, 'leave stings' in the minds of the spectators! There is, I grant, the same personal appeal, the same point-blank look in some of Raphael's portraits (see those of a Princess of Arragon and of Count Castiglione, No. 1150 and 1151) as in Titian: but they want the texture of the skin and the minute individual details to stamp them with the same reality. And again, as to the uniformity of outline in the features, this principle has been acted upon and carried to excess by Kneller and other artists. The eyes, the eyebrows, the nose, the mouth, the chin, are rounded off as if they were turned in a *lathe*, or as a peruke-maker arranges the curls of a wig. In them it is vile and mechanical, without any reference to truth of character or nature; and instead of being pregnant with meaning and originality of expression, produces only insipidity and monotony.

Perhaps what is offered above as a key to the peculiar expression of Titian's heads may also serve to explain the difference between painting or copying a portrait. As the perfection of his faces consists in the entire unity and coincidence of all the parts, so the difficulty of ordi-

nary portrait-painting is to bring them to bear at all, or to piece one
feature, or one day's labour onto another. In copying, this difficulty
does not occur at all. The human face is not one thing, as the vulgar
suppose, nor does it remain always the same. It has infinite varieties,
which the artist is obliged to notice and to reconcile, or he will make
strange work. Not only the light and shade upon it do not continue
for two minutes the same: the position of the head constantly varies
(or if you are strict with a sitter, he grows sullen and stupid), each
feature is in motion every moment, even while the artist is working
at it, and in the course of a day the whole expression of the countenance undergoes a change, so that the expression which you gave to
the forehead or eyes yesterday is totally incompatible with that which
you have to give to the mouth today. You can only bring it back
again to the same point or give it a consistent construction by an
effort of imagination, or a strong feeling of character; and you must
connect the features together less by the eye than by the mind. The
mere setting down what you see in this medley of successive, teasing,
contradictory impressions, would never do; either you must continually efface what you have done the instant before, or if you retain
it, you will produce a piece of patchwork, worse than any caricature.
There must be a comprehension of the whole, and in truth a *moral
sense* (as well as a literal one) to unravel the confusion, and guide you
through the labyrinth of shifting muscles and features. You must feel
what *this* means, and dive into the hidden soul, in order to know
whether *that* is as it ought to be; for you cannot be sure that it remains as it was. Portrait-painting is, then, painting from recollection
and from a conception of character, with the object before us to
assist the memory and understanding. In copying, on the contrary,
one part does not run away and leave you in the lurch, while you are
intent upon another. You have only to attend to what is before you,
and finish it carefully a bit at a time, and you are sure that the whole
will come right. One might parcel it out into squares, as in engrav-
ing, and copy one at a time, without seeing or thinking of the rest. I
do not say that a conception of the whole, and a feeling of the art
will not abridge the labour of copying, or produce a truer likeness;
but it is the changeableness or identity of the object that chiefly constitutes the difficulty or facility of imitating it, and, in the latter case,
reduces it nearly to a mechanical operation. It is the same in the

imitation of *still life*, where real objects have not a principle of motion in them. It is as easy to produce a *facsimile* of a table or a chair as to copy a picture, because these things do not stir from their places any more than the features of a portrait stir from theirs. You may therefore bestow any given degree of minute and continued attention on finishing any given part without being afraid that when finished it will not correspond with the rest. Nay, it requires more talent to copy a fine portrait than to paint an original picture of a table or a chair, for the picture has a soul in it, and the table has not.

It has been made an objection (and I think a just one) against the extreme high-finishing of the drapery and backgrounds in portraits (to which some schools, particularly the French, are addicted), that it gives an unfinished look to the face, the most important part of the picture. A lady or a gentleman cannot sit quite so long or so still as a lay-figure, and if you finish up each part according to the length of time it will remain in one position, the face will seem to have been painted for the sake of the drapery, not the drapery to set off the face. There is an obvious limit to everything, if we attend to common sense and feeling. If a carpet or a curtain will admit of being finished more than the living face, we finish them less because they excite less interest, and we are less willing to throw away our time and pains upon them. This is the unavoidable result in a natural and well regulated style of art; but what is to be said of a school where no interest is felt in anything, where nothing is known of any object but that it is there, and where superficial and petty details which the eye can explore, and the hand execute, with persevering and systematic indifference, constitute the soul of art?

The expression is the great difficulty in history or portrait-painting, and yet it is the great clue to both. It renders forms doubly impressive from the interest and signification attached to them, and at the same time renders the imitation of them critically nice, by making any departure from the line of truth doubly sensible. Mr Coleridge used to say that what gave the romantic and mysterious interest to Salvator's landscapes was their containing some implicit analogy to human or other living forms. His rocks had a latent resemblance to the outline of a human face; his trees had the distorted jagged shape of a satyr's horns and grotesque features. I do not think this is the case; but it may serve to supply us with an illustration of the present question. Suppose a given outline to represent a human face, but to be so disguised by circumstances and little interruptions as to be mistaken for a projecting fragment of a rock in a natural scenery. As long as we conceive of this outline merely as a representation of a rock or other inanimate substance, any copy of it, however rude, will seem the same and as good as the original. Now let the disguise be removed and the general resemblance to a human face pointed out, and what before seemed perfect, will be found to be deficient in the most essential features. Let it be further understood to be a profile of a particular face that we know, and all likeness will vanish from the want of the individual expression, which can only be given by being felt. That is, the imitation of external and visible form is only correct or nearly perfect, when the information of the eye and the direction of the hand are aided and confirmed by the previous knowledge and actual feeling of character in the object represented. The more there is of character and feeling in any object, and the greater sympathy there is with it in the mind of the artist, the closer will be the affinity between the imitation and the thing imitated; as the more there is of character and expression in the object without a proportionable sympathy with it in the imitator, the more obvious will this defect and the imperfection of the copy become. That is, expression is the great test and measure of a genius for painting and the fine arts. The mere imitation of *still life*, however perfect, can never furnish proofs of the highest skill or talent; for there is an inner sense, a deeper intuition into nature that is never unfolded by merely mechanical objects, and which, if it were called out by a new soul being suddenly infused into an inanimate substance, would make the former unconscious representation appear crude and vapid. The eye is sharpened and the hand made more delicate in its tact,

> While by the power
> Of harmony, and the deep power of joy,
> We see into the life of things.

We not only *see*, but *feel* expression, by the help of the finest of all our senses, the sense of pleasure and pain. He then is the greatest painter who can put the greatest quantity of expression into his works, for this is the nicest and most subtle object of imitation; it is that in which any defect is soonest visible, which must be able to stand the severest scrutiny, and where the power of avoiding errors, extravagance, or tameness can only be supplied by the fund of moral feeling, the strength or delicacy of the artist's sympathy with the ideal object of his imitation. To see or imitate any given sensible object is one thing, the effect of attention and practice; but to give expression to a face is to collect its meaning from a thousand other sources, is to bring into play the observation and feeling of one's whole life, or an infinity of knowledge bearing upon a single object in different degrees and manners, and implying a loftiness and refinement of character proportioned to the loftiness and refinement of expression delineated. Expression is of all things the least to be mistaken, and the most evanescent in its manifestations. Pope's lines on the character of women may be addressed to the painter who undertakes to embody it.

> Come then, the colours and the ground prepare,
> Dip in the rainbow, trick it off in air;
> Chuse a firm cloud, before it falls, and in it
> Catch, ere it change, the Cynthia of the minute.

It is a maxim among painters that no one can paint more than his own character, or more than he himself understands or can enter into. Nay, even in copying a head, we have some difficulty in making the features unlike our own. A person with a low forehead or a short chin puts a constraint on himself in painting a high forehead or a long chin. So much has sympathy to do with what is supposed to be a mere act of servile imitation! To pursue this argument one step farther. People sometimes wonder what difficulty there can be in painting, and ask what you have to do but to set down what you see? This is true, but the difficulty is to see what is before you. This is at least as difficult as to learn any trade or language. We imagine that we see the whole of nature, because we are aware of no more than we see of it. We also suppose that any given object, a head, a hand, is one thing, because we see it at once, and call it by one name. But how little we see or know, even of the most familiar face, beyond a vague abstraction, will be evident to everyone who tries to recollect distinctly all its component parts, or to draw the most rude outline of it for the first time; or who considers the variety of surface, the numberless lights and shades, the tints of the skin, every particle and pore of which varies, the forms and markings of the features, the combined expression, and all these caught (as far as common use is concerned) by a random glance, and communicated by a passing word. A student, when he first copies a head, soon comes to a stand, or is at a loss to proceed from seeing nothing more in the face than there is in his copy. After a year or two's practice he never knows when to have done, and the longer he has been occupied in copying a face or any particular feature, sees more and more in it, that he has left undone and can never hope to do. There have been only four or five painters who could ever produce a copy of the human countenance really fit to be seen; and even of these few none was ever perfect, except in giving some single quality or partial aspect of nature, which happened to fall in with his own particular studies and the bias of his genius, as Raphael the drawing, Rembrandt the light and shade, Vandyke ease and delicacy of appearance, etc. Titian gave more than anyone else, and yet he had his defects. After this, shall we say that any, the commonest and most uninstructed spectator sees the whole of nature at a single glance, and would be able to stamp a perfect representation of it on the canvas, if he could embody the image in his mind's eye?

I have in this essay mentioned one or two of the portraits in the Louvre that I like best. The two landscapes which I should most covet, are the one with a rainbow by Rubens, and the *Adam and Eve in Paradise* by Poussin. In the first, shepherds are reposing with their flocks under the shelter of a breezy grove, the distances are of air, and the whole landscape seems just washed with the shower that has passed off. The Adam and Eve by Poussin is the full growth and luxuriant expansion of the principle of vegetation. It is the first lovely dawn of creation, when nature played her virgin fancies wild; when all was sweetness and freshness, and the heavens dropped fatness. It is the very *ideal* of landscape-painting, and of the scene it is intended to represent. It throws us back to the first ages of the world, and to the only period of perfect human bliss, which is, however, on the point of being soon disturbed.[1] I should be contented with these four or five pictures, the *Lady* by Vandyke, the Titian, the *Presentation in the Temple*, the Rubens, and the Poussin, or even with faithful copies of them, added to the two which I have of a young Neapolitan Nobleman and of the Hippolito de Medici; and which, when I look at them, recall other times and the feelings with which they were done. It is now twenty years since I made those copies, and I hope to keep them while I live. It seems to me no longer ago than yesterday. Should the next twenty years pass as swiftly, forty years will have glided by me like a dream. By this kind of speculation I can look down as from a slippery height on the beginning, and the end of life beneath my feet, and the thought makes me dizzy!

My taste in pictures is, I believe, very different from that of rich and princely collectors. I would not give twopence for the whole gallery at Fonthill. I should like to have a few pictures hung round the room, that speak to me with well-known looks, that touch some string of memory – not a number of varnished, smooth, glittering gewgaws. The taste of the great in pictures is singular, but not unaccountable. The King is said to prefer the Dutch to the Italian school of painting; and if you hint your surprise at this, you are looked upon as a very Gothic and *outrè* sort of person. You are told, however, by way of consolation, 'To be sure, there is Lord Carlisle likes an Italian picture – Mr Holwell Carr likes an Italian picture – the Marquis of Stafford is fond of an Italian picture – Sir George Beaumont likes an

---

1   I may be allowed to mention here (not for the sake of invidious comparison, but to explain my meaning) Mr Martin's picture of Adam and Eve asleep in Paradise. It has this capital defect, that there is no *repose* in it. You see two insignificant naked figures, and a preposterous architectural landscape, like a range of buildings overlooking them. They might as well have been represented on the top of the pinnacle of the Temple, with the world and all the glories thereof spread out before them. They ought to have been painted imparadised in one another's arms, shut up in measureless content, with Eden's choicest bowers closing round them, and Nature stooping to clothe them with vernal flowers. Nothing could be too retired, too voluptuous, too sacred from 'day's garish eye'; on the contrary, you have a gaudy panoramic view, a glittering barren waste, a triple row of clouds, of rocks, and mountains, piled one upon the other, as if the imagination already bent its idle gaze over that wide world which was so soon to be our place of exile, and the aching, restless spirit of the artist was occupied in building a stately prison for our first parents, instead of decking their bridal bed, and wrapping them in a short-lived dream of bliss.

Italian picture!' These, notwithstanding, are regarded as quaint and daring exceptions to the established rule; and their preference is a species of *leze majesté* in the Fine Arts, as great an eccentricity and want of fashionable etiquette, as if any gentleman or nobleman still preferred old claret to new, when the King is known to have changed his mind on this subject; or was guilty of the offence of dipping his forefinger and thumb in the middle of a snuff-box, instead of gradually approximating the contents to the edge of the box, according to the most approved models. One would imagine that the great and exalted in station would like lofty subjects in works of art, whereas they seem to have an almost exclusive predilection for the mean and mechanical. One would think those whose word was law, would be pleased with the great and striking effects of the pencil;[2] on the contrary, they admire nothing but the little and elaborate. They have a fondness for cabinet and *furniture* pictures, and a proportionable antipathy to works of genius. Even art with them must be servile, to be tolerated. Perhaps the seeming contradiction may be explained thus. Such persons are raised so high above the rest of the species, that the more violent and agitating pursuits of mankind appear to them like the turmoil of ants on a molehill. Nothing interests them but their own pride and self-importance. Our passions are to them an impertinence; an expression of high sentiment they rather shrink from as a ludicrous and upstart assumption of equality. They therefore like what glitters to the eye, what is smooth to the touch; but they shun, by an instinct of sovereign taste, whatever has a soul in it, or implies a reciprocity of feeling. The gods of the earth can have no interest in anything human; they are cut off from all sympathy with the 'bosoms and businesses of men'. Instead of requiring to be wound up beyond their habitual feeling of stately dignity, they wish to have the springs of over-strained pretension let down, to be relaxed with 'trifles light as air', to be amused with the familiar and frivolous, and

2   The Duke of Wellington, it is said, cannot enter into the merits of Raphael; but he admires 'the spirit and fire' of Tintoret. I do not wonder at this bias. A sentiment probably never dawned upon his Grace's mind; but he may be supposed to relish the dashing execution and *hit or miss* manner of the Venetian artist. Oh, Raphael! well is it that it was one who did not understand thee, that blundered upon the destruction of humanity!

to have the world appear a scene of *still life*, except as they disturb it! The little in thought and internal sentiment is a natural relief and set off to the oppressive sense of external magnificence. Hence kings babble and repeat they know not what. A childish dotage often accompanies the consciousness of absolute power. Repose is somewhere necessary, and the soul sleeps while the senses gloat around! Besides, the mechanical and high-finished style of art may be considered as something *done to order*. It is a task to be executed more or less perfectly, according to the price given, and the industry of the artist. We stand by, as it were, to see the work done, insist upon a greater degree of neatness and accuracy, and exercise a sort of petty, jealous jurisdiction over each particular. We are judges of the minuteness of the details, and though ever so nicely executed, as they give us no ideas beyond what we had before, we do not feel humbled in the comparison. The artisan scarcely rises into the artist; and the name of genius is degraded rather than exalted in his person. The performance is so far ours that we have paid for it, and the highest price is all that is necessary to produce the highest finishing. But it is not so in works of genius and imagination. Their price is above rubies. The inspiration of the Muse comes not with the *fiat* of a monarch, with the donation of a patron; and, therefore, the great turn with disgust or effeminate indifference from the mighty masters of the Italian school, because such works baffle and confound their self-love, and make them feel that there is something in the mind of man which they can neither give nor take away.

Quam nihil ad tuum, Papiniane, ingenium!

Madame Pasta and Mademoiselle Mars

FIRST PUBLISHED *NEW MONTHLY MAGAZINE*, JANUARY 1825

I liked Mademoiselle Mars exceedingly well, till I saw Madame Pasta whom I liked so much better. The reason is, the one is the perfection of French, the other of natural acting. Madame Pasta is Italian, and she might be English – Mademoiselle Mars belongs emphatically to her country; the scene of her triumphs is Paris. She plays naturally too, but it is French nature. Let me explain. She has, it is true, none of the vices of the French theatre, its extravagance, its flutter, its grimace, and affectation, but her merit in these respects is as it were negative, and she seems to put an artificial restraint upon herself. There is still a pettiness, an attention to *minutiae*, an etiquette, a mannerism about her acting: she does not give an entire loose to her feelings, or trust to the unpremeditated and habitual impulse of her situation. She has greater elegance, perhaps, and precision of style than Madame Pasta, but not half her boldness or grace. In short, everything she does is voluntary, instead of being spontaneous. It seems as if she might be acting from marginal directions to her part. When not speaking, she stands in general quite still. When she speaks, she extends first one hand and then the other, in a way that you can foresee every time she does so, or in which a machine might be elaborately constructed to develop different successive movements. When she enters, she advances in a straight line from the other end to the middle of the stage with the slight unvarying trip of her countrywomen, and then stops short, as if under the drill of a *fugal man*. When she speaks, she articulates with perfect clearness and propriety, but it is the facility of a singer executing a difficult passage. The ease is that of habit, not of nature. Whatever she does, is right in the intention, and she takes care not to carry it too far; but she appears to say beforehand, '*This* I will do, I must not do *that*'. Her acting is an inimitable study or consummate rehearsal of the part as a preparatory performance: she hardly yet appears to have assumed the character; something more is wanting, and that something you find in Madame Pasta. If Mademoiselle Mars has to smile, a slight and evanescent expression of pleasure passes across the surface of her face; twinkles in her eyelids, dimples her chin, compresses her lips, and plays on each feature: when Madame Pasta smiles, a beam of joy seems to have struck upon her heart, and to irradiate her countenance. Her whole face is bathed and melted in expression, instead of its glancing from particular points. When she speaks, it is in music. When she moves, it is without thinking whether she is graceful or not. When she weeps, it is a fountain of tears, not a few trickling drops, that glitter and vanish the instant after. The French themselves admire Madame Pasta's acting (who indeed can help it?), but they go away thinking how much one of her simple movements would be improved by their extravagant gesticulations, and that her noble, natural expression would be the better for having twenty airs of mincing affectation added to it. In her Nina there is a listless vacancy, an awkward grace, a want of *bienseance*, that is like a child or a changeling, and that no French actress would venture upon for a moment, lest she should be suspected of a want of *esprit* or of *bon mien*. A French actress always plays before the court; she is always in the presence of an audience, with whom she first settles her personal pretensions by a significant hint or side-glance, and then as much nature and simplicity as you please. Poor Madame Pasta thinks no more of the audience than Nina herself would, if she could be observed by stealth, or than the fawn that wounded comes to drink, or the flower that droops in the sun or wags its sweet head in the gale. She gives herself entirely up to the impression of the part, loses her power over herself, is led away by her feelings either to an expression of stupor or of artless joy, borrows beauty from deformity, charms unconsciously, and is transformed into the very being the represents. She does not act the character – she *is* it, looks it, breathes it. She does not study for an effect, but strives to possess herself of the feeling which should dictate what she is to do, and which gives birth to the proper degree of grace, dignity, ease, or force. She makes no point all the way through, but her whole style and manner is in perfect keeping, as if she were really a lovesick, care-crazed maiden, occupied with one deep sorrow, and who had no other idea or interest in the world. This alone is true nature and true art. The rest is sophistical; and French art is not free from the imputation; it never places an implicit faith in nature but always ways mixes up a certain portion of art, that is, of consciousness and affectation with it. I shall illustrate this subject from a passage in Shakespeare.

> *Polixenes.* Shepherdess,
> (A fair one are you) well you fit our ages
> With flow'rs of winter.
> *Perdita:*   Sir, the year growing ancient,
> Not yet on summer's death, nor on the birth
> Of trembling winter, the faires flowers o'th' season
> Are our carnations and streak'd gilliflowers,
> Which some call nature's bastards; of that kind
> Our rustic garden's barren, and I care not
> To get slips of them.
> *Polix:*   Wherefore, gentle maiden,
> Do you neglect them?
> *Perdita:*   For I have heard it said,
> There is an art which in their piedness shares
> With great creating nature.
> *Polix:*   Say, there be,
> Yet nature is made better by no mean,
> But nature makes that mean; so o'er that art,
> Which you say adds to nature, is an art,
> That nature makes; you see, sweet maid, we marry
> A gentle scyon to the wildest stock,
> And make conceive a bark of baser kind
> By bud of nobler race. This is an art,
> Which does mend nature, change it rather; but
> The art itself is nature.
> *Perdita:*   So it is.
> *Polix:* Then make your garden rich in gilliflowers,
> And do not call them bastards.
> *Perdita:* I'll not put

A dibble in earth, to set one slip of them;
No more than, were I painted, I should wish
This youth to say, 'twere well; and only therefore
Desire to breed by me. (*Winter's Tale*, Act IV)

Madame Pasta appears to be of Perdita's mind in respect to her acting, and I applaud her resolution heartily. We English are charged unjustly with wishing to disparage the French: we cannot help it; there is a natural antipathy between the two nations. Thus unable to deny their theatrical merit, we are said insidiously to have invented the appellation, *French nature*, to explain away or throw a stigma on their most successful exertions:

> Though that their art be nature,
> We throw such changes of vexation on it,
> As it may lose some colour.

The English are a heavy people, and the most like a stone of all others. The French are a lively people, and more like a feather. They are easily moved and by slight causes, and each part of the impression has its separate effect: the English, if they are moved at all (which is a work of time and difficulty), are moved altogether, or in mass, and the impression, if it takes root, strikes deep and spreads wide, involving a number of other impressions in it. If a fragment of a rock wrenched from its place rolls slowly at first, gathers strength and fury as it proceeds, tears up everything in its way, and thunders to the plain below, there is something noble and imposing in the sight, for it is an image of our own headlong passions and the increasing vehemence of our desires. But we hate to see a feather launched into the air and driven back on the hand that throws it, shifting its course with every puff of wind, and carried no farther by the strongest than by the slightest impulse. It is provoking (is it not?) to see the strength of the blow always defeated by the very insignificance and want of resistance in the object, and the impulse received never answering to the impulse given. It is the very same fluttering, fidgeting, tantalizing, inconsequential, ridiculous process that annoys us in the French character. There seems no *natural* correspondence between objects and feelings, between things and words. By yielding to every impulse at once, nothing produces a powerful or permanent impression; nothing produces an aggregate impression, for every part tells separately. Every idea turns off to something else, or back upon itself; there is no progress made, no blind impulse, no accumulation of imagination with circumstances, no absorption of all other feelings in one overwhelming one, that is, no keeping, no *momentum*, no integrity, no totality, no inflexible sincerity of purpose, and it is this resolution of the sentiments into their detached points and first impressions, so that they do not take an entire and involuntary hold of them, but either they can throw them off from their lightness, or escape from them by reason of their minuteness, that we English complain of as French nature or a want of nature, for by nature is only meant that the mind identifies itself with something so as to be no longer master of itself, and the French mind never identifies itself with anything, but always has its own consciousness, its own affectation, its own gratification, its own slippery inconstancy or impertinent prolixity interposed between the object and the impression. It is this theatrical or artificial nature with which we cannot and will not sympathize, because it circumscribes the truth of things and the capacities of the human mind within the petty round of vanity, indifference, and physical sensations, stunts the growth of imagination, effaces the broad light of nature, and requires us to look at all things through the prism of their petulance and self-conceit. The French in a word leave *sincerity* out of their nature (not moral but imaginative sincerity), cut down the varieties of feeling to their own narrow and superficial standard, and having clipped and adulterated the current coin of expression, would pass it off as sterling gold. We cannot make an exchange with them. They are affected by things in a different manner from us, not in a different degree; and a mutual understanding is hopeless. We have no dislike to foreigners as such: on the contrary, a rage for foreign artists and works of art is one of our foibles. But if we give up our national pride, it must be to our taste and understandings. Nay, we adopt the manners and the fashions of the French, their dancing and their cooking – not their music, not their painting, not their poetry, not their metaphysics, not their style of acting. If we are sensible of our own stupidity, we cannot admire *their* vivacity; if we are sick of our own awkwardness, we like it better than their grace; we cannot part with our grossness for their refinement; if we would be glad to have our lumpish clay animated, it must be with true Promethean heat, not with painted phosphorus: they are not the Frankensteins that must perform this feat. Who among us in reading Schiller's *Robbers* for the first time ever asked if it was German or not? Who in reading Klopstock's *Messiah* did not object that it was German, not because it was German, but because it was heavy; that is, because the imagination and the heart do not act like a machine, so as to be wound up or let down by the pulleys of the will? Do not the French complain (and complain justly), that a picture is English, when it is coarse and unfinished, and leaves out the details which are one part of nature? Do not the English remonstrate against this defect too, and endeavour to cure it? But it may be said we relish Schiller, because he is barbarous, violent, and like Shakespeare. We have the cartoons of Raphael then, and the Elgin marbles; and we profess to admire and understand these too, and I think without any affectation. The reason is that there is no affectation in them. We like those noble outlines of the human face at Hampton Court; the sustained dignity of the expression; the broad, ample folds of the drapery; the bold, massive limbs; there is breath and motion in them, and we would willingly be so transformed and spiritualized: but we do not want to have our heavy, stupid faces flittered away into a number of glittering points or transfixed into a smooth petrifaction on French canvas. Our faces, if wanting in expression, have a settled purpose in them; are as solid as they are stupid; and we are at least flesh and blood. We also like the sway of the limbs and negligent grandeur of the Elgin marbles; in spite of their huge weight and manly strength, they have the buoyancy of a wave of the sea, with all the ease and softness of flesh: they fall into attitudes of themselves: but if they were put into attitudes by the genius of opera-dancing, we should feel no disposition to imitate or envy them, any more than we do the Zephyr and Flora graces of French statuary. We prefer a single head of Chantrey's to a quarry of French sculpture. The English are a modest people, except in comparing themselves with their next neighbours, and nothing provokes their pride in this case, so much as the self-sufficiency of the latter. When Madame Pasta walks in upon the stage, and looks about her with the same unconsciousness or timid wonder as the young stag in the forest; when she moves her limbs as carelessly as a tree its branches; when she unfolds one of her divine expressions of countenance, which reflect the inmost feelings of the soul, as the calm, deep lake reflects the face of heaven; do we not sufficiently admire her, do we not wish her ours, and feel, with the same cast of thought and character, a want of glow, of grace, and ease in the expression of what we feel? We bow, like Guiderius and Arviragus in the cave when they saw Imogen, as to a thing superior. On the other hand, when Mademoiselle Mars comes on the stage, something in the manner of a fantoccini figure slid along on a wooden frame, and making directly for the point at which her official operations commence – when her face is puckered into a hundred little expressions like the wrinkles on the skin of a bowl of cream, set in a window to cool, her eyes peering out with an ironical meaning, her nose pointing it, and her lips confirming it with a dry pressure – we admire indeed, we are delighted, we may envy, but we do not sympathize or very well know what to make of it. We are not electrified, as in the former instance, but *animal-magnetized*.[1] We can manage pretty well with any one feeling or expression (like a clown that must be taught his letters one at a time) if it keeps on in the same even course, that expands and deepens by degrees, but we are distracted and puzzled, or at best only amused with that sort of expression which is hardly itself for two moments together, that shifts from point to point, that seems to have no place to rest on, no impulse to urge it forward, and might as well be twenty other things at the same time – where tears come so easily they can hardly be real, where smiles are so playful they appear put on, where you cannot tell what you are to believe, for the parties themselves do not know whether they are in jest or earnest, where the whole tone is ironical, conventional, and where the difference between nature and art is nearly imperceptible. This is what we mean by French nature, *viz.* that the feelings and ideas are so slight and discontinuous that they can be changed for others like a dress or vizor; or else, to make up for want of truth and breadth, are caricatured into a mask. This is the

---

1 Even her *j'existe* in *Valeria* (when she first acquires the use of sight) is pointed like an epigram, and *put in italics* like a technical or metaphysical distinction, instead of being a pure effusion of joy. Accordingly a French pit-critic took up the phrase, insisting that *to exist* was common to all things, and asked what the expression was in the original German. This treatment of passion is *topical* and extraneous, and seldom strikes at the seat of the disorder, the heart.

defect of their tragedy, and the defect and excellence of their comedy; the one is a pompous abortion, the other a *facsimile* of life, almost too close to be agreeable. A French comic actor might be supposed to have left his shop for half an hour to show himself upon a stage – there is no difference, worth speaking of, between the man and the actor – whether on the stage or at home, he is equally full of gesticulation, equally voluble, and without meaning – as their tragic actors are solemn puppets, moved by rules, pulled by wires, and with their mouths stuffed with rant and bombast. This is the harm that can be said of them: they themselves are doubtless best acquainted with the good, and are not too diffident to tell it. Though other people abuse them, they can still praise themselves! I once knew a French lady who said all manner of good things and forgot them the next moment; who maintained an argument with great wit and eloquence, and presently after changed sides, without knowing that she had done so; who invented a story and believed it on the spot; who wept herself and made you weep with the force of her descriptions, and suddenly drying her eyes, laughed at you for looking grave. Is not this like acting? Yet it was not affected in her, but natural, involuntary, incorrigible. The hurry and excitement of her natural spirits was like a species of intoxication, or she resembled a child in thoughtlessness and incoherence. She was a Frenchwoman. It was nature, but nature that had nothing to do with truth or consistency.

In one of the Paris journals lately, there was a criticism on two pictures by Girodet of Bonchamps and Cathelineau, Vendean chiefs. The paper is well written, and points out the defects of the portraits very fairly and judiciously. These persons are there called 'Illustrious Vendeans'. The dead dogs of 1812 are the illustrious Vendeans of 1824. Monsieur Chateaubriand will have it so, and the French are too polite a nation to contradict him. They split on this rock of complaisance, surrendering every principle to the fear of giving offence, as we do on the opposite one of party spirit and rancorous hostility, sacrificing the best of causes, and our best friends to the desire of giving offence, to the indulgence of our spleen, and of an ill tongue. We apply a degrading appellation, or bring an opprobrious charge against an individual; and such is our tenaciousness of the painful and disagreeable, so fond are we of brooding over grievances, so incapable are our imaginations of raising themselves above the lowest scurrility or the dirtiest abuse, that should the person attacked come out an angel from the contest, the prejudice against him remains nearly the same as if the charge had been fully proved. An unpleasant association has been created, and this is too delightful an exercise of the understanding with the English public easily to be parted with. John Bull would as soon give up an estate as a bugbear. Having been once gulled, they are not soon *ungulled*. They are too knowing for that. Nay, they resent the attempt to undeceive them as an injury. The French apply a brilliant epithet to the most vulnerable characters; and thus gloss over a life of treachery or infamy. With them the immediate or last impression is everything: with us, the first, if it is sufficiently strong and gloomy, never wears out! The French critic observes that M. Girodet has given General Bonchamps, though in a situation of great difficulty and danger, a calm and even smiling air, and that the portrait of Cathelineau, instead of a hero, looks only like an angry peasant. In fact, the lips in the first portrait are made of marmalade, the complexion is cosmetic, and the smile ineffably engaging; while the eye of the peasant Cathelineau darts a beam of light, such as no eye, however illustrious, was ever illumined with. But so it is, the senses, like a favourite lapdog, are pampered and indulged at any expense: the imagination, like a gaunt hound, is starved and driven away. Danger and death, and ferocious courage and stern fortitude, however the subject may exact them, are uncourtly topics and kept out of sight: but smiling lips and glistening eyes are pleasing objects, and there you find them. *The style of portrait requires it.* It is of this varnish and glitter of sentiment that we complain (perhaps it is no business of ours) as what must forever intercept the true feeling and genuine rendering of nature in French art; as what makes it spurious and counterfeit, and strips it of simplicity, force and grandeur. Whatever pleases, whatever strikes, holds out a temptation to the French artist too strong to be resisted, and there is too great a sympathy in the public mind with this view of the subject, to quarrel with or severely criticize what is so congenial with its own feelings. A premature and superficial sensibility is the grave of French genius and of French taste. Beyond the momentary impulse of a lively organization, all the rest is mechanical and pedantic; they give you rules and theories for truth and nature, the unities for poetry, and the dead body for the living soul of art. They colour a Greek statue ill and call it a picture: they paraphrase a Greek tragedy, and overload it with long-winded speeches, and think they have a national drama of their own. Any other people would be ashamed of such preposterous pretensions. In invention, they do not get beyond models; in imitation, beyond details. Their microscopic vision hinders them from seeing nature. I observed two young students the other day near the top of Montmartre, making oil sketches of a ruinous hovel in one corner of the road. Paris lay below, glittering grey and gold (like a spider's web) in the setting sun, which shot its slant rays upon their shining canvas, and they were busy in giving the finishing touches. The little outhouse was in itself picturesque enough: it was covered with moss, which hung down in a sort of drooping form as the rain had streamed down it, and the walls were loose and crumbling in pieces. Our artists had repaired everything: not a stone was out of its place: no traces were left of the winter's flaw in the pendent moss. One would think the bricklayer and gardener had been regularly set to work to do away everything like sentiment or keeping in the object before them. Oh, Paris! it was indeed on this thy weak side (thy inability to connect any two ideas into one) that thy barbarous and ruthless foes entered in!

The French have a great dislike to anything obscure. They cannot bear to suppose for a moment there should be anything they do not understand: they are shockingly afraid of being *mystified*. Hence they have no idea either of mental or aerial perspective. Everything must be distinctly made out and in the foreground; for if it is not so clear that they can take it up bit by bit, it is wholly lost upon them, and they turn away as from an unmeaning blank. This is the cause of the stiff, unnatural look of their portraits. No allowance is made for the veil that shade as well as an oblique position casts over the different parts of the face; every feature, and every part of every feature is given with the same flat effect, and it is owing to this perverse fidelity of detail, that that which is literally true, is naturally false. The side of a face seen in perspective does not present so many markings as the one that meets your eye full: but if it is put into the *vice* of French portrait, wrenched round by incorrigible affectation and conceit (that insist upon knowing all that is there, and set it down formally, though it is not to be seen), what can be the result, but that the portrait will look like a head stuck in a vice, will be flat, hard, and finished, will have the appearance of reality and at the same time look like paint; in short, will be a French portrait? That is, the artist, from a pettiness of view and want of more enlarged and liberal notions of art, comes forward not to represent nature, but like an impertinent commentator to explain what she has left in doubt, to insist on that which she passes over or touches only slightly, to throw a critical light on what she casts into shade, and to pick out the details of what she blends into masses. I wonder they allow the existence of the term *clairobscur* at all, but it is a word; and a word is a thing they can repeat and remember. A French gentleman formerly asked me what I thought of a landscape in their exhibition. I said I thought it too clear. He made answer that he should have conceived that to be impossible. I replied that what I meant was, that the parts of the several objects were made out with too nearly equal distinctness all over the picture; that the leaves of the trees in shadow were as distinct as those in light, the branches of the trees at a distance as plain as of those near. The perspective arose only from the diminution of objects, and there was no interposition of air. I said, one could not see the leaves of a tree a mile off, but this, I added, appertained to a question in metaphysics. He shook his head, thinking that a young Englishman could know as little of abstruse philosophy as of fine art, and no more was said. I owe to this gentleman (whose name was Merrimee, and who I understand is still living) a grateful sense of many friendly attentions and many useful suggestions, and I take this opportunity of acknowledging my obligations.

Someone was observing of Madame Pasta's acting, that its chief merit consisted in its being natural. To which it was replied, 'Not so, for that there was an ugly and a handsome nature'. There is an old proverb, that 'Home is home, be it never so homely': and so it may be said of nature; that whether ugly or handsome, it is nature still. Besides beauty, there is truth, which is always one principal thing. It doubles the effect of beauty, which is mere affectation without it, and even reconciles us to deformity. Nature, the truth of nature in imitation, denotes a given object, a 'foregone conclusion' in reality, to which the artist is to conform in his copy. In nature real objects exist, real causes act, which are only supposed to act in art; and it is in the subordination of the uncertain and superficial combinations of fancy to the more stable and powerful law of reality that the perfection of art consists. A painter may arrange fine colours on his palette; but if he merely does this, he does nothing. It is accidental or arbitrary. The difficulty and the charm of the combination begins with the truth of imitation, that is, with the resemblance to a given object in nature, or in other words, with the strength, coherence, and justness of our impressions, which must be verified by a reference to a known and determinate class of objects as the test. Art is so far the development or the communication of knowledge, but there can be no knowledge unless it be of some given or standard object which exists independently of the representation and bends the will to an obedience to it. The strokes of the pencil are what the artist pleases, are mere idleness and caprice without meaning, unless they point to nature. Then they are right or wrong, true or false, as they follow in her steps and copy her style. Art must anchor in nature, or it is the sport of every breath of folly. Natural objects convey given or intelligible ideas which art embodies and represents, or it represents nothing, is a mere chimera or bubble; and, farther, natural objects or events cause certain feelings, in expressing which art manifests its power, and genius its prerogative. The capacity of expressing these movements of passion is in proportion to the power with which they are felt; and this is the same as sympathy with the human mind placed in actual situations, and influenced by the real causes that are supposed to act. Genius is the power which equalizes or identifies the imagination with the reality or with nature. Certain events happening to us naturally produce joy, others sorrow, and these feelings, if excessive, lead to other consequences, such as stupor or ecstasy, and express themselves by certain signs in the countenance or voice or gestures; and we admire and applaud an actress accordingly, who gives these tones and gestures as they would follow in the order of things, because we then know that her mind has been affected in like manner, that she enters deeply into the resources of nature, and understands the riches of the human heart. For nothing else can impel and stir her up to the imitation of the truth. The way in which real causes act upon the feelings is not arbitrary, is not fanciful; it is as true as it is powerful and unforeseen; the effects can only be similar when the exciting causes have a correspondence with each other, and there is nothing like feeling *but* feeling. The sense of joy can alone produce the smile of joy; and in proportion to the sweetness, the unconsciousness, and the expansion of the last, we may be sure is the fullness and sincerity of the heart from which it proceeds. The elements of joy at least are there, in their integrity and perfection. The death or absence of a beloved object is nothing as a word, as a mere passing thought, till it comes to be dwelt upon, and we begin to feel the revulsion, the long dreary separation, the stunning sense of the blow to our happiness, as we should in reality. The power of giving this sad and bewildering effect of sorrow on the stage is derived from the force of sympathy with what we should feel in reality. That is, a great histrionic genius is one that approximates the effects of words, or of supposed situations on the mind, most nearly to the deep and vivid effect of real and inevitable ones. Joy produces tears: the violence of passion turns to childish weakness; but this could not be foreseen by study, nor taught by rules, nor mimicked by observation. Natural acting is therefore fine, because it implies and calls forth the most varied and strongest feelings that the supposed characters and circumstances can possibly give birth to: it reaches the height of the subject. The conceiving or entering into a part in this sense is everything: the acting follows easily and of course. But art without nature is a nickname, a word without meaning, a conclusion without any premises to go upon. The beauty of Madame Pasta's acting in *Nina* proceeds upon this principle. It is not what she does at any particular juncture, but she seems to be the character, and to be incapable of divesting herself of it. This is true acting: anything else is playing tricks, may be clever and ingenious, is French opera-dancing, recitation, heroics or hysterics – but it is not true nature or true art.

Appendix I: Advertisement to Hazlitt's *Table Talk* (Paris, 1825)

Hazlitt left England for France with his second wife, Isabella, on 1 September 1824, and arrived in Paris a week later. At some point in mid-October he began negotiations with the Galignani brothers[1] for an edition of *Table Talk*. With him in Paris he had copies of the English edition of *Table Talk* (2 vols, 1821–2), as well as proof sheets for volume one of the 1826 London edition of *The Plain Speaker* (as yet unpublished).[2] It was from these materials that he made up the text of the Paris *Table Talk*.[3] The only piece of writing executed solely for the Paris volume was its advertisement, which we present here.

1 Jean-Antoine (1796–1873) and Guillaume (1798–1882), for more on whom see Giles Barber, 'Galignani and the Publication of English Books in France from 1800 to 1852', *The Library*, 5th ser., 16 (1961) 267–86, and James J. Barnes, 'Galignani and the Publication of English Books in France: A Postscript', *The Library*, 5th ser., 25 (1970) 294–313.
2 The first volume of *The Plain Speaker* was originally intended to be the third volume of *Table Talk*.
3 Full and detailed accounts of the publication of this work can be found in Stanley Jones, *Hazlitt: A Life* (Oxford, 1989), pp. 367–8 and *William Hazlitt to his Publishers, Friends, and Creditors: Twenty Seven New Holograph Letters*, ed. Charles E. Robinson (York, 1987), pp. 22–6.

Advertisement

The work here offered to the public is a selection from the four volumes of *Table-Talk*, printed in London. Should it meet with success, it will be followed by two other volumes of the same description, which will include all that the author wishes to preserve of his writings in this kind. The title may perhaps serve to explain what there is of peculiarity in the style or mode of treating the subjects. I had remarked that when I had written or thought upon a particular topic, and afterwards had occasion to speak of it with a friend, the conversation generally took a much wider range and branched off into a number of indirect and collateral questions, which were not strictly connected with the original view of the subject, but which often threw a curious and striking light upon it, or upon human life in general. It therefore occurred to me as possible to combine the advantages of these two styles, the *literary* and *conversational*; or after stating and enforcing some leading idea, to follow it up by such observations and reflections as would probably suggest themselves in discussing the same question in company with others. This seemed to me to promise a greater variety and richness, and perhaps a greater sincerity, than could be attained by a more precise and scholastic method. The same consideration had an influence on the familiarity and conversational idiom of the style which I have used. How far the plan was feasible, or how far I have succeeded in the execution of it, must be left to others to decide. I am also afraid of having too frequently attempted to give a popular air and effect to subtle distinctions and trains of thought; so that I shall be considered as too metaphysical by the careless reader, while by the more severe and scrupulous enquirer my style will be complained of as too light and desultory. To all this I can only answer that I have done not what I wished, but the best I could do; and I heartily wish it had been better.

Appendix II:
'A Half-length':
an uncollected Hazlitt
portrait

John Wilson Croker (1780–1857) was a British politician and writer famous for his critical severity as a reviewer and for his rigid adherence to Tory principle. He was born at Galway in Ireland, and after graduating from Trinity College, Dublin, was called to the Irish bar in 1802, and entered Parliament as member for Downpatrick in 1807. From the first he was a close ally of Wellington, then Sir Arthur Wellesley, and within a few years he had been appointed to the office of Secretary to the Admiralty, a post he held until the Whigs came to power in 1830. Had Croker been of no further significance to Hazlitt, he would have been an object of contempt simply for the fact that he was an Irishman who served the Tory cause. And indeed, Hazlitt had already sniped at Croker on purely political grounds in *The Examiner* in January 1814.[1]

But Croker was also a literary man, and had been involved in the establishment and running of the government-funded *Quarterly Review*, edited by William Gifford. The *Quarterly* was the scourge of liberal writers, and in its pages Croker was responsible for the scathing review of *Endymion* later held, by Shelley, to have been the direct cause of Keats's premature death. The *Quarterly* also published several reviews of Hazlitt's works, all of them withering in their contempt. More importantly, Croker may have played a key role in a particularly damaging review of Hazlitt's *Liber Amoris*.

1 'Mr W. Pole and Mr Croker', *The Examiner*, 9 January 1814, pp. 27–8.

Liber Amoris describes, in intimate detail, the story of Hazlitt's futile, failed passion for his landlady's daughter, Sarah Walker; he chose to publish it, inadvisedly, in 1823. Although it was published anonymously, his identity was soon revealed by his enemies, and an onslaught of abuse followed. Of these severe and unforgiving reviews, the worst came from *John Bull*, a newspaper edited by Theodore Hook. Hook named not only Hazlitt, but Sarah Walker as well. And, with a degree of vituperation and ridicule that surpassed anything thus far administered, it published the text of an original love letter from Hazlitt to Sarah that had fallen into the reviewer's hands.[2] Hazlitt believed the culprit to have been Croker, · and he took his revenge by writing 'A Half-length'.

Stanley Jones was the first scholar to argue for Hazlitt's authorship of this 'half-length' portrait of John Wilson Croker; his arguments are conclusive, and we refer the reader to his article for details as to attribution.[3] 'A Half-length' was published only a few weeks after Hazlitt's *Spirit of the Age* portrait of Canning, and it may be regarded as a kind of coda to that volume, and a prelude to *The Plain Speaker*. It shares with *The Plain Speaker* a concern with portraiture. From his deep love of Fielding and Smollett, as well as his early career as an artist, Hazlitt had imbibed a fascination with the art of sketching human beings in words, and it is a skill which he practises throughout *The Plain Speaker*.

It seems likely that Dickens recognized that aspect of Hazlitt's writing, and learnt from it.[4] In *The Spirit of the Age* Hazlitt's essay on Sir James Mackintosh mentions 'the inexhaustible stores of his memory and reading';[5] as a kind of extrapolation of that phrase, Dickens describes Bradley Headstone in *Our Mutual Friend* as follows:

---

2 For a much fuller account of the review, see Stanley Jones, *Hazlitt: A Life*, pp. 339–42.

3 'Three Additions to the Canon of Hazlitt's Political Writings', *Review of English Studies* 38 (1987), pp. 355–63 (hereafter, Jones 1987).

4 There can be little doubt that Dickens knew, and admired, Hazlitt's writing. He was a friend and colleague of Hazlitt's son on the *Morning Chronicle*.

5 See *Selected Writings of William Hazlitt* ed. Duncan Wu (9 vols, London, 1998), vol. vii, p. 154.

From his early childhood up, his mind had been a place of mechanical stowage. The arrangement of his wholesale, so that it might be always ready to meet the demands of retail dealers – history there, geography there, astronomy to the right, political economy to the left – natural history, the physical sciences, figures, music, the lower mathematics, and what not, all in their several places – this care had imparted to his countenance a look of care.[6]

If Bradley Headstone was a character who embodied traits described by Hazlitt in the essay on Mackintosh, it is even more likely that Hazlitt's account of Croker influenced the character of Krook, the 'dealer in Marine Stores' in *Bleak House*, who disintegrates in an act of spontaneous combustion: 'He was short, cadaverous, and withered; with his head sunk sideways between his shoulders, and the breath issuing in visible smoke from his mouth, as if he were on fire within.'[7] Croker in 'A Half-length' is not, admittedly, an old man, but he is as disreputable and repulsive as his Dickensian alter ego, and he too might be caricatured as a dealer in marine stores (a vulgarization of his job as Secretary to the Admiralty).

Here, then, is Hazlitt's portrait of Croker, which should win pride of place in any anthology of invective – impassioned, biting and funny. No doubt, as Jones has suggested, Hazlitt did not consider it 'to be suitable for inclusion among the more judicious studies that made up *The Spirit of the Age*', but it serves as a beautiful illustration of his technique.[8] It is uncollected, and the present text comes from *The Examiner*, 1 August 1824, page 484.

---

6   *Our Mutual Friend* (London, 1966), Book 2, chapter 1, p. 217.
7   *Bleak House* (London, 1966), p. 49.
8   Jones, *Hazlitt*, p. 361.

A Half-length

Hic niger est: hunc tu, Romane, caveto.[1]

Who is it that you meet sauntering along Pall-mall with fleering eyes, and nose turned up, as if the mud and the people offended him, – that has the look of an informer, or the keeper of a bagnio, or a dealer in marine stores, or an attorney struck off the list, – a walking nuisance, with the sense of smell added to it, a moving *nausea*, with whose stomach nothing agrees, and that seeks some object to vent its spleen and ill-humour upon, that turns another way, afraid to express it –

> A dog, in forehead; and in heart, a deer;[2]

that stops to look at a print-shop with a supercilious air of indifference, as if he would be thought to understand, but scorned to approve anything – that finds fault with Hogarth, and can see no grace in Raphael; with his round shoulders, *hulking* stoop, slouching great-coat, and unwashed face, like the smut of his last night's conversation – that's let in and out of Carlton House,[3] like a night-cart, full of filth, and crawling with lies – the Thersites of modern politics, the ring-leader of the Yahoos of the Press, the *goul* of the Boroughmongers; that preys on the carcase of patriot reputation; the Probert[4] of the Allies, that 'bags the game' of liberty in the *Quar-*

---

1 From Horace, *Satires*, I. iv. 85.
2 From Pope, *Homer's Iliad*, i. 297–8:

> O Monster, mix'd in Insolence and Fear,
> Thou Dog in Forehead, but in Heart a Deer!

3 The *Examiner* text is more diplomatic; it reads '—— House'. Carlton House was the residence of George IV, where Croker was a visitor.
4 A reference to William Probert, a well-known villain of the day, believed to have been involved in the murder of Weare, but for which Thurtell was executed. Probert was hanged for horse-stealing in 1825.

terly that Duke Humphrey[5] slew in the field – a Jack-pudding in wit,[6] a pretender to sense, a tool of power, who thinks that a nickname implies disgrace, as a title confers honour, that to calumniate is to convince, and whose genius is on an exact par with the taste and understanding of his employers; – whose highest ambition is to be a *cat's-paw*, whose leading principle is to advocate his own interest by betraying his country and his species; to whom the very names of LIBERTY, HUMANITY, VIRTUE, PATRIOTISM, are a byword from the want of a single generous or manly feeling in his own breast; whose only pleasure is in malignity, and whose only pride is in degrading others to his own level; who affects literature, and fancies he writes like Tacitus, by leaving out the conjunction *and*; who helps himself to English out of Lindley Murray's Grammar,[7] and maintains, with a pragmatical air, that no one writes it but himself; who conceals his own writings and publishes those of other people, which he procures from his relations at a lodging-house; who frightens elderly gentle-women who ask him to dinner, by pleasantly offering to carve a 'Holy-Ghost Pye', that is, a Pigeon-Pye, and gallantly calling for a bit of the 'Leg of the Saviour', that is, a leg of Lamb; who afterwards props the Bible and the Crown with ribaldry and slander, but who has no ob-jection to the Pope, the Turk or the Devil, provided they are on the side of his LEGITIMATE Patrons, and who keeps a fellow even more impudent than himself,[8] who, whenever the cause of humanity is mentioned, sticks his hands in his sides, and cries HUMBUG, and while nations are massacring, and the hopes of earth withered, plays a tune on the salt-box for the amusement of the Ladies and Gentlemen of Great Britain, and in honour of Great Fûm?[9]

5   The Duke of Wellington (by reference to *1 Henry VI*, I. i. 75–103).
6   In a footnote to an article in *The Liberal*, Hazlitt quotes Croker's father on the Tories' choice of his son as Parliamentary candidate: 'They wanted a Jack-pud-ding, and so they chose my son'.
7   Lindley Murray (1745–1826) was an American who settled in England in 1785. His *English Grammar* (1795), despite Hazlitt's reservations about it, was for a long time accepted as a standard textbook; it had reached its fifth edition by 1824.
8   Theodore Hook, editor of *John Bull*, which had launched one of the bitterest attacks against Hazlitt for *Liber Amoris*.
9   George IV (by reference to Byron, *Don Juan*, xi. 78).

Appendix III:
— Reynolds's account of —
Hazlitt, 28 April 1817

In this Appendix we present another portrait in words: this time it is not by Hazlitt, but describes him. Hitherto unpublished, it comes from a letter by John Hamilton Reynolds to Mary Leigh, 28 April 1817, now preserved at Keats House, Hampstead. Reynolds (1794–1852) was one of Keats's dearest friends, and, like Keats, was a particular admirer of Hazlitt. His friendship with Taylor and Hessey meant that he saw proof sheets of Hazlitt's *Lectures on the English Poets* as it was being set up in 1818.[1] A year before that, shortly after publication of *The Round Table*, the two men dined together, and some days later Reynolds recalled him in a written portrait that shows how charismatic and charming Hazlitt could be – the archetypal plain speaker. We wish to thank Tina Gee, Curator of Keats House, Hampstead, for bringing the passage to our attention, and The Corporation of London for permission to publish.

> On Thursday last Hazlitt was with me at home, and remained with us till 3 o'clock in the morning! – full of Eloquence, – Warm, lofty, & communicative on everything Imaginative & Intelligent, – breathing out with us the peculiar & favourite beauties of our best Bards, – Passing from grand & comma[n]ding argument to the gaieties & graces of wit and humour, – and the Elegant and higher beauties of Poetry. He is indeed *great* company, and leaves a weight on the mind, which

1   See Reynolds's letter to Hessey of March 1818, now preserved at Keats House, Rome.

'it can hardly bear.' He is full of what D^r. Johnson terms 'good talk.'[2] His countenance is also extremely fine: – a sunken & melancholy face, – a forehead lined with thought and bearing a full & strange pulsation, – on exciting subjects, – an eye, dashed in its light with sorrow, but kindling & *living* at intellectual moments, – and a stream of coal-black hair dropping around all. Such a face, so silent and so sensitive, is indeed the Banner of the Mind. 'It is as a book, in which Men may read strange things.'[3] He would have become the pencil of Titian, and have done justice to the soul-fed colours of that bold & matchless Italian. I fear you will be tired with this long *personality*, but I remember having read a few papers of his to you, and therefore imagine you will not be wholly uninterested in him.

---

2   Reynolds is recalling Boswell's *Life of Johnson*: ' "Well, (said he,) we had good talk." Boswell: "Yes, Sir; you tossed and gored several persons" ' (*Boswell's Life of Johnson* ed. George Birkbeck Hill, rev. L.F. Powell, 6 vols, Oxford, 1934–50, ii. 66). The phrase is frequently used by Hazlitt.
3   From *Macbeth*, I. v. 62–3.

Index